God in Our Hands

Graham Shaw

God in Our Hands

SCM PRESS LTD

British Library Cataloguing in Publication Data

Shaw, Graham, *1944-*
God in our hands.
1. Theology
I. Title

230   BR118

ISBN 0-334-02033-6

First published 1987
by SCM Press Ltd
26-30 Tottenham Road London N1

Typeset at The Spartan Press Ltd
Lymington, Hants
and printed in Great Britain by
Richard Clay Ltd, Bungay, Suffolk

CONTENTS

PART THREE: THE USE OF GOD IN A RELIGION OF PEACE

PREFACE

Four years ago in a book called *The Cost of Authority* I undertook a close examination of the Pauline letters and the Gospel according to Mark in order to discern their function in the assertion and exercise of authority. Eventually I found that my own understanding of God had been changed. I described this development in a section entitled:

A God for whom We are Responsible to Each Other

'Emphasis on the function of doctrines, on asking questions about the use to which human beings are putting their religious claims and language, makes possible a new understanding of the reality of God, modified and more intelligible. For the logical consequence of this approach to scripture is that the only reality of God lies in the use of that word by human beings. It does not refer to some supernatural or mysterious or special being; it is instead a word of the creative imagination by which we construct first in imagination and ultimately in reality a new and different world. The only significance of the word 'God' is its purely verbal function; that is not necessarily disparaging, for its function is uniquely precious: it is an integral part of human freedom, a means by which we transcend the given and transform ourselves and the world.

'All attempts to objectify God, to attribute to God an assured metaphysical reality, have therefore to be abandoned; and that for religious as well as for philosophical reasons. The intellectual difficulties of such objectification are a commonplace of the modern philosophy of religion. The religious objections are rather different, and lie in the acceptance and evasion of responsibility. A God objectively or supernaturally conceived connives too easily with our attempts to evade responsibility for our constructions which are thus removed from the possibility of criticism. Moreover the unchanging metaphysical God, whose relationship to the world is fundamentally non-reciprocal, has always been associated with the construction and preservation of equally unbalanced social relationships . . .

'The God implied by the gospel of the New Testament is necessarily a criticism of other possibilities. Such a God cannot simply sanctify the given and celebrate the world as it is, as the best possible world; for that God is quite redundant, just because he makes no difference. Indeed the only function of that God is to deter change; he is the classic ally of the privileged and powerful for whom alone such a vision of reality is plausible. His praise represents the triumphant expression of their own power and dominance. By contrast the God of the New Testament is abused the moment he is identified with human structures of authority and social control. Far from legitimating those structures, the Christian account of God emerged in bloody conflict with them. It is true that in the New Testament itself the process has begun by which Jesus merely sanctions one system of social control as opposed to another, but I hope I have convincingly demonstrated that that is a betrayal of the possibilities which the gospel creates, and to which the New Testament itself also witnesses.

'The God of the gospel sustains human freedom first of all by providing a vocabulary which readily challenges all human structures of authority and control. This subversive character is not temporary and circumstantial, something which is relevant to one society but not to another; it is one of the intrinsically Christian uses of the word God. The appeal to God negates all existing human claims – it places them in question, and thus enables the individual to resist them. Secondly, it provides a language which enables human beings to transcend the given, to achieve imaginative detachment. Without such a possibility, the scientific description of reality will only reinforce present oppression and inequality. By contrast the language of religion facilitates the creative redescription of reality. Thirdly, this is no substitute for action, but a preparation for it. A religion confined to the imagination, be it the awareness of the mystic or the consciousness of grace, remains in the most negative sense unreal. Once the imagination has been detached from action, the way is open to religious fantasy and every kind of dishonest compensation. The God of the Christian gospel frees precisely because he calls to action. Objective benefits which are passively received easily rob their beneficiaries of initiative. By contrast, the gifts of the Christian gospel are obtained only in use.

'Such a God gives no sanction for a timid retreat into arbitrary and isolated subjectivity. The exercise of freedom is private in origin, but ultimately it is accessible and public. The believer in the Christian God must subject himself to the discipline of communication, which involves listening as well as speaking. The believer must therefore always be prepared to give reasons, to share his understanding, to listen to criticism and thus to achieve a greater intelligibility; for once he takes refuge in a believing circle his freedom is divisive and becomes an expression and instrument of alienation. The privileged proclamation of the pulpit is no satisfactory substitute for mutual discussion. The exercise of our freedom, which is also our discovery of the will of God, is necessarily co-operative with others. Ultimately, however, it is the need to exercise freedom in action which ensures that religion cannot be a matter of private fancy. The believer may challenge the world as he finds it, and use his imagination to construct a different world, but when he proceeds to act on that vision he cannot evade the recognition of constraint. The need for action ensures that beliefs about God are incarnated, and in that incarnation they are tested and explored. For the writers of the Gospels, the actual fate of Jesus in suffering and death was clearly intolerable; they could only affirm it if it was vindicated and reversed by a miraculous resurrection; but it is far from clear that Jesus himself shared their assessment of his freedom. By contrast he appears to have acknowledged and accepted the risks of his own action, and thus invites us to do the same.

'We may use God to challenge other men and the world as we perceive it, but we cannot use the word to evade our ultimate engagement with them. God enables us to defy social constraint and to remould reality; he does not enable us to deny our dependence on others or to lie about what is true. A God who sustains our freedom is also a God for whom we have to recognize our responsibility. We have to acknowledge our creativity in his construction, and our responsibility to each other for the ways in which we invoke him.'[1]

It may seem self-absorbed and self-indulgent to begin one book by quoting from the closing passages of another, but two reasons have led me to take this step. First, it provides my starting point by its emphasis on the need to take responsibility for the God we worship. I want to explore what happens to religion as we begin to take a more mature responsibility for our God, recognizing how intimately our identity and our portrayal of God are related to each other. As will become apparent I am not entirely happy with that first sketch of 'a God for whom we are responsible to each other', but I remain convinced that we have to take responsibility for our God, that we have to repudiate all those accounts of God which help us to evade that responsibility, and that such an understanding of God represents the future of theology.

The Charge of Atheism

To affirm the future of theology leads me to my second reason, for beginning with a lengthy quotation from my previous book – it is the charge of atheism. For many readers such an account of God was tantamount to disbelief. Ronald Preston in an otherwise sympathetic review put the case most cogently:

'All attempts to objectify God, to attribute to God an assured, metaphysical reality, have therefore to be abandoned' p. 282. A good deal hangs on what weight is given to 'assured' – for we live as Christians by faith – but the general drift suggests the most negative sense. Shaw's position seems like Ernst Bloch's atheism in Christianity. In that case we must say firmly to Shaw that it is *not* a logical consequence of his approach; that this is a different question which it is quite proper to raise, but that he has not written anything in this book to justify his answer; that there is much more to be said about metaphysical theism and it cannot be so easily dismissed; and that it is a great pity he has included these remarks, because it will lead to his book being dismissed on the grounds that it leads to atheism by those who most need to read it.[2]

To ignore such an indictment would do violence to the very notion of responsibility which I tried to outline.

In so far as Professor Preston is suggesting a lack of prudence, he may well be right. It was probably a mistake at the end of a highly controversial argument to introduce a new note of discord for which I had not adequately prepared the reader. I returned to the question of God, because I thought it would be cowardly not to give some indication of how I proposed to deal with the destructive implications of my own argument. I was not, however, raising a new question, but returning to acknowledge the agnostic nature of the theological method which I had indicated in the introduction:

> No prior positions need to be taken on the existence of God or the possibility of revelation. No special pleading is required to rehabilitate the miraculous, far less a commitment to some version of infallibility. It is enough that the reader admits the possibility of human freedom and of reconciliation between men, and does not regard these possibilities as mutually incompatible.[3]

In the intervening pages I never directly considered the philosophical arguments against traditional metaphysical theism, but the pervading attitude was clearly stated at the outset:

> The appeal to God distracts attention from the human speaker. Heaven is silent, and when men's attention is directed towards it, we easily fail to notice that human lips are moving. This is not to dismiss all talk of God as deceit, but it does suggest that we fix our eyes most carefully on the human speaker, and treat with caution any confusion of identity between man and God. Wherever a man cannot speak in his own name, but buttresses his speech with divine authorship, suspicion is certainly in order. Is the human speaker benefitting by this device, and if so, how?[4]

If the basic approach was sound, as Professor Preston seemed prepared to grant, it had profoundly disturbing implications for traditional theism. I hoped by anticipating them, if not to forestall criticism, at least to demonstrate that I was conscious of the difficulties.

I regard the charge of atheism as a serious one, which I do not wish to pass unchallenged. In the ancient world of polytheism Jews and Christians were often suspected of the same impiety. The vigorous repudiation of some accounts of God may be a necessary tribute to other accounts of God, and stem not from irreligion, but from a genuinely religious commitment. In today's context I run the risk of being dismissed as an atheist because I believe that a great deal of the modern critique of religion will have to be accepted, and this in two important respects. First, the metaphysical arguments for the existence of God the creator have not, and probably cannot, recover from the objections of modern philosophy. Secondly, the human origins of religious belief and the continuing human creativity in their development have therefore to be honestly acknowledged, and indeed the future of religion depends upon this being done. This means that the distinction between the real God who exists and the man-made gods which must be repudiated is false. It is a distinction we can no longer make, and in so far as the Christian tradition has used that distinction in the past it was mistaken. In this book I shall suggest that this does not mean the end of religion, but demands instead its radical transformation. Atheism can only be answered by a theology which is convincingly and consistently self-critical.

The immediate response may well be one of impatience. Why not simply dismiss the whole religious enterprise? Here as so often the conservative believer and the modern unbeliever are in unholy collusion. The conservative insists on objectivity, returning to the ancient distinction between the real God and sham fabrications. The unbeliever is not dissatisfied with such an insistence – it provides the presupposition which justifies his repudiation. It is important to note the contradiction. The total denial of religious activity is a paradoxical tribute to the account of true religion it is denying. The disappointment in discovering the human origin of all religion is only intelligible in terms of the long polemic of the Judaeo-Christian tradition against idolatry. It is from that polemic that the modern unbeliever has derived his principle that a man-made God is no God.

I want to suggest that there is an alternative. Once we have recognized that all religion is man-made, instead of repudiating it with a misplaced sense of disappointment, we might still choose to affirm religious activity as something which enriches our lives and which like other forms of art is inextricably intertwined with human creativity and freedom. For it must be something of an embarrassment to all but the most complacent atheist that so much of man's social organization and artistic achievement has been associated with religion. Beliefs about God, words spoken in his name, aspirations addressed to him, have exercised enormous power through generations of human life. Particularly striking is the ability of religion, with all its mistakes and deceits, to elicit a wealth of artistic creativity, which contrasts sadly with the drab secularized society which is its successor. Throughout the world there is a depressing pattern of urban development which surrounds a historic and usually religious heart with a vast, anonymous and functional sprawl: entirely parasitic for its identity and its values on a tradition to which it has ceased to contribute and can barely conserve.

It is not therefore quixotic to look at our religious creativity with a friendly eye, for much within it deserves our affirmation. In future religious people will have to be more humble about the claims they make, just because they cannot ignore that it is they who make them rather than God. That calls for a very different style – relaxed rather than authoritarian. It invites us to discover in our religion a new playfulness, as we admit and celebrate the human creativity at work in all religious activity. It remains necessary to make distinctions. Although we can no longer say that this religion is true and that is false, we must continue to make moral distinctions about the ways in which particular religions function. There are important differences between religions which enslave or liberate, which alienate or reconcile, which mislead or foster honesty. To adjure such criticism would mean to stay silent in the face of cruelty, intolerance, domination and deceit. We may know enough of atheistic societies to realize that atheism does not remove such evils, but we also have to recognize that not only in the past, but in the present, much religious activity has a similar cost.

This book falls therefore into three parts. The first, if read in isolation, would deserve to be considered an exercise in atheism. It consists of a description and repudiation of those elements in traditional theism which promise power while evading responsibility. Inevitably it will offend some religious people, but I hope they may persevere at least to read the second part which, although it is brief, is the hinge on which my whole argument turns. Very simply it claims that the crucified Christ represents a critique of the religions of power which is far more radical than that of modern atheism, and invites his followers to take account of that. In the last part of the book I have outlined an approach to religion which is not concerned with power but with peace, in the hope that such a religion can give an account of God that is neither mistaken nor deceptive.

Walton-on-the-Hill,
The Circumcision of Christ, 1987.

INTRODUCTION

Prayer and the Functions of Belief

'Close your eyes. Keep quiet. Say after me.' These are probably the earliest lessons in prayer that most of us receive, and those of us who continue to pray learn them all too well. They place us in a private world where we cannot see what other people are doing. Opening our eyes during prayer, catching the eye of another, is both distracting and subversive. The quiet, which is conducive to concentration, also inhibits dissent. To question is to disturb. All prayer begins in imitation, and the conformity which it demands at its outset is often never outgrown. It is not therefore surprising that many of those who practice prayer should think that it defies analysis, and insist that it participates in the mystery of the God to whom it is addressed. It might be said that those who continue to pray are selected by their tolerance of those first lessons, and are likely to be unwilling and ill-equipped to give an account of what they are doing.

Both the devout and the irreligious will probably agree that prayer is fundamental to any kind of religion. The practice of prayer distinguishes those who believe from those who disbelieve. The regularity and persistence of prayer is probably the most reliable measure of religious commitment. It is nevertheless a human activity. It is something we can choose to do or not to do, and as a human activity it invites question. We are answerable to other people for our actions, and prayer has its place among them. I shall argue that the study of prayer is important because it is an essential preliminary to understanding the historical development of doctrine and to appreciating the metaphysical difficulties of belief today. The attempts to rehabilitate a religious metaphysic or to ground

Christian beliefs in history will only prove sterile if they neglect the context of prayer in which those beliefs have their place. In this I entirely agree with the emphasis of Professor D. Z. Phillips in *The Concept of Prayer*. In that perceptive work published twenty years ago he challenged the usual assumption that the philosophical discussion of prayer was a secondary matter, which could be postponed until the question of God's existence had first been settled. Instead he insisted that we must *begin* by asking what it means to confess to God, to thank him, to petition or intercede. There is much in his development of those subjects which I wish to question, but his emphasis on prayer as a primary object of religious study is one that I endorse. It is that direction rather than his precise positions, which gives his work its pioneering character and its continuing importance.

The Person who Prays and the Possibility of Self-Deception

Although piety often resents curiosity, there are two intrinsic reasons why prayer merits careful reflection. The first concerns the person who prays, and the ever present possibility of self-deception. It is therefore a question of personal integrity. If we simply take refuge in the activity of praying, and refuse to question or probe it, we are at the very least creating conditions which are conducive to dishonesty. For all the mystique with which it is surrounded prayer is subject to very special temptations. Prayer is not some generalized phenomenon, which can be properly discussed in the abstract. It is a personal and often a private activity. Even when I am using the most formal prayers there is a vital element of individual appropriation, by which I make my own the prayer of the church. More frequently prayer has an intuitive, spontaneous character, which reflects and forms my own identity. This very intimacy has specific dangers. It removes the person who prays from the observation of other people, and the healthy disciplines of communication and criticism. It is this solitude and secrecy of prayer which can be so easily abused.

The focus of prayer on God often conceals from us what we contribute to our prayer and what we gain from it. It also facilitates false assumptions about the identity of the person who prays. Misleading over-simplifications are introduced which are only remedied with difficulty. Do we possess an integrated, continuous personality? How conflict-laden is our identity? How much self-knowledge do we possess? The simple and apparently uncomplicated personal pronouns which we use in prayer only reinforce the problem. The 'I' of prayer should never be taken for granted. Indeed much of the agenda of prayer comes from the burden of being who I am: a person with radically conflicting desires, subject to changing moods and sometimes quite lacking in self-knowledge. Often when I pray it is these incoherences in myself that I am trying to order and overcome.

Critical reflection cannot of course guarantee an end to self-deception; deviousness and evasiveness are often too deeply rooted to yield any easy victory. Such habits are slow to die, and often successfully defend themselves by subtly adopting new strategies of surprise and disguise. Reflection is, however, a necessary first step towards a greater honesty. In this process writing provides a form of discipline, a means of focussing attention. It represents an attempt to fix and so to understand impressions, which would otherwise be too elusive to analyse. In prayer which is confined to consciousness the mind is too fugitive – it runs on, giddy and uncomprehending. It leaves no trace, and confusion closes in behind it. The pen on paper is often painfully slow, but it makes possible correction. It provides its own fixed points in relation to which it may be possible to steer a new course. It also creates the possibility of public examination and debate. At the least it expresses a commitment to a clearer understanding. It will be for the reader to judge the extent to which the commitment is matched by achievement.

Prayer and the Functions of Belief

The second intrinsic reason why prayer deserves careful examination has to do with the assumed beliefs which any prayer implies. The simplest prayer makes very complex assumptions about God and his relation to the world. The very utterance of prayer suggests a God who is attentive and responsive. It may be that the conviction that God exists owes more to the persistent practice of prayer than to the changing arguments of religious philosophers. The mere existence of people and communities which pray, which continue to use language addressed to God, makes a powerful impact on our imagination. As conclusive evidence for the truth of religious beliefs, it is obviously inadequate, but as *prima facie* evidence it is undeniable. Does God exist? What difference does God make to us? How is God at work? All these metaphysical questions are not posed by the existence of the world, but by the existence of people who obstinately continue to pray. As the fact of prayer invites questions about the God to whom it is addressed, those who pray have to be prepared to take responsibility for their beliefs: for their prayer is always their most eloquent statement of beliefs.

While the customary wording of the Credo insists that we say 'I believe', two recent evasions of that uncompromising language have become widespread. Often the defensive words 'I happen to believe' are used as an apologetic preface to religious belief: as if it was analogous to the accidental possession of red hair or buck-teeth. Equally revealing has been the return to the conciliar 'we believe' in the liturgical use of the Nicene Creed. Belief is thus identified with collective conformity. What both these developments share is an avoidance of personal responsibility for what we believe – instead history or the community become responsible. This is only to confuse beliefs with prejudices. Certainly I harbour all manner of prejudices because I have a particular history and belong to certain groups within society, and for that reason I have to try to overcome them. What distinguishes my beliefs from my prejudices is precisely that I am prepared to take full responsibility for them, and only for that reason am I in a position to insist upon them. I and I alone am answerable for my beliefs and must be prepared to give an account of them. It is insufficient to point to what has happened to me or to the shared convictions of the community to which I belong. Taking responsibility for my beliefs means being prepared to articulate them and to commend them to other people – not just to other people who already share them, but to the sceptical and the critical. Anything less robust is a form of special pleading.

Theology and Prayer: the Conservative Approach

I began by making large claims for the contribution which the study of prayer can make to theology. I ought however to make it plain that I have little sympathy for the conservative theologians and exponents of spirituality who are prone to lament the modern division between theology and spirituality. Andrew Louth in *Discerning the Mystery* provides an elegant example:

> For us there is an almost unconscious division between theology and spirituality; even if we feel they belong together, we have to relate them to each other, and not all theologians want to relate them too closely. The commitment that prayer implies seems to some to compromise the 'objectivity' of theology as a rational study. The centre does not hold; the object of theology retreats, and is displaced. Theologians become more concerned with one another, and less with God who is the traditional object of their study.[1]

The rapprochement which he then advocates has the happy consequence of disarming the modern theologian of most of his critical weapons: the way is even opened for a return to allegory. The satire is entertaining, but unconvincing. Mr Louth is himself preoccupied by the views of other theologians whom he quotes at length. The insistence on spirituality in theology does not ensure an uncluttered attention to God. Instead the note of commitment or prior assumption which it introduces has the effect of foreclosing some basic areas of theological debate. The exponents of spirituality seek to protect themselves from disturbance by theologians in the name of reverence for God and a humility towards the religious tradition. Conservative theologians seek a certainty in the prayerful encounter with God which can no longer be provided by a confident metaphysic. In both the association of theology and spirituality serves to beg questions rather than to answer them.

Sadly much of D. Z. Phillips' work must be included in this criticism. It is one thing to demand that the study of religious beliefs begins with the way in which they function in prayer, but it is difficult to avoid the impression that D. Z. Phillips would also end the discussion there. This gives to *The Concept of Prayer* an irritatingly evasive character. Only in the final pages does he begin to face the implications which his analysis has suggested. Following Simone Weil he outlines the philosophical version of the naturalistic fallacy:

If a philosopher is aware that the God of whom he is giving an account is a natural God, an existent among existents, and an agent among agents, there is no philosophical objection to what he is doing. On the other hand, if he thinks that this conception of God is the only possible one, the only intelligible notion of divinity, he is making a mistake. Furthermore, if the philosopher proceeds to give an account of *all* conceptions of God in terms of a natural God, he is guilty of the naturalistic fallacy.[2]

It is by no means clear, however, that what he dismisses as the natural God is not the supernatural God. To invoke Simone Weil's notion of the supernatural without facing or justifying the radical revision of the traditional concept which it implies is unsatisfactory. To define the supernatural as that pure generosity which forbears to command where it possesses the power to do so, is a fascinating reinterpretation of the religious tradition; but it is a reinterpretation which requires examination and justification. This ultimate impression of arbitrary assertion is only strengthened by Phillips' later work, *Religion without Explanation*. There he explicitly denies that the philosopher can answer the question 'Does God exist?'[3]

> To ask whether God exists is not to ask a theoretical question. If it is to mean anything at all, it is to wonder about praising and praying; it is to wonder whether there is anything in all that.[4]

Such a position is unconvincing. To ask whether God exists may not simply be a theoretical question, but that it is at least in part a theoretical question is indicated by Phillips' own elucidation. 'To wonder about praising and praying' is to ask questions both about the activity and its assumptions. Wonder is not merely an attitude of awed acquiescence; it has often expressed itself in questions, and has not always been afraid to supply answers. 'What is man that thou shouldst remember him?' the psalmist asks and then proceeds to tell us. Ultimately it is impossible to disagree with J. L. Mackie's harsh verdict:

> Phillips has given no grounds for denying that 'the God of religion' is a possible subject of simple truth or falsehood; in consequence what he offers is either disguised atheism or

unsupported theism – since he declines to support its factual claims – or else an unresolved hesitation between the two.[5]

This is perhaps the most fitting epitaph for what might be described as the vulgar use of Kierkegaard.

Theology and Prayer: the Philosophical Approach

I would argue that the study of prayer is important for theology, not because it introduces an element of surreptitious commitment, but precisely because in prayer the human activity, which is at work in all religion, cannot be concealed. By contrast theology, particularly as represented in the philosophy of religion, appears not only more abstract but also more objective. The doctrines of creation and providence are represented as abstract propositions for debate: believers who worship God make claims about him: worship depends on first assenting to those claims. Only when we have satisfied ourselves about those claims will we condescend to pray. Apart from the comical and entirely irreligious nature of such a procedure, it invites deception and misunderstanding. Religious claims are much more intimately related to human aspirations than such a view allows. Indeed in some of the basic texts of Judaism and Christianity it is very difficult to distinguish assertions about God from the desires and hopes that God is as the assertions claim. A few examples from the psalter will suffice.

The most familiar of all Psalms, the twenty-third, the surprising accompaniment of both weddings and funerals, begins with the appearance of a description of God, 'The Lord is my shepherd', but immediately proceeds to specify very personal benefits:

> I shall want nothing.
> He makes me lie down in green pastures,
> and leads me beside the waters of peace.

Only the most insensitive ear could fail to catch the anxiety, which such assured language paradoxically articulates:

> Even though I walk through a valley as dark as death
> I fear no evil, for thou art with me,
> thy staff and thy crook are my comfort.

The words may be uttered with perfect conviction, and yet inevitably they function as an invocation as much as a description. We speak of God in this way, not simply because we know that he is like this, but because we hope and pray that he is so. Our language therefore goes far beyond our actual experience:

> Goodness and love unfailing, these will follow me
>   all the days of my life,
>   and I shall dwell in the house of the Lord
>   my whole life long.

When we speak of 'all the days of my life', we are unavoidably speaking the language of hope.

Repeatedly in the psalter descriptions of God alternate with invocations so that it is difficult to distinguish them apart from their grammatical form, which is often in itself misleading:

> Rise up, Lord; save me, O my God.
>   Thou dost strike all my foes across the face
>   and breakest the teeth of the wicked (Ps. 3.7).

Here the appeal for divine vengeance and intervention is supported by a rehearsal of the divine record, yet as so often in the Psalms the enemies of God and the enemies of the psalmist have an embarrassing identity – 'my foes' are 'the wicked'. Simply to abstract from such language the notion of a vindictive and interventionist God, apart from the human context of fear and hatred in which it has its origin, is to conceal something important about the belief. I am not suggesting that the belief itself should not be examined and questioned; instead I am asking that the circumstances of its origin be considered as relevant to its truth.

For instance the unremitting partiality of God as he is represented in the psalter is most readily explained and understood by the situation and interest of the psalmist. The explicit description of God as judge in Psalm 7 helps to make this clear:

> God, the High God is my shield
>   who saves men of honest heart.
> God is a just judge,
>   every day he requites the raging enemy (Ps. 7.10f.).

The belief that God is a righteous judge is intertwined with the assertion of the psalmist's righteousness. The flattery of the judge is also a very personal plea for justice. The obsession with legal processes which the psalter displays is eloquent testimony to the inadequacy of contemporary human justice, which it both reflects and transcends. The beliefs about divine justice seem rooted in frustrating human experience of judicial delay and misrepresentation. To concentrate on the beliefs and ignore the social context in which they were developed and the intentions of those who developed them is a procedure to which the psalter gives no encouragement. There theology and spirituality are brought into a juxtaposition which is both revealing and disturbing.

In the psalter the language of prayer compels the theologian and particularly the philosopher of religion to recognize that assertions about God reflect specific historical circumstances and often have their origin in human aspirations. To isolate the assertion from the aspiration and then to seek for evidence that the assertion is true rests on a misunderstanding and invites disappointment. The misunderstanding lies in the failure to perceive that although believers make statements about God, which have the appearance of straightforward descriptions, they are led to make them not because of what they know, but because they have certain hopes and desires. Thus an analysis of the hopes and desires of the person who prays is a necessary preliminary to understanding his statements of belief. Isolated from that context of aspiration those beliefs may well appear curiously groundless. The breakdown of metaphysical theology in modern times represents the bankruptcy of such a procedure to establish the truth of religious beliefs. If religious beliefs are examined in that way, a negative verdict is probably inevitable, and religious beliefs are reduced to a series of almost unintelligible and therefore stupid mistakes. If instead religious beliefs are approached by examining the aspirations with which they are associated, the verdict may be rather different. This is not a road which will lead to the restoration of the whole range of traditional orthodoxy. Some of the most widespread traditional beliefs may still be dismissed as mistaken though understandable; but on these terms some religious beliefs may be vindicated. To do this they will correspond to our deepest aspirations; they will mediate that hunger for salvation which is the knowledge of God. That, however, is to anticipate.

The Activity of Prayer: Learning and Reassessment

It is my starting point that both theology and spirituality, whatever else they may be, are complementary forms of human activity. Theology consists in the first place of what human beings say and think about God. Spirituality likewise consists of the speech and attention to God of those who believe in him. If the interrelation is complicated there is some clarification in remembering that human beings are at work in both. That is not necessarily to rule out the possibility of divine intervention or dialogue, but to point out that our access to the human activity involved is always less problematic.

Just as we have to learn theology, so the activity of prayer is something we learn to do. This is described with precision in the *Confessions* of Augustine:

> But we found that some men prayed to you, Lord, and we learned from them to do the same, thinking of you in the only way that we could understand, as some great person who could listen to us and help us, even though we could not see you or hear you or touch you.[6]

In the first place we see and hear other people pray and imitate their language and gestures. Equally we will probably begin to pray before we have any well constructed beliefs about God, and our religious beliefs will be strongly marked by the assumptions of the prayers we are taught. Those who learn prayers which propitiate an angry deity and those who are encouraged to thank the God of beauty in creation, will not simply learn different prayers, they will acquire radically different impressions of God. What Augustine does not realize is that in this process of imitation our perception of ourselves is subtly modified. The phrases we learn will not simply express our condition, indeed it may be many years before we have the confidence and freedom to pray from our immediate experience. Instead we learn prayers which teach us that we are weak, sinful, needy and dying. One of the greatest difficulties in learning to pray is learning to discover ourselves in the categories that are offered to us.

So for most people learning to pray will at first be a matter of more or less unwilling imitation, but we only persist in that activity if we envisage some benefit from it, and we learn what to expect at first from the prayers we are taught.

Prayer therefore is like music – a part of our acquired culture. If it was simply natural or innate, it would not invite reassessment. Instead each generation has to learn the art of prayer anew. Old habits and assumptions are necessarily challenged in the process of appropriation by which the practice of prayer is transmitted. Like all such processes of transmission the tradition of prayer is generally conservative. Indeed in its liability to preserve archaic language and formulae and sometimes to retain a language which has no surviving secular use, it is perhaps the most conservative of all human cultural traditions. Hebrew and Aramaic, Greek and Latin survive into the modern world principally as vehicles of prayer. Just as most theological traditions like to see themselves as unchanging, and so participating in the eternity of the God to whom they refer, so the tradition of prayer gains much of its prestige from an impression of unchanging continuity. The themes are brought together and celebrated in one of the most successful Victorian hymns:

> We thank Thee that Thy Church unsleeping,
> > While earth rolls onward into light,
> Through all the world her watch is keeping,
> > And rests not now by day or night.

> As o'er each continent and island
> > The dawn leads on another day,
> The voice of prayer is never silent,
> > Nor dies the strain of praise away.

> So be it, Lord; Thy Throne shall never,
> > Like earth's proud empires, pass away;
> Thy Kingdom stands, and grows for ever,
> > Till all Thy creatures own Thy sway.

Only the consciously global imperialism betrays its specifically English and nineteenth-century origin.

Nevertheless, there is a continuous if unacknowledged process of reassessment. Our generation with its recent liturgies and translations of the Bible is most aware of it in the search for a convincing modern language in which to express religious belief. Even in that attenuated linguistic form the process of reassessment has been far from painless. The changes of emphasis and content in the tradition of belief have only reluctantly been acknowledged, and in so far as they continue are fiercely contested. Equally profound shifts have taken place in the tradition of prayer. The most obvious occasion was at the Protestant Reformation which not only emphasized the use of the vernacular, but ruthlessly obliterated some of the most popular forms of medieval devotion – most strikingly those Marian prayers associated with the rosary. But many of the changes have been much less self-conscious and deliberate. To take an example from the Psalms, few religious people are now happy to recite:

Happy is he who shall seize your children
    and dash them against the rock (Ps. 137.9).

The change of religious sensibility, which introduced brackets into the psalter, was only gradual. Equally the Alternative Service Book has not found it necessary to modernize the Commination, 'or denouncing of God's anger and judgments against sinners'. In all Protestant forms of Christianity there has been a move away from the psalter to the more exciting and rhapsodic sentiments of Christian hymnody. Very ancient forms of prayer like exorcism occupy an ambiguous position in modern piety, neglected in some denominations, cherished in others. A service like the Churching of Women is only retained with a quite different rationale. With such a history behind us we cannot deny that a powerful process of reassessment has marked even this most conservative of traditions.

It would be wrong to think that the continuous reassessment of the tradition of prayer was simply a matter of adjusting to changing beliefs about God. At times such doctrinal changes have influenced prayer profoundly. Most recently, weakened convictions about the wrath of God, the punitive aspect of his providence and the eternity or even the existence of hell have all diminished the propitiatory elements in prayer. In the confession at the Communion the Book of

Common Prayer speaks of 'Provoking most justly thy wrath and indignation against us'. The ASB is innocent of such fears, reflecting a church which is more preoccupied by problems of theodicy than with the doctrine of the atonement. Good Friday now brings the consolation that God suffers with us – 'He opened wide his arms for us on the cross' – where once it was 'a full, perfect, and sufficient sacrifice, oblation and satisfaction, for the sins of the whole world'. But quite as influential as changing beliefs about God have been the fluctuating preoccupations of human beings: menaced by demons, doomed to decay, guilty or grieving, weak or selfish, anticipating the delights of the heavenly court, or continually tempted to disobey the commandments of God, sometimes sinful, more recently simply confused. These varying assessments of our position have not only changed the self-understanding that prayer forms; they have also affected the portrayal of God and our changing expectations of what prayer achieves. For the most crucial reassessment must concern the difference that we believe prayer makes, and each generation reinterprets its hopes with at least one eye to its experience. In a world of lightning conductors the Litany – *pace* York minster – has ceased to ask the good Lord to deliver us from lightning. Learning to pray has always involved an element of complicated reassessment. If some of the changes which I shall suggest seem outrageous, I can only say that they are not designed to shock but to conserve. If some of the changes seem so radical as to threaten their religious identity, that is perhaps a measure of the threat to the immemorial tradition of prayer which the indifference and triviality of a secularized world represent.

Prayer in the Horizontal Mode

Much that passes for prayer is no such thing. I am not referring to the day-dreaming with which we fill the boredom of church services, but to those prayers which from their form of address seem directed towards a divine audience, yet betray in their detail a desire to communicate not so much with God as with men. This possibility is inherent in all public prayer, where the congregation can easily become the significant audience. In some of the Psalms the congregation is directly addressed:

Mark my teaching, O my people,
listen to the words I am to speak (Ps. 78.1).

The lengthy recital of the Lord's 'wonderful acts' which follows may
be for God's honour, but it is also for our instruction and edification.
Similarly in the many declaratory hymns of praise there is an
ambivalence between the worship overtly offered to God and the
formation of the congregation, whose attitude is being deliberately
shaped by such exercises:

Alleluia, Alleluia, Alleluia.
 The strife is o'er, the battle done;
 Now is the Victor's triumph won;
 O let the song of praise be sung.

Such praise is represented as a duty, an obligation: but a rationale for
such tributes to an all-knowing ear is not easy to devise. There is,
however, an immediate human audience for such language in the
congregation whose faith can usually profit from reinforcement. We
also show a touching confidence that we share the Almighty's taste in
music. From this it is naive to think that only the lessons and the
sermon are addressed to the pew.

Nowhere is this substitution of a human audience for the divine
more obvious than in the Book of Common Prayer. The use of the
vernacular which made possible the intelligent participation of the
congregation, also provided the royal authority, which framed the
prayer book, with an unprecedented opportunity both to communicate directly to the nation, and to form its attitudes in an effective and
insidious manner. The most blatant examples are the prayers for the
monarch. Consider for instance the rolling periods of 'A Prayer for
the Queen's Majesty'. 'O Lord our heavenly Father, high and
mighty, King of Kings, Lord of Lords.' In these words God is
exalted as the heavenly apex of an earthly hierarchy, which he
sanctifies and sanctions. This culminates in words which place the
human monarch safely beyond all human accountability: God is 'the
only Ruler of Princes'. The point is underlined by stressing the ever
present divine eye – 'Who dost from thy throne behold all the
dwellers upon earth'. Such a potentate it is only prudent to obey,
both in his person and in his deputies. Just as the subject must not

presume on the favour of earthly majesty, 'our most gracious Sovereign Lady' is shown to be equally deferential before her heavenly Sovereign: 'Most heartily we beseech thee with thy favour to behold . . .' The petitions which are thus prefaced are a curious mixture of political and spiritual blessings: 'heavenly gifts' and 'everlasting joy' are juxtaposed with prosperity and victory. It is not surprising that Tudor and Stuart monarchs looked askance at *ex tempore* prayer: they had every motive to maintain a jealous monopoly of such exalted propaganda. Even at the eucharist the subject is encouraged to take her Majesty's view of his condition by praying, 'that under her we may be godly and quietly governed: and grant unto her whole Council, and to all that are put in authority under her, that they may truly and indifferently minister justice, to the punishment of wickedness and vice, and to the maintenance of thy true religion and virtue'.

Except on state occasions most governments today do not manage their publicity through a nation's prayers. This kind of horizontal prayer has become the mark of evangelical and charismatic prayer groups. As 'Amen' is the only permitted response, it remains a powerful instrument of conformity and control. Equally the 'we' of such prayer is often tendentious, suppressing conflicts and cloaking the assertiveness of the leader in prayer with an inclusiveness which it is usually embarrassing to disclaim. When the human audience has substantially displaced the divine, prayer is only parodied. Such illicit forms deserve to be treated with critical reserve. Jesus' concern to rule out the possibility of such a distortion of prayer is fully vindicated by the public worship that has been offered in his name.

> When you pray, do not be like the hypocrites: they love to say their prayers standing up in synagogue and at the street-corners, for everyone to see them. I tell you this: they have their reward already. But when you pray, go into a room by yourself, shut the door, and pray to your Father who is there in the secret place; and your Father who sees what is secret will reward you (Matt. 6.5f.).

The teaching of the Lord's Prayer that God's name should be hallowed also acquires in this context a clear relevance. For the reverence and docility which accompany prayer give dangerous opportunities for unscrupulous manipulation. I have devoted some

attention to the horizontal mode of prayer, because it is so
widespread and requires recognition. It is, however, a perverted
form of prayer and therefore need occupy us no further.

The Dynamics of Prayer and the Functions of Belief

The mark of all true prayer is that it is addressed to God, but it also
articulates the identity of the person who prays. A consideration of
prayer, which confines itself to God and the possibility of his
intervention, is therefore necessarily inadequate. Prayer is directed
towards God, but it originates in the person who prays. This analysis
of prayer will therefore constantly examine the ways in which we
shape our perception of ourselves in prayer. These perceptions are
not primarily explanatory; that is the task of the psychologist. The
widely differing perceptions of the self in prayer find their common
ground in the drama that they make possible. The available roles are
many: the weak calling for rescue, the threatened hoping for victory,
the sick searching for healing, the sinful asking for forgiveness, the
guilty appealing for reconciliation. Self-portrayal in prayer is seldom
simply descriptive, rather it places the soul in a dramatic setting.
Every prayer contains strong narrative possibilities. The encounter
with God is one way in which we can transform the fragmentary
confusion of our lives into story. In doing so we achieve not only a
measure of self-respect, but an unexpected joy.

Nothing shows more clearly the faithfulness of Augustine to the
religion of the scriptures and of the Psalms than his recognition of
the importance of narrative both in our relation to God and in the joy
that we find in that relationship. The abstract neo-platonist in him
would much prefer simply to dwell on the unchanging nature of God:

> For you are always the same, because all those things which are
> neither unchangeable nor endure for ever are for ever known to
> you and your knowledge of them is unchangeable.

Instead he is impelled to recognize a quite different kind of delight:

> What is it then that makes the soul rejoice more over things which
> it finds or regains than it would if it had always had them? There is
> proof of this in worldly things as well and the evidence that

proclaims the truth of it is all around us. The victorious general marches home in triumph, but there would have been no victory if he had not fought, and the greater the danger in the battle, the greater the joy of the triumph.

Augustine tries to rationalize this in terms of a general law which demands that joy be preceded by pain:

It is always the case that the greater the joy, the greater is the pain which precedes it.

But he remains unconvinced. Instead he allows the surprise to remain unexplained, ending the passage not by denying the experience, but with a series of unanswered questions:

Why should this be, O Lord my God, when you are your own eternal joy, you are Joy itself and you are always surrounded by creatures which rejoice in you? Why is it that in this part of your creation which we know there is this ebb and flow of progress and retreat, of hurt and reconciliation? Is this the rhythm of our world? Is this what you prescribed when from the heights of heaven to the depths of earth . . . you allotted a proper place and a proper time to good things of every kind and to all your just works?[7]

Once we have grasped the dramatic character of the way we present ourselves in prayer, the portrayal of God, implicit or explicit in our prayers, becomes more readily understandable. Systematic theology speaks of the divine attributes, and seeks to establish their appropriateness, their intelligibility and the grounds for asserting them. In prayer, however, we see their assertion at first hand. It is not the case that prayer simply applies beliefs, which already exist and are accepted. Living prayer would seem to make its claims about God, not on the basis of an assured theology, but as the dramatic complement to the portrayal of the self. I am perishing, God is immortal. I am weak, God is almighty. I am wicked, God is holy. I am in conflict, God is one. My view is partial, God is omniscient. I am self-preoccupied, God is love. The striking contrasts between God and man with which prayer abounds are invariably complementary. The relationship between God and the soul is far from reciprocal, but they are always well adapted to each other. The attributes of God are not therefore primarily abstract descriptions of God. Like the portrayal of the self to which they are so closely linked they are dramatic. They make it possible for God to have a role in the stories we tell about ourselves.

In this preliminary analysis of prayer I have used the concepts of drama and story, emphasizing the implicit narrative quality of prayer. In that sense prayer is historic, it promises to every one that in relation to God we have a history. In one crucial sense, however, this literary understanding of prayer is unsatisfactory. In drama at its most trivial we are entertained, at its most profound we are enabled to confer meaning on our lives. Prayer, however, moves beyond dramatic affirmation. In prayer we seek a change; it is part of the conviction that sustains prayer that it can make a difference. Augustine's memories of childhood are a cogent reminder of this:

> I was still a boy when I first began to pray to you, my Help and my Refuge. I used to prattle away to you, and though I was small, my devotion was great when I begged you not to let me be beaten at school.[8]

Contemplation by contrast is content to say, yes: the simplicity of its affirmation requires acquiescence rather than utterance. Prayer is spoken because it always envisages a transaction. The person who prays seeks a benefit. It is significant of the aristocratic land-holding past of the church and its modern bureaucratic present that it still has a certain distaste for the lively commercial and litigious spirit exemplified in the Jewish covenant, and culminating in the teaching of Jesus. The transactions of prayer, like those of commerce, are profit-oriented. The New Testament is vitally concerned with reward, just because it is a testament, a bargain between two parties, where man has everything to gain and God has everything to give.

The dramatic portrayal of God and the soul in prayer sets the terms of the hoped for transaction. The strident theologians of grace will, of course, declaim that in prayer as elsewhere – all is of God; he takes the initiative, he elicits our response, and we are entirely dependent on his favour. This stress on the non-reciprocal character of God is both an accurate and yet misleading description of the kind of transaction that prayer envisages. It certainly attributes all the power, the responsibility and the initiative to God – that indeed is part of the deal. The only hint that the soul is creative in this process comes from a consideration of the beneficiary. In prayer the advantage always goes to the person who offers the prayer, or his designated beneficiaries. In placing God beyond reward, we put ourselves in a position where we cannot lose. The language of prayer appears a model of humility. The person who prays is disparaged, God is extravagantly exalted; but prayer does not stop there. In prayer we always seek to appropriate something of the excellence we have disclaimed for ourselves and attributed to God. This aspect of the transaction suggests that we are much more assertive in prayer than we imagine. To point out the discrepancy between the rhetoric in which prayer is expressed and the benefit which it envisages, and to suggest that the latter is the key to the process, is prudent rather than paranoid.

The academic and scientific milieu of most theologians suggests to them that beliefs about God are primarily explanatory and descriptive. So for instance we are asked to assent to the doctrine of creation and the associated beliefs in God's existence and omnipotence, as providing the only satisfactory explanations of the world and accounts of God. The prayers, which are addressed to the Creator God, open up a quite different understanding of the beliefs. Such prayers highlight the function of those beliefs and suggest that the function is both the origin and the basis of the doctrine. On such an account we believe in the power which we attribute to God, because we hope to appropriate some of it to ourselves; it is that hope which leads us to assert or entertain the belief in the first place. Our experience of prayer in that belief then provides us with the rational basis for maintaining the belief, or revising it. If prayers for rain had never succeeded; if human society was continually disrupted by earthquakes and eruptions we may doubt whether the doctrine of creation would have retained its hold for so long. Spasmodic disaster gave urgency to prayers for protection: the underlying regularity of nature gave us confidence that our prayers were effective. In this respect it has to be remembered that prayer and belief belong to the living. Just as history is written by the victors, so prayer is offered by the survivors – it is not perhaps surprising that we have found accounts of an interventionist God both appealing and convincing: our presence is evidence both of his power and of the delicacy of his discrimination.

The Future of Prayer

Such an analysis of prayer obviously places its future in question, for several reasons. Is prayer intrinsically dishonest? Is prayer necessarily self-deceiving? The discrepancy between the rhetoric of prayer and the transactions it serves must raise acute misgivings. Is such an account of the origin of religious beliefs compatible with continuing to hold them? Many will see such an approach to religion as nothing more than the triumph of atheism. What are the valid transactions in prayer and how can they be distinguished from the false? For this analysis places great weight on the experience of prayer to provide the rational grounds both for continuing to pray and for continuing to believe.

I shall make no attempt to disguise or evade the negative implications of this analysis. I believe that prayer only has a future if religious people are prepared to listen very seriously to the atheists' criticisms, in much the same way that the religion of the ancient world was only able to survive in Christianity, by absorbing and making its own the philosophers' criticisms of idolatry and sacrifice. The extent of the atheists' victory is best defined as the end of the God of power who promised privilege to his people. The God of creation and providence not only promised power to his people, he possessed awesome sanctions to enforce obedience. The existence of such a God was the essential precondition of his power. Only a God who existed over and against the world could intervene decisively within it. Because the world existed and was the theatre of his actions, it was necessary that such a God also existed. Such a view of God implied a religious preoccupation with man's weakness. The philosophical objections to such a religion are overwhelming, and are well stated in J. L. Mackie's *The Miracle of Theism*. A certain kind of prayer has no future. As a Christian I am able to listen to the atheists' objections to the God of power, because I believe that they were anticipated in the crucifixion of Jesus. The Gospels try to rehabilitate the God of nature in veiling the sun as Jesus died, and attempt to restore the God of providence in the miraculous reversal of resurrection. Our task as Christians today is to learn to affirm the crucified Christ without resort to those evasions of his story.

In retrospect I believe that the religions of power came to their end at Calvary, but not all religions are of that type. Preoccupied by our weakness we came to God, hungry for power and survival. In weakness and death the man of God came to us, and showed us that our hunger was misplaced. We thought we were desperate because we were weak and dying – in the mirror which the crucifixion holds up to us we lack not power but pity and peace. For us the cross remains a haunting symbol not least because it reflects our ruthless and destructive possibilities. Mankind with nuclear power in its possession no longer kneels to an Almighty God. As we come to recognize our real needs the religions of power must give way to a religion of peace. It is from ourselves and each other that we seek deliverance in prayer; the God of power has been disarmed; he exists only in our phantasies of overwhelming destruction and total security. The God of grace lives in the life of prayer and feeds those who learn to hunger for him.

Method and Sources

Because I believe that prayer throws light not simply on the application of doctrine, but on its origins, I shall devote much attention in the first three chapters to the Psalms. In approaching the doctrines of God's omniscience, providence and creation in this way, I hope to make good the most surprising omission from D. Z. Phillips' work. Understandably he was reluctant to embark on 'a survey of Hebrew and Christian prayers',[9] but in view of the stress which his argument places on the use of the concept of God in prayer, one might have expected much closer attention to the structures of prayers than he provides. It is difficult to avoid the impression that he first formulated his attitudes to confession, thanksgiving, and petitionary prayer and then selected some examples to illustrate his point of view. Instead he quotes at length from other writers on prayer. That helps to place his own somewhat idiosyncratic account of prayer in a wider context, but I doubt whether it is any substitute for a more disciplined attention to the actual language of prayer.

The psalter and other early Jewish sources show very clearly the relation of prayer to doctrine. Moreover, they are among the earliest religious texts we possess. They are far older than any works of more abstract theology, which represent a later rationalization, an attempt to justify beliefs which were first articulated for quite different reasons. In the Psalms we see that primary assertion of belief. We can learn to understand its attractiveness, even when we conclude that it is bankrupt.

The same qualities, which commend the psalter, have suggested the two Christian texts, apart from scripture,[10] to which most frequent reference will be made: the *Confessions* of St Augustine and the *Proslogion* of St Anselm. Both are the work of men whose imagination was steeped in the language of the Psalms. Perhaps for that reason they share a style which holds together prayer to God and rational reflection on that prayer. In many ways the God of power, who dominates the Psalms, continues to live in their minds, but we can also hear a different note, the beginnings of a new theology. For they are on the far side of the cross, and however confused and inconsistent they may be, the God of peace has begun to replace the God of power. In reading Augustine and Anselm in that way I am doubtless reading them in a manner which they would neither have anticipated nor approved. I doubt, however, whether I am doing any more violence to them than they themselves did to the Psalms in their search for the living God:

> How I cried out to you, my God, when I read the Psalms of David, those hymns of faith, those songs of a pious heart in which the spirit of pride can find no place! . . . How they set me on fire with love of you! I was burning to echo them to all the world, if only I could, so that they might vanquish men's pride. And indeed they are sung throughout the world and just as none can hide away from the sun *none can escape your burning heat.*[11]

Part One

THE ABUSE OF GOD:
AN IRRESPONSIBLE EXERCISE
IN POWER

I

The All-Seeing Eye

Almighty God, unto whom all hearts be open, all desires known, and from whom no secrets are hid: Cleanse the thoughts of our hearts by the inspiration of thy Holy Spirit, that we may perfectly love thee, and worthily magnify thy holy Name, through Christ our Lord.

The doctrine of God's omniscience, the belief that God knows all things, may seem at first sight the abstract product of speculative theology. It invites teasing questions about the reality of human freedom, the responsibility for evil, and the significance of prayer. Orthodox theologians are unanimous that omniscience is one of the divine attributes. In philosophical reflection this is usually justified as an inference from the notion of creation. The Creator of the world is inadequately pictured as a blind force, when at least one of his creatures has some knowledge of what he is doing. On such an account the beautiful words of the collect for purity are only the most intimate application of a belief which has its basis in religious cosmology. The reality is rather different.

The Preoccupation with Judgment

Two collections of texts in the Old Testament are much concerned with the question of God's omniscience – Job and the Psalms. Both are dominated, not by the modern philosopher of religion's concern to explain the world, but by a strikingly litigious relationship with God. The judgment of God is being examined throughout the book of Job and supplies the imagined context for perhaps the majority of Psalms. Modern Christians who are the heirs of a medieval terror of hell and an enlightenment distaste for the vindictiveness of such teaching have considerable difficulty in giving any clear account of their beliefs about God's judgment. On the one hand they have been educated not to be too complacent that they will be found among the sheep rather than the goats; on the other hand they are uneasy that God's justice should be marked by a brutality which makes the regime of the Ayatollah appear humane. The thirst for judgment which marks the ancient Jewish scriptures is altogether more urgent and optimistic. In the first place the predominant tone is one of outraged innocence. That is the picture which the prose introduction to the book of Job creates; it is reflected in the astounding self-righteousness of many of the Psalms:

> Hear, Lord, my plea for justice,
>   give my cry a hearing,
>   listen to my prayer,
>   for it is innocent of all deceit.
> Let judgment in my cause issue from thy lips,
> let thine eyes be fixed on justice.
> Thou hast tested my heart and watched me all night long;
> thou hast assayed me and found in me no mind to evil.
> I will not speak of the deeds of men;
>   I have taken good note of all thy sayings.
> I have not strayed from the course of duty;
>   I have followed thy path and never stumbled (Ps. 17.1–5).

To the Christian reader this vehement assertion of innocence sounds extravagant, reared as we are on the doctrine of original sin. For us such language is only appropriate on the lips of Jesus, the sinless, holy one. It can only apply to us insofar as we are found in him. The writers of the Psalms do not share such inhibitions. They look forward to God's judgment with enthusiasm, because they entertain no doubts as to its vindicating outcome.

Such confidence reflects the hopes and disappointments of their experience of human justice. In our society where the expense and delay of litigation are proverbial, most people hope to pass their lives without becoming the objects of the law's attention. In the society which produced the Psalms oppression was immediate and recurrent, justice while distant and spasmodic represented the only hope of relief. The Psalms are full of a lively sense of grievance:

> I have seen violence and strife in the city;
> > day and night they encircle it,
> > all along its walls;
> it is filled with trouble and mischief,
> > alive with rumour and scandal,
> and its public square is never free
> > from violence and spite.
> It was no enemy that taunted me,
> > or I should have avoided him;
> no adversary that treated me with scorn,
> > or I should have kept out of his way.
> It was you, a man of my own sort,
> > my comrade, my own dear friend,
> with whom I kept pleasant company
> > in the house of God (Ps. 55.9–15).

Neighbours are almost always objects of suspicion. At times the alienation verges on paranoia:

> I looked for consolation and received none,
> > for comfort and did not find any.
> They put poison in my food
> > and gave me vinegar when I was thirsty (Ps. 69.20f.).

Not surprisingly such feelings issue in uncontrollable anger; no devotional literature can contain more unbridled vindictiveness:

> May their settlements be desolate,
> and no one living in their tents;
> for they pursue him whom thou hast struck down
> and multiply the torments of those whom thou hast wounded.
> Give them the punishment their sin deserves;

exclude them from thy righteous mercy;
let them be blotted out from the book of life
and not enrolled among the righteous (Ps. 69.25–28).

Just as human justice took place in a court where vindication was
sweet and the fear of shame never absent, so God's justice is the
object of lively social concern and comment:

Let all who seek my life be brought to shame and dismay,
let all who love to hurt me shrink back disgraced;
let those who cry 'Hurrah' at my downfall
turn back at the shame they incur (Ps. 70.2f.).

In neither court can the attention of the judge be taken for granted;
for the judge simply to listen to the plaintiff is a matter of favour, it
demands the most careful solicitation. At times the compassion of
the judge is engaged by the misery of the plaintiff's condition; at
times flattery and hopefulness are combined to secure a decision:

But I am poor and needy;
    O God, hasten to my aid.
Thou art my help, my salvation;
    O Lord, make no delay (Ps. 70.5).

The Psalms which rehearse the majesty of God are perhaps to be
understood as only the obsequious overtures to a judge who must be
properly appreciated if his justice is to be relied upon.

The All-Seeing Judge: Every Action Noted

It is in this context that the omniscience of God is expounded in
scripture. Human judges have only limited knowledge; they have to
rely on human evidence and use their frail wisdom to make sense of
conflicting testimony. God is quite differently placed, literally:

The Lord is in his holy Temple,
The Lord's throne is in heaven,
His eye is upon mankind, he takes their measure at a glance,
The Lord weighs just and unjust,
and hates with all his soul the lover of violence (Ps. 11.4f.).

The extent to which God's omniscience is secured by the elevation of his viewpoint is given vivid expression by Eliphaz, who doubtless spoke for a certain kind of orthodoxy:

> Surely God is at the zenith of the heavens
> and looks down on all the stars, high as they are (Job 22.12).

Characteristically he envisages Job's objection in the same literal terms:

> You say 'What does God know?
> Can he see through thick darkness to judge?
> His eyes cannot pierce the curtain of the clouds
> As he walks to and fro on the vault of heaven' (Job 22.13f.).

What distinguishes the omniscience of God in all these texts is its preoccupation with the behaviour and disposition of men:

> His eyes are on the ways of men,
> and he sees every step they take;
> there is nowhere so dark, so deep in shadow,
> that wrongdoers may hide from him (Job 34.21f.).

In the psalter the denial of God's omniscience is several times put into the mouths of the wicked. Indeed this gives them the confidence to behave as they do. They believe that they have nothing to fear.

> 'What does God know? The Most High neither knows nor cares'
> (Ps. 73.11).

By characterizing such thoughts as the mark of the 'wicked', the reader is effectively forbidden to entertain them.

The All-Seeing Judge: The Secrets of the Heart

Appearances can of course deceive. People say things they do not mean. They disguise their intentions. The possibility of dissimulation haunts every courtroom. So the psalter develops an intimate conception of God's omniscience, which far exceeds mere external behaviour. The divine judge is conceived as having direct access to the consciousness of the suppliant:

Thou hast tested my heart and watched me all night long;
thou hast assayed me and found in me no evil (Ps. 17.3).

The divine judge is sensitive to every nuance of the suppliant's grief:

O Lord, all my lament lies open before thee
and my sighing is no secret to thee (Ps. 38.9).

Indeed at times such knowledge verges on the brink of sympathy:

Thou knowest what reproaches I bear,
all my anguish is seen by thee (Ps. 69.19).

This intimate knowledge of man is usually understood as the prerogative of the Creator:

It is he who fashions the hearts of all men alike,
who discerns all that they do (Ps. 33.15).

Or:

Does he that planted the ear not hear,
he that moulded the eye not see?
Shall not he that instructs the nations correct them?
The teacher of mankind has he no knowledge?
The Lord knows the thoughts of man,
that they are but a puff of wind (Ps. 94.9–11).

It is significant that this teaching which emphasizes the transparency of man's thoughts to God also insists on their insignificance. The consciousness which can be hidden from men and sustains human freedom is thus powerfully disparaged:

As a father has compassion on his children,
so has the Lord compassion on all who fear him.
For he knows how we were made,
He knows full well that we are dust (Ps. 103. 13f.).

The most powerful exposition of this intimate divine knowledge is to be found in Psalm 139. The knowledge is absolute:

Lord, thou hast examined me and knowest me.
Thou knowest all, whether I sit down or rise up;
    thou hast discerned my thoughts from afar.
Thou hast traced my journey and my resting places,
    and art familiar with all my paths.
For there is not a word on my tongue
    but thou, Lord, knowest them all (Ps. 139.1–4).

Significantly the first response is one of flight, a doomed attempt at
self-preservation:

Where can I escape from thy spirit?
    Where can I flee from thy presence?
If I climb up to heaven, thou art there;
if I make my bed in Sheol, again I find thee.
If I take my flight to the frontiers of the morning
    or dwell at the limit of the western sea,
even there thy hand will meet me
    and thy right hand will hold me fast.
If I say, 'Surely darkness will steal over me,
    night will close around me',
darkness is no darkness for thee
    and night is luminous as day;
    to thee both dark and light are one (Ps. 139.7–12).

The omniscience of God is experienced at first as claustraphobic
constraint. The soul is trapped in conditions curiously prophetic of
the modern floodlit concentration camp. It is indeed in the total
elimination of concealing darkness that the attitude of the psalmist is
transformed. In one of those reversals with which the technique of
brainwashing has made us so familiar, what he at first feared, he now
affirms. The divine omniscience ceases to be a threat and becomes
the object of wonder and praise. In attributing to God his formation
in the womb, the psalmist gives God a knowledge which transcends
even the maternal:

Thou it was who didst fashion my inward parts;
thou didst knit me together in my mother's womb.
I will praise thee, for thou dost fill me with awe;
wonderful thou art, and wonderful thy works.

Thou knowest me through and through:
  my body is no mystery to thee,
how I was secretly kneaded into shape
  and patterned in the depths of the earth.
Thou didst see my limbs unformed in the womb,
  and in thy book they are all recorded;
  day by day they were fashioned,
  not one of them was late in growing.
How deep I find thy thoughts, O God,
  how inexhaustible their themes!
Can I count them? They outnumber the grains of the sand;
to finish the count, my years must equal thine (Ps. 139.13–18).

To the modern reader it is something of a surprise to turn from such rhapsody to a vehement call for vengeance. Modern liturgical use prefers to stop at verse 18, but what follows is no extraneous insertion. The total transparency of the innocent and aggrieved party to the knowledge of God necessarily commits the Almighty to his cause. My enemies and God's become identical:

O God, if only thou wouldst slay the wicked!
If those men of blood would but leave me in peace –
those who provoke thee with deliberate evil
  and rise in vicious rebellion against thee!
How I hate them, O Lord, that hate thee!
I am cut to the quick when they oppose thee;
I hate them with undying hatred;
  I hold them all my enemies (Ps. 139.19–22).

The Attitude of the Divine Judge

In the psalter the attitude towards the divine judge is almost invariably optimistic. It may contain moments of self-abasement, but there is an underlying confidence in the God who is being invoked:

Be gracious to me, O God, in thy true love;
in the fullness of thy mercy blot out my misdeeds (Ps. 51.1).

However, once such intimate knowledge and brutal sanctions had been attributed to God, his good favour became an object of increasing anxiety. The psalmist is only happy to equip God with a horrifying array of punishments, because he is confident that they will apply to other people:

> When judgment is given, that rascal will be exposed
>   and his follies accounted a sin.
> May his days be few;
>   may his hoarded wealth fall to another!
> May his children be fatherless,
>   his wife a widow!
> May his children be vagabonds and beggars,
>   driven from their homes!
> May the money-lender distrain on all his goods
>   and strangers seize his earnings!
> May none remain loyal to him,
>   and none have mercy on his fatherless children!
> May his line be doomed to extinction,
>   may their name be wiped out within a generation!
> May the sins of his forefathers be remembered
>   and his mother's wickedness never be wiped out!
> May they remain on record before the Lord,
>   but may he extinguish their name from the earth!
> (Ps. 109.7–15)

The attitude of Job, however, is far more equivocal: the collusion between God and his prosecutor Satan in the prose introduction is faithfully reflected in the exacting and almost malignant nature of the divine attention. It is not simply that like the psalmist he can imagine God luring the wicked to their ruin:

> He lulls them into security and confidence;
> but his eyes are fixed on their ways (Job 24.23).

Job even suspects the intention which underlies God's creation. He never questions the power of the Creator; he is uncertain of his goodwill:

> Thy hands gave me shape and made me;
> and dost thou at once turn and destroy me? (Job 10.8)

In the psalter such a question would be entirely rhetorical; the creature has a natural claim on the mercy and care of his maker. Job by contrast conceives the sovereignty of God in much more ambiguous terms. He can articulate the position of a creature with the same apparent piety as the psalmist:

> Thou hast given me life and continuing favour,
> and thy providence has watched over my spirit (Job 10.12).

In the psalter such language would lead to an expression of trust, made perhaps more urgent by the description of present misery. In Job it only makes the depth of his suspicion more devastating:

> Yet this was the secret purpose of thy heart,
> and I know that this was thy intent:
> that, if I sinned, thou wouldst be watching me
> and wouldst not acquit me of my guilt (Job 10.13f.).

The omniscience of God is in no way denied, but it has ceased to be the property of the vindicating judge; it has become the sinister instrument of a remorseless prosecutor:

> Thou dost count every step I take,
> watching all my course.
> Every offence of mine is stored in thy bag;
> thou dost keep my iniquity under seal (Job 14.16f.).

It is not surprising that there are times when Job seeks to escape from such scrutiny. Man's condition is such that it would be better for him to be without such a God:

> The days of his life are determined,
> and the number of his months is known to thee;
> thou hast laid down a limit, which he cannot pass.
> Look away from him therefore and leave him alone
> counting the hours day by day like a hired labourer (Job 14.5f.).

The Disparity between the Judge and his Suppliants

In these texts the omniscience of God is one of his attributes which ensures that the relationship between God and man is non-reciprocal. His knowledge enables him to control the whole judicial proceeding:

> The day of reckoning is no secret to the Almighty,
> though those who know him have no hint of its date (Job 24.1).

Most significantly for us God knows the length of our lives. The discrepancy is most powerfully expressed in Psalm 39:

> Lord, let me know my end
> and the number of my days;
> tell me how short my life must be.
> I know thou hast made my days a mere span long,
> and my whole life is nothing in thy sight.
> Man, though he stands upright, is but a puff of wind,
> he moves like a phantom;
> the riches he piles up are no more than vapour,
> he does not know who will enjoy them (Ps. 39.4–6).

The contrast between the omniscience of God and the limited and gloomy knowledge of man is abrupt, but this is not merely a moving meditation on mortality. Christians with their later beliefs about the after-life can only be surprised that such a passage does not prepare for a proclamation of resurrection. Instead we are back in the litigious world of the courtroom. The frailty of man is only an argument to enlist the judge's intervention and mitigation:

> And now, Lord, what do I wait for?
> My hope is in thee.
> Deliver me from all who do me wrong,
> and make me no longer the butt of fools.
> I am dumb, I will not open my mouth,
> because it is thy doing.
> Plague me no more;
> I am exhausted by thy blows (Ps. 39.7–10).

The Omniscience of God in Religious Metaphysics

The omniscience of God as it is elaborated in the Book of Job and the Psalms is a keynote of the portrayal of Yahweh throughout the

Old Testament. When Adam and Eve eat the forbidden fruit, when
Cain slays Abel, God's knowledge is taken for granted, and issues in
their speedy punishment. Because most modern readers inherit at
least something of the achievement of medieval natural theology, we
tend to equate the omniscience of God in scripture with the
omniscience of God as it was later understood as a metaphysical
attribute of God the Creator. It is true that on some occasions God's
omniscience was grounded in that belief (e.g. Ps. 94.9–11), but the
interest of scripture is not in any explanatory account of creation.
That seems quite secondary to its interest in divine judgment. If we
tend to discount the discrepancy as insignificant, that is because we
possess assumptions and arguments which assist that process. We
tend to argue that God exists, he is omnipotent and omniscient, and
that those attributes were always implicit in the concept of God,
because they were grounded in the reality of God. It may be that in
early Jewish religion certain aspects of his nature received an
attention, which seems to us rather curious, but that is merely to be
explained by their particular situation. With time and reflection later
philosophical theologians were able to give these notions a clearer
expression and a more all-embracing justification. The kind of
analogy behind all such thinking is the belief that God exists rather
like an undiscovered continent. The accounts of the first explorers
may be confused and partial in their insights. Later acquaintance
enables us to make sense of their anticipations.

If, however, we suppose that such a God may not exist, we see the
position very differently. As long as such a God is supposed to exist
we can understand previous accounts, however partial or inadequate,
as responses to that reality. They are like the early maps of
America or Australia, where the gaps may be made up by
imagination, but where the subsequently charted continent vindicates
some features and exposes others as fanciful. On such a view
we might in this instance choose to affirm the account of God's
omniscience as it is found in Psalm 139, based on the Creator's
knowledge of his creature, while being rather less committed to the
God's eye-view found in the speech of Eliphaz. Belief in the
existence of such a God functions therefore as a powerful means of
reconciling and making sense of divergent accounts of his attributes.
It is very different if we suppose that such a God does not exist. If the

concept of God does not refer to a reality which determines its content, but is a construction of the human imagination, then the position is transformed. In the first place, we are freed to accept that human beings may have radically different conceptions of God, and that this may be the case not only between different religions, but within the same religion in different contexts and at different times. The element of identity can no longer be supplied by a shared reference, it can only be achieved by shared human traditions. Moreover, historical traditions only work one way. In the twentieth century my conception of God may be shaped by that of Jesus, but Jesus' conception of God cannot have been shaped by mine. An imaginative construction has no reality before it has been imagined. So for instance the metaphysical God of the high middle ages literally did not exist in Old Testament times, and we should be extremely wary of reading him back, so to say, as the constraining or originative power behind the Old Testament texts.

It is one of the great merits of Emil Brunner's theology that he is so sensitive to the radically different concept of omniscience in the Bible and in later metaphysical theology:

The Biblical testimony to revelation shows that this natural, 'objective' ability to 'know everything' is not the actual subject of this article of faith. Here, too, where the Knowledge of God is mentioned . . . everything is viewed in the closest connexion with His aim in revelation and in redemption. Certainly, God knows everything that happens in the world of Nature – He knows 'the ordinances of the heavens' (Job 38.33); He knows the 'rising and the going down of the sun' (Ps. 104.19); He knows 'the balancings of the clouds' (Job 37.16); – but all this is not at the centre of the Biblical point of view, but at the circumference; at the centre there stands all that refers to the realization of His purpose for the Kingdom. God's knowledge is not objective and impersonal but 'interested'.[1]

I do not share the biblical positivism with which he later concludes that 'the Biblical idea of an Attribute scatters all rational and metaphysical definitions to the four winds like chaff'.[2] Nevertheless he has performed a most valuable service in underlining the

difference between biblical conceptions and those of later philosophical religion.

All too easily a process of unconscious assimilation takes place,
which conceals from us the very distinctive form of the biblical
attributes. What misleads Brunner is that he uses his insight for
undeclared apologetic purposes. Underlying his whole dogmatic
work is the suspicion that metaphysics has collapsed, and the hope
that nevertheless biblical ideas can emerge unscathed. He does not
appreciate that although metaphysical conceptions of God are not to
be equated with biblical ones, they are nevertheless a response to
them – a subsequent rationalization with an apologetic purpose.
Medieval schoolmen constructed a metaphysical theology not to
create a new religion, but in an attempt to conserve an old one with
new methods. It was precisely the incoherences in the biblical ideas
which drove them to elaborate their theology. If their rationalization
no longer convinces, biblical ideas cannot be rehabilitated by mere
reassertion. Only a more convincing rationale can save them.

It is not the intention of this book to dwell on the inherent
contradictions in the traditional metaphysical account of God's
attributes. To conduct the debate at that level prevents one from
perceiving how the belief actually functions in religion and so
understanding its origin. However, it may be worthwhile to remind
the reader of the difficulties of the traditional account of that belief,
in the words of the most influential of all modern theologians:

> Religion has no hesitation in attributing to God himself the nobler
> senses: God sees and hears all things. But the divine omniscience
> is a power of knowing through the senses while yet the necessary
> quality, the essential determination of actual knowledge through
> the senses is denied to it. My senses present sensible objects to me
> only separately and in succession; but God sees all sensible things
> at once, all locality in an unlocal manner, all temporal things in an
> untemporal manner, all objects of sense in an unsensational
> manner. That is to say: I extend the horizon of my senses by the
> imagination; I form to myself a confused conception of the whole
> of things; and this conception, which exalts me above the limited
> standpoint of the senses, and therefore affects me agreeably, I
> posit as a divine reality. I feel the fact that my knowledge is tied to a

local standpoint, to sensational experience as a limitation; what I feel as a limitation I do away in my imagination, which furnishes free space for the play of my feelings. This negativing of limits by the imagination is the positing of omniscience as a divine power and quality. But at the same time there is only a *quantitative* distinction between omniscience and my knowledge; the *quality* of the knowledge is the same.[3]

It is not therefore surprising that more recent theologians have approached the subject of God's omniscience with a certain caution. Tillich begins by totally repudiating the traditional conception:

Omniscience is not the faculty of a highest being who is supposed to know all objects, past, present, and future, and, beyond this, everything that might have happened if what has happened had not happened. The absurdity of such an image is due to the impossibility of subsuming God under the subject-object scheme, although this structure is grounded in the divine life.[4]

He completes this breathtaking piece of theological effrontery by asking us to equate the doctrine of omniscience with the doctrine that God is 'present spiritually'. As so often with Tillich he evades engaging with the difficulties of traditional theology by proclaiming its absurdity, while nevertheless continuing to use its language in a quite different sense. Even so self-consciously orthodox a theologian as Professor Keith Ward is forced to admit a surprising degree of agnosticism:

(God) must be conceived as all-knowing and all-powerful to enable us to accept the hope for a moral fulfilment of reality; but in saying these things we in no way increase our theoretical knowledge – i.e. we do not understand what God's 'knowledge' or 'causality' is like.[5]

Professor Ward, as befits a philosopher, chooses his words with care; he speaks of us being enabled 'to accept the hope for a moral fulfilment of reality'. It seems unnecessarily churlish even to question whether we want such a hope. The use of the gentle word 'enable' is particularly seductive. One might never guess that morality is usually imposed, and is often the instrument by which one human being controls another.

My starting point is that the traditional concept of divine omniscience as elaborated by the schoolmen of the high middle ages is deeply flawed. In part this is a matter of internal contradiction, which has led modern theologians to be extremely wary of the doctrine; and even a sympathetic philosopher like F. R. Tennant has to modify the doctrine and its implications considerably in order to defend it.[6] The other weakness relates to the grounds for believing that an omniscient God exists; at the very least it is difficult to believe that the authors of Job or the Psalms could have given any more satisfactory an answer to that problem than we can. It is not likely to be the case that they possessed a coherent and philosophically well-grounded concept of God's omniscience which they were simply applying to their particular situation. The muddles which mark later thought are already present in theirs. They made very powerful assertions about the omniscience of God, but nowhere felt it necessary to defend them.

The Function of Omniscience in the Early Accounts of God

We cannot therefore avoid wondering whether the omniscient God exists, and once we ask that question the biblical examples of the belief begin to look very different. If God does not exist, then the varied talk of God's omniscience cannot be understood simply as differing if inadequate responses to the reality of God. Instead the picture of an omniscient God must be the work of human imagination, a human construction for which those who framed it are responsible. It is not simply a mistake. There is enough contrary evidence to have ensured that it was long ago discarded, if it was simply a mistaken perception or inference. Human beings have clung to God because he was useful to them, or at least to some of them. That is why it is so important to study carefully the functions of the belief in early texts like Job and the Psalms. For on this account those functions are not secondary but primary. They reveal the human intentions which led to the fabrication and which sustain it. It is no accident that the belief emerges before any attempt at rational justification. In the Psalms we see not the application, but the origin of the belief. Very simply the assertion is made, not because men knew that it was true, but because they sensed that it was useful.

At this stage a parallel in imaginative literature may be helpful. George Orwell in his novel, *Nineteen Eighty-Four*, portrays a nightmare of totalitarian control. A crucial part of that control is the attempt to achieve at least the semblance of an omniscient ruler. The propaganda is unremitting:

> On each landing, opposite the lift shaft, the poster with the enormous face gazed from the wall. It was one of those pictures which are so contrived that the eyes follow you about when you move. BIG BROTHER IS WATCHING YOU, the caption beneath it ran.[7]

The main instrument of this omniscience was the two-way tele-screen:

> Behind Winston's back the voice from the telescreen was still babbling away about pig-iron and the overfulfilment of the Ninth Three-Year Plan. The telescreen received and transmitted simultaneously. Any sound that Winston made, above the level of a very low whisper, would be picked up by it; moreover, so long as he remained within the field of vision which the metal plaque commanded, he could be seen as well as heard. There was of course no way of knowing whether you were being watched at any given moment. How often, or on what system, the Thought Police plugged in on any individual wire was guesswork. It was even conceivable that they watched everybody all the time. But at any rate they could plug in your wire whenever they wanted to. You had to live – did live, from habit that became instinct – in the assumption that every sound you made was overheard, and, except in darkness, every movement scrutinized.[8]

The figure of Big Brother is obviously something of a parody of the traditional God. It is revealing, however, that even in this phantasy of authoritarian power, Big Brother's omniscience, dependent as it is on propaganda and technology, is relatively limited. Darkness checks the mechanical vision. Places may exist where there are no transmitters. Fundamentally such supervision only monitors external behaviour. The consciousness of human beings, while not immune from the effect of such scrutiny, nevertheless remains hidden. It is also worth noting that Orwell does not think that continuous observation is necessary to ensure fairly effective control. It was enough that there was 'no way of knowing whether you were being watched at any given moment'.

This literary parallel enables us to appreciate the subtlety and power of the imaginative construction of the omniscient God. Orwell's leadership has available to it many of the resources of modern technology. The early religious leaders of mankind did not have such instruments to hand. Instead they appealed to the imagination and sustained their message by all the means of propaganda that were available to them: art, architecture, ritual, music and literature. As we have seen, they were able to abolish the security of privacy by suggesting that every thought and feeling was known to God. Consciousness was no longer concealed but transparent. Whereas technology could only create inescapable uncertainty, whoever believed in the omniscient God acquired the conviction that his every thought was known. Inevitably that was a powerful inducement to obedience to God, and the control of men with whom God was identified. The placing of the collect for purity in the Book of Common Prayer service of Holy Communion is well judged. The worshipper is reminded first of a God 'unto whom all hearts be open, all desires known, and from whom no secrets are hid'. Immediately there follows a rehearsal of that God's commandments. The worshipper has every incentive to utter a heart-felt, 'Lord, have mercy upon us.'

The Human Use of God's Omniscience

Jews, Christians and Muslims are sometimes referred to as the people of the book, but it is a mark of all religions in literate societies that they are highly literary phenomena. One of the reasons for this is that the text functions in a way which resembles the mask in less sophisticated cultures. It conceals the agent, and the philosophers of religion have usually been duped by this procedure. The survival of the text encourages them to concentrate on the content of what is said and believed, without asking who is speaking and why. Orwell conceives behind his apparatus of control a vast bureaucracy. The people associated with our scriptures are perhaps more varied: early Jewish priests and prophets, scribes and rabbis, Christian martyrs, feudal bishops, anxious magistrates, preaching clergy, modern school masters. Until the advent of printing the scriptures were the almost exclusive possession of a tiny elite, who justified and modelled their leadership on whatever selective use of the texts suited their purpose. The users of scripture have been varied, but throughout the divine judge with his ever open eye has been in collusion with some system of human control.

The religious texts demand certain forms of behaviour. The Psalms are only an appendix to the Law. The religious leadership gains its status and prestige from effectively enforcing that behaviour. Always the position of the religious leader is ambiguous. In part he is an example, a fellow subject, a model of obedience; but the obedience he exemplifies, he also commands. In our secularized society that command may now be very weak, but that simply reflects a crisis of religious leadership. Wherever religious leadership is effective, it has the confidence not simply to commend, but to command. The other respect in which the religious leader occupies a curious position is in the matter of jurisdiction. He proclaims a God, who knows all things, and judges behaviour in terms of the standards that he has set, and which the religious leader merely passes on. Nevertheless, few religious leaders are content to leave the control of behaviour entirely in God's hands. Human discipline seems always to accompany the divine. In secular societies where civil law protects most people from such interference, religious leaders are reduced to asserting themselves largely in relation to their clergy. It is the mark of religious societies that the control endeavours to be all-embracing.

In one respect, however, the parallel of *Nineteen Eighty-Four* is deeply misleading. Big Brother is a deliberately fabricated apparatus of control. The manipulation may be cynical but it is conscious. Religious leadership is in an altogether more complicated situation. It possesses a rhetoric which not only conceals motivation from its subjects, but to a considerable extent conceals from the leadership its own motivations. Religious leaders not only demand to be called servants, they see themselves as servants. In religion responsibility always lies elsewhere. Initiative is with God; the prophet is merely one whom God calls. The implication is: Don't blame me, blame God (if you dare). It is true that there are considerable advantages from occupying such a position, otherwise no one would become a clergyman. But the effective religious leader is marked by the extent to which he exemplifies the beliefs he commends. He does not consciously exploit the system of beliefs in which he lives. He commits himself to them, and finds that they sustain him. His attention like that of his followers is directed away from himself towards God. It doubtless strengthens his picture of God that he finds himself clothed and fed, paid and housed, obeyed and honoured, but he is always able to repress the consciousness of privilege. In this way religious leadership not only defuses conflict, it also overcomes the guilt and many of the anxieties which surround secular leadership. Because that confidence is convenient, that is no reason to doubt its reality. The antiquity, the inherited character of so much religious organization, also means that it is not properly understood as cold hearted deceit. Religious leaders are usually neither inventive nor deliberate. Instead they assent and commit themselves to a structure which pre-exists them. As much as the most credulous of their followers, they are impressed by its apparent objectivity. The difference between priest and layman is not one of credulity. It is rather that one is persuaded to pay tithe, and the other is content to receive it; but both perceive the exchange as entirely natural.

We are now in a position to understand the function of the doctrine of the omniscience of God in the system of religious control. It did not originate as the result of philosophical speculation, it was asserted in relation to a particular code of law, attributed to God while propagated by men. In the first place, because God sees every action, punishment is inescapable. It may be delayed to bring out the worst in the sinner, or to provide an opportunity for change. It may be averted by subsequent behaviour or by a plea for mercy, but unlike human systems of justice it is utterly reliable. Human systems of justice have to be policed to be effective and the police have to be incorruptible. Moreover, there are never enough police to be entirely effective. Much crime goes unpunished by human systems of retribution, and such evasions of penalty discredit and so weaken the entire system. The structure of religious control can afford to be much more economical in its means of enforcement: once the wrong-doer is convinced that every action is seen by God, he can never be certain that he has 'got away with it'. To believe in an omniscient God is inevitably to carry round with one a burden of anxiety and unexpiated guilt. Any subsequent disaster, no matter how long delayed, can then be interpreted as deserved retribution. This is not to say that human punishment has no place in such a system: it has both an exemplary and a disinfecting role. God may use it as an instrument of his righteousness, but he is in no way dependent on it. Moreover the human contribution is thus marked by tenderness. Although it may seem brutal, its savage penalties are a warning to others; it is a far worse thing to have to do with God. If stern measures have sometimes to be taken, that is not to maintain the prestige of the system: God will look after that. However, the misdeeds of any member of the community, if they are not publicly repudiated by punishment, may render the entire community liable to penalty. Religious systems of justice are marked by the quality, 'more in sorrow than in anger'. Anger belongs to God. His human representatives merely act in sorrow. The pathos of this situation is given eloquent expression in the letter to the Hebrews:

> For we know who it is that has said, 'Justice is mine: I will repay'; and again, 'The Lord will judge his people'. It is a terrible thing to fall into the hands of the living God (10.30f.).

By contrast the writer of the letter appears a mild and gentle person.

The Credibility of the Divine Judge

The extension of the range of God's knowledge from action to consciousness gives religious control opportunities which are not open to any other human system. Once we believe that our minds are transparent to our judge, we have every incentive to root out even the thought of disobedience. In the control of action, it is always possible that those who conform externally are nursing resentment and disaffection. Where the disposition is also examined the person can only secure his innocence by the constant repression of dissent. It is the beauty and economy of this system that it needs no police at all:

every person has to police his own thoughts. The potential rebel can only obtain security if he becomes a perpetual spy, monitoring and suppressing every wayward thought and feeling. It also makes the entire system much more difficult to discredit.

We only know the external actions of other people: we may guess their motives, but God knows them with more clarity than we know ourselves. If therefore his dealings do not always seem to be marked by justice, that is only because we judge by externals, while he knows the heart. Before we rail against the justice of God, we do well to remember that he knows other people far better than we do. While other human systems of justice often make mistakes, releasing the guilty and punishing the innocent, in God's justice all suffering is the consequence of guilt. In scripture this is maintained in a variety of ways. Most simple is the insistence that the unlucky person is always guilty. That is why Job is urged by his friends to more self-scrutiny, and eventually concedes to God what he refused to concede to them. The only way in which purely innocent suffering can be admitted is as vicarious. So in the case of the servant of God in Second Isaiah, God is pleased to accept his suffering in lieu of ours:

> Yet on himself he bore our sufferings,
>   our torments he endured,
> while we counted him smitten by God,
>   struck down by disease and misery;
> but he was pierced for our transgressions,
>   tortured for our iniquities;
> the chastisement he bore is health for us
>   and by his scourging we are healed.
> We had all strayed like sheep,
> each of us had gone his own way;
> but the Lord laid upon him
>   the guilt of us all (Isa. 53.4–5).

The atoning suffering of the innocent Christ is an integral part of the grammar of divine justice. In that way innocent suffering, which would otherwise discredit the system, becomes the highest mark of God's mercy and kindness.

The extension of God's scrutiny from behaviour to consciousness has furthermore the effect of making innocence impossible. The self-righteous professions of innocence, which the psalter contains, relate to a religious view which confines God's interest to behaviour. Once righteousness becomes a matter of disposition, the religious person can never be certain how he stands with God. There is always the suspicion that he suffers the temptations of imagination, because he is in secret collusion with them, however much he may consciously resist them. This produces the doctrine of universal sin:

Bring not thy servant to trial before thee;
against thee no man on earth can be right (Ps. 143.2).

The elaboration of a doctrine of original sin may be a particularly Christian development: it goes hand in hand with the Christian ethical preoccupation with intention. It would seem, however, that some version of universal sin is necessary if belief in divine justice is to be sustained. It is no accident that as modern Christians have become less preoccupied by divine judgment, their theology has met with insoluble problems of theodicy.

The Beneficiaries of God's Omniscience

It is easy to see that once the notion of an omniscient God became embedded in the mind it was extremely difficult to remove. Its omniscient character deters the sacrilege of scepticism. We may wonder how it was ever plausible. In addition to the devices of propaganda already aluded to, it must be remembered that at least in part this omniscience seemed to be delegated. Total delegation was not to be expected, but God's representatives did seem to possess some access to the omniscience with which they credited him. God's prophets, like God himself, possessed an uncanny knowledge of guilty action. Nathan is quite undeceived by all the precautions that David takes to hide his responsibility for the death of Uriah the Hittite (II Sam. 11 and 12). When Elijah goes to rebuke Ahab, he acts on information, which God has given him, and so cuts through the misleading machinations of Jezebel:

Then the word of the Lord came to Elijah the Tishbite: 'Go down
at once to Ahab king of Israel, who is in Samaria; you will find him
in Naboth's vineyard, where he has gone to take possession. Say to
him, "This is the word of the Lord: Have you killed your man, and
taken his land as well?" Say to him, "This is the word of the Lord:
Where dogs licked the blood of Naboth, there dogs shall lick your
blood"' (I Kings 21.17–19).

God tells Elijah both of the crime and where the criminal is to be
found. Equally when Gehazi lies to Elisha he discovers that the
prophet's vision is no more limited by place than God's:

Elisha said, 'Where have you been, Gehazi?' 'Nowhere', said
Gehazi. But he said to him, 'Was I not with you in spirit when the
man turned back from his chariot to meet you? Is it not true that
you have the money? You may buy gardens with it, and olive-trees
and vineyards, sheep and oxen, slaves and slave-girls; but the
disease of Naaman will fasten on you and on your descendants for
ever.' Gehazi left his presence, his skin diseased, white as snow (II
Kings 5.25–27).

Such stories represent the most effective propaganda: in dealing
with God's representatives one could never be sure that God
would not give to them something of his knowledge – and his
power.

It is entirely consistent with such a view that the most detailed
account of God's foreknowledge comes in the prophetic literature.
The knowledge of the future attributed to God is claimed by his
prophets; not surprisingly the person who makes the attribution also
claims to be the beneficiary:

Thus says the Lord, Israel's King,
the Lord of Hosts, his ransomer:
I am the first and I am the last,
    and there is no god but me.
Who is like me? Let him stand up,
let him declare himself and speak and show me his evidence,
let him announce beforehand things to come,
let him declare what is yet to happen.

> Take heart, do not be afraid.
> Did I not foretell this long ago?
> I declared it, and you are my witnesses (Isa. 44.6ff.).

The prestige of God and the prestige of the prophet stem alike from the foreknowledge that they share. It is this which establishes the superiority of Yahweh over the empty claims of the idols; it also inculcates a healthy respect for his prophets.

The human intuition of motive, which provides the analogy for God's knowledge of our hearts is not explicitly claimed in the Old Testament. The nearest example is the ability of Daniel to tell Nebuchadnezzar the content of his dream:

> The secret about which your majesty inquires no wise man, exorcist, magician or diviner can disclose to you. But there is in heaven a god who reveals secrets, and he has told King Nebuchadnezzar what is to be at the end of this age. This is the dream and these the visions that came into your head . . . This secret has been revealed to me not because I am wise beyond all living men, but because your majesty is to know the interpretation and understand the thoughts which have entered your mind (Dan. 2.27–30).

In the New Testament, however, it is precisely this kind of omniscience which is frequently claimed for Jesus. The writers of the Gospels are not concerned to claim for him the infallibility of an encyclopaedia, but a very specific form of omniscience. He is able to divine the thoughts of his enemies:

> Now there were some lawyers sitting there and they thought to themselves, 'Why does the fellow talk like that? This is blasphemy! Who but God alone can forgive sins?' Jesus knew in his own mind that this was what they were thinking (Mark 2.6ff.).

When the disciples quarrel, Jesus may ask about the cause; but when they are silent, he makes it plain that he knows the reason (Mark 9.33ff.). The treachery of Judas is transparent to Jesus, and he knows the cowardice of Peter, better than Peter knows himself. The claim is put most succinctly in St John's Gospel:

He knew men so well, all of them, that he needed no evidence from others about a man, for he himself could tell what was in a man (John 2.25).

The Omniscience of God and the Evasion of Responsibility

The belief in divine omniscience was therefore an integral part of a system of religious control and leadership. There remains one further characteristic contribution of the doctrine which has not been properly considered: the question of responsibility. Secular systems of control and leadership always involve an exchange of responsibility and accountability in return for power. In the most personal systems the will of the individual can be sufficient reason. 'Because I say so', the exasperated parent tells the erring child. In saying this the parent not only tries to exact obedience; he lays himself open to blame, if the outcome is unfortunate. As much of the art of leadership involves asserting control while evading blame, most political structures operate on a more complicated and devious model. The first person plural is particularly popular for this purpose. By including the audience the politician spreads the responsibility should things go ill. Moreover, in so far as it reflects a genuinely shared leadership, in the event of disaster, the leaders can always find among themselves a scape-goat who absolves the rest of blame. In the event of disaster every leader will hope to blame his followers. In his last bunker Hitler dwelt on the extent to which the German people had failed him. The verb of government is therefore highly irregular: I have my way, we share responsibility , you take the blame.

Religious control is quite different. The religious leaders place all positive responsibility on God. God is King, God is the judge: all men are only his servants. God takes responsibility for his commands: his prophets have no responsibility for the content of their message: all that is asked of them is that they faithfully and truthfully convey the message which God has entrusted to them. God takes full responsibility both for his blessings and his judgments. The faithful prophet has no responsibility for them: if disaster follows it can only be because of the people's disobedience. In religious systems of control therefore the only human initiative and responsibility which are allowed are sin and guilt. For these reasons it is extremely difficult to discredit. A secular leader can be discredited by his failures. Disasters to the religious mind are only a sign of divine wrath: they point to unrepented or undiscovered sin. Just because religious structures are so difficult to discredit, they are also singularly prone to be cruel. Harsh discrimination and savage penalties are not something for which the religious person has to accept any responsibility. The Jew refusing to countenance inter-marriage with Gentiles, the Muslim using punishments of amputation, Protestants stigmatizing Roman Catholics, the Roman Catholic demanding a Roman upbringing for the children of mixed marriages, are in the words with which Nazi Germans have made us so familiar, 'only obeying orders' – in their case the orders not of men, but of God.

Once of course we question the existence of that God who is purported to issue such instructions, the whole procedure looks somewhat disreputable. The omniscience of God is one of the means by which men are taught to see themselves as having an all-demanding non-reciprocal obligation to God. The propaganda of religion in insisting on our responsibility to God distracts attention from the question as to whether anybody is responsible for God. This is not of course deliberate deception, but it is very useful nevertheless. It is the religious equivalent of President Kennedy's 'Ask not what your country can do for you. Ask, what can you do for your country?' (A singularly impertinent comment from a newly elected democratic leader: many found their answer in Vietnam.) The religious leader declines any responsibility and attributes all to God. In reality he contributes far more than he realizes or acknowledges to that God. His assent, his interpretation of the religious tradition, is what gives that God vitality. He tells himself of course that he believes and behaves as he does because God exists. It is the existence of God, which absolves him of responsibility. If such a God does not exist, then it is the religious leaders who have to accept full responsibility for the conflicts they create in his name. As a matter of fact it is the leaders of religions who elaborate beliefs about God and claim to know his will. By inculcating the most widespread guilt and responsibility towards God, they inhibit the perception that their will and God's will may have a rather different relationship to each other than they claim.

2

The Lord of History

O God, whose never-failing providence ordereth all things both
in heaven and earth: We humbly beseech thee to put away from us
all hurtful things, and to give us those things which be profitable
for us; through Jesus Christ our Lord.

In the first chapter I argued that the doctrine of God's omniscience,
as developed by the later Christian theologians is only a subsequent
metaphysical rationale for beliefs which had a quite different origin
and justification. The portrayal of God, who knows every action,
thought and feeling, and the successful implanting of that belief in
the minds of religious people, formed part of a subtle and successful
system of religious leadership and control. Just as the doctrine of
omniscience must primarily be understood in that context, so the
doctrine of divine providence plays an essential part in the same
system. While the doctrine of omniscience secured the most
intimate sense of accountability, the doctrine of providence provided
the sanctions of reward and punishment on which the system
depended. Threats and promises are essential to any system of
control, and of all the systems devised by men that of religious
control has always been the most pervasive, embracing the whole of
society and every facet of individual behaviour and disposition.

The Doctrine of Providence Prior to that of Creation

Such an approach to the doctrine of divine providence helps to
make sense of what is otherwise a rather puzzling feature of the
belief as it is first found in scripture. Christian creeds with their

starting point in the doctrine of creation, and classical metaphysical theology arguing from the existence of the world to the existence of a Creator, both conceived the doctrine of God as having its corrollary in the doctrine of creation. It is true that the book of Genesis begins with accounts of creation, and that references to God's creative activity recur in some of the Old Testament books. Detailed attention to that will be given in the following chapter. Here it will suffice to point out the discrepancy between the religion of the Bible and later speculative theology. Once again Emil Brunner is perceptive:

> To know the Creator thus, means to know, first and foremost, that God, because He is Sovereign Lord, is Creator. Thus from the outset this idea of Creation is clearly distinguished from all the various theories about the way in which the world came into existence. Before Israel knew Yahweh as *Creator*, it knew Him as *Lord*. It is not forbidden, and indeed it is inevitable, that, as human beings, on the basis of our knowledge of the world, we must ask questions about its origin, and certainly it is not unimportant that to-day leading physicists once more point to a divine reason as the basis of the world which they discover through science. But this has a very remote and indirect relation to the Christian doctrine of Creation . . . This truth comes to man as a personal summons; it is not a truth which is the fruit of reflection; hence it is truth which, from the very outset, makes me directly responsible.[1]

I do not share Brunner's confidence in a truth which is not the fruit of reflection, but I believe he is correct in pointing out that the biblical doctrine of creation is quite different from what we often imagine.

Interest in God the creator was a relatively late development within Judaism. Jews came to place great emphasis on God's creation, but it does not seem to have been at the origin of their faith. Indeed it appears to have been the part of their religion where they were most indebted to surrounding cultures. So while we tend to come to belief in God through being persuaded of the cogency of belief in creation, and subsequently acquire some convictions about God's providence, their development was the reverse. They began with very strong beliefs in God's intervention and leadership on their behalf, and slowly came to see that this demanded an account of his creation of the world. If their God had been primarily an explanatory concept, such a procedure would be incomprehensible, but once we see that the primary function of their God was political, in the sense of legitimating and effecting control, the development of their beliefs in that order makes sense. In this respect they follow an alternative natural theology, which is given succinct expression in the letter to the Hebrews:

> Anyone who comes to God must believe that he exists and that he rewards those who search for him (Heb. 11.6).

Of course where there is reward there is also punishment. So the mark of scriptural religion is primarily the rehearsal of threats and promises in the name of God, who has governed history in the past, and will do so in the future. It is elaborated in both collective and individual terms.

The Court of the Divine King

It is entirely consistent therefore that the dominant image of God throughout scripture is that of King, not Creator. Many of the psalms are devoted to proclaiming the royal sovereignty of God:

> The Lord has established his throne in heaven,
>   his kingly power over the whole world.
> Bless the Lord, all his angels,
>   creatures of might who do his bidding.
> Bless the Lord, all his hosts,
>   his ministers who serve his will.
> Bless the Lord, all created things,
>   in every place where he has dominion (Ps. 103.19–22).

The divine court is an idealized version of a human palace. The king is surrounded by his obedient and dutiful servants who are the agents of his power. While human courts are rent by faction and intrigue, the divine court is a model of order and obedience.

Another significant difference was its cost. The Jews were remarkably clear-sighted about the human and financial price of earthly courts. They understood the fiscal reality behind royal pomp. Others might be overawed by conspicuous expenditure, they were prepared to be critical. Samuel's warning was specific, and remains a telling indictment of royal magnificence:

> This will be the sort of king who will govern you. He will take your sons and make them serve in his chariots and with his cavalry, and will make them run before his chariot. Some he will appoint officers over units of a thousand and units of fifty. Others will plough his fields and reap his harvest; others again will make weapons of war and equipment for mounted troops. He will take your daughters for perfumers, cooks, and confectioners, and will seize the best of your cornfields, vineyards, and oliveyards, and give them to his lackeys. He will take a tenth of your grain and your vintage to give to his eunuchs and lackeys. Your slaves, both men and women, and the best of your cattle and your asses he will seize and put to his own use. He will take a tenth of your flocks, and you yourselves will become his slaves (I Sam. 8.11–17).

For all their splendour human courts are dependent upon exactions to maintain their state. God may require an even greater obedience, but at least he provides the equipment for his own throne-room:

> Cloud and mist enfold him,
>   righteousness and justice
>   are the foundation of his throne.
> Fire goes before him
> and burns up his enemies all around.
> The world is lit up beneath his lightning-flash;
> the earth sees it and writhes in pain.
> The mountains melt like wax as the Lord approaches,
>   the Lord of all the earth.
> The heavens proclaim his righteousness,
>   and all peoples see his glory (Ps. 97.2–6).

He may demand sacrifice, but it is only a token of obedience: unlike human kings, he is not in any way dependent on the tribute he levies:

> I need take no young bull from your house,
>   no he-goat from your folds;
> for all the beasts of the forest are mine
>   and the cattle in thousands on my hills.

I know every bird on those hills,
    the teeming life of the fields is my care.
If I were hungry, I would not tell you,
    for the world and all that is in it are mine.
    Shall I eat the flesh of your bulls
        or drink the blood of he-goats? (Ps. 50.9–13)

The propagandists of the divine court were not blind to some of its very basic advantages.

Just as human kings are approached with an elaborate and careful etiquette, the worshipper of God should take nothing for granted. In Psalm 145 we have an example of how the commonplaces and expectations, which surrounded human monarchs are used in negotiating with God. What in a human context might be suspected of flattery, when applied to God, may still sound obsequious, but not inappropriate:

I will extol thee, O God my king,
    and bless thy name for ever and ever.
Every day will I bless thee
    and praise thy name for ever and ever.
Great is the Lord and worthy of all praise;
    his greatness is unfathomable.
One generation shall commend thy works to another
    and set forth thy mighty deeds.
My theme shall be thy marvellous works,
    the glorious splendour of thy majesty.
Men shall declare thy mighty acts with awe
    and tell of thy great deeds.
They shall recite the story of thy abounding goodness
    and sing of thy righteousness with joy (Ps. 145.1–7).

An Egyptian Pharaoh would have easily recognized the sentiments. The psalmist envisages that God's prestige is as precious to him, as to any human ruler, who has constantly to project the correct image. As at human courts the hopeful description functions as an implicit request:

The Lord is gracious and compassionate,
    forbearing, and constant in his love.

The Lord is good to all men,
and his tender care rests upon all his creatures (Ps. 145.8f.).

A recurrent anxiety of ancient courts was the sense of impermanence: the whole structure of favour and patronage rested on a frail human life. This haunting fear found utterance in such expressions as 'May the King live for ever': today we still sing, 'Long live the Queen'. While monarchs might leave their favourites bereft, at the mercy of a successor with quite different friends, the immortality of the divine king could be affirmed with conviction:

Thy kingdom is an everlasting kingdom,
and thy dominion stands for all generations (Ps. 145.13).

Equally human kings had to be kept to their word, and there was always the possibility of evil counsellors changing their minds; God by contrast is utterly reliable:

In all his promises the Lord keeps faith,
he is unchanging in all his works (Ps. 145.14).

The Perquisites of a Courtier

This elaborate rehearsal of the divine perfections is not disinterested. The psalmist makes us aware of what can be expected from such a paragon of royal power:

The Lord holds up those who stumble
and straightens backs which are bent.
The eyes of all are lifted to thee in hope,
and thou givest them their food when it is due;
with open and bountiful hand
thou givest what they desire to every living creature
(Ps. 145.14ff.).

One might compare this with the more selective catering arrangements made by King Nebuchadnezzar for his distinguished captives (Dan. 1.5). The condition for access to all this bounty is reverence, which if it is not given voluntarily makes the rebel liable to punishment:

> He fulfils their desire if only they fear him;
>   he hears their cry and saves them.
> The Lord watches over all who love him
>   but sends the wicked to their doom (Ps. 145.19f.).

Perhaps the most significant feature of the divine king is his accessibility. While in most human courts access to the monarch, the fount of justice and favour, is closely guarded and carefully rationed, the divine king is immediately available:

> Very near is the Lord to those who call to him,
>   who call to him in singleness of heart (Ps. 145.18).

Such beliefs made the humblest believer a courtier in a palace which deprived all human establishments of their significance. Quite apart from any benefits actually conferred, that status alone was precious.

The dream of a universal jurisdiction has always been a part of the rhetoric of human monarchs and has lured them to overextend their power. At the coronation the Queen may no longer be the Empress of India, but she still holds the orb in her hand. Within the terms of a rather different cosmology the Jews did not hesitate to claim for their God an empire on which the sun never set:

> Let all the ends of the earth remember and turn again to the Lord;
> let all the families of the nations bow down before him.
>   For kingly power belongs to the Lord,
>   and dominion over the nations is his (Ps. 22.27f.).

Just as the Pharaohs of Egypt and the kings of Assyria surrounded themselves with pictures of tributaries bringing gifts, the psalmist used language to project the same imagery of divine power:

> Ascribe to the Lord, you families of the nations,
>   ascribe to the Lord glory and might;
> ascribe to the Lord the glory due to his name,
>   bring a gift and come into his courts (Ps. 96.7f.).

The supremacy is ascribed to God, but it is noticeable that those who ascribe such sovereignty to God themselves participate in its benefits. Psalm 47 provides a clear example of the delicate transition:

Clap your hands, all you nations;
acclaim our God with shouts of joy.
How fearful is the Lord Most High,
great sovereign over all the earth!
He lays the nations prostrate beneath us,
    he lays peoples under our feet;
he chose our patrimony for us,
the pride of Jacob whom he loved (Ps. 47.1–4).

We see here an exchange which is at the heart of the belief in divine omnipotence. In ascribing power to God the believer seems to be abasing himself, but in the prayer which follows he then appropriates to himself the very power which he has only appeared to decline. Perhaps the classic brief example of this occurs in the Christian hymn:

I am weak, but thou art mighty,
Hold me with thy powerful hand.

So in the psalter the blessings which God's worshippers expect are never distant from their praise:

The Lord is king above the flood,
The Lord has taken his royal seat as king for ever.
The Lord will give strength to his people;
The Lord will bless his people with peace (Ps. 29.10f.).

It may be doubted whether the power of God has ever been celebrated by people who did not hope to participate in it. Such at least is the evidence of the psalms. So for all the tone of obsequious humility the exaltation of God becomes a disguised form of national self-aggrandisement:

Acclaim our God, all men on earth;
    let psalms declare the glory of his name,
    make glorious his praise.
Say unto God, 'How fearful are thy works!
Thy foes cower before the greatness of thy strength.
    All men on earth fall prostrate in thy presence,
and sing to thee, sing psalms in honour of thy name' (Ps. 66.1–4).

The imperialist tone is unmistakable. Our God only becomes your God on terms of abject surrender.

The military basis of royal power was not something that the Jews concealed from themselves. While surrounding kings legitimated themselves by claiming descent from the gods, or identity with them, the account of the origin of the monarchy in I Samuel makes it plain that it is a military expedient. While subsequent experience proved that human kings could often be discredited by defeat, the divine king lived in an atmosphere of perpetual triumph:

> Lift up your heads, you gates,
>> lift yourselves up, you everlasting doors,
> that the king of glory may come in.
>> Who is the king of glory?
>> The Lord strong and mighty,
>> the Lord mighty in battle (Ps. 25.7f.).

The worship of such a God had the overtones of a victory-parade:

> Sing a new song to the Lord,
>> for he has done marvellous deeds;
> his right hand and holy arm have won him victory.
>> The Lord has made his victory known;
>> he has displayed his righteousness to all the nations.
>> He has remembered his constancy,
>> his love for the house of Israel.
> All the ends of the earth have seen
>> the victory of our God (Ps. 98.1ff.).

Alliance with such a power had quite tangible benefits; it was conceived as securing the land from invasion and occupation:

> The Lord is king for ever and ever;
>> the nations have vanished from his land.
>> Thou hast heard the lament of the humble, O Lord,
>> and art attentive to their heart's desire,
>> bringing justice to the orphan and the downtrodden
> that fear may never drive men from their homes again (Ps. 10.16ff.).

The generalship of God was one which any commander might envy. Every victory was ascribed to God; but defeats neither destroyed nor discredited him. A human king might fall in battle. The divine king never experienced defeat: disaster was only a sign of his displeasure. His people in their disobedience had failed him:

> If my people would but listen to me,
> if Israel would only conform to my ways,
> I would soon bring their enemies to their knees
> and lay a heavy hand upon their persecutors (Ps. 81.13f.).

The tone of regretful sorrow is also one of promise.

The Justice of the Divine King

The triumph of God is also the triumph of justice, which both legitimates God's rule and reminds the worshipper of the obedience which is God's due. Beside the justice of God, all human systems of justice are disparaged:

> Answer, you rulers: are your judgements just?
> Do you decide impartially between man and man?
> Never! Your hearts devise all kinds of wickedness
> and survey the violence that you have done on earth
> (Ps. 58.1f.).

Although the impartiality of God is emphasized it is seen from a very interested point of view. Gentiles are unlikely to be so convinced about the fairness of the treatment which they can expect. The justice of God is celebrated from a viewpoint of confident grievance; and there is no sense that such justice need be mitigated by humanity:

> O God, break the teeth in their mouths.
> Break, O Lord, the jaws of the unbelievers.
> May they melt, may they vanish like water,
> may they wither like trodden grass,
> like an abortive birth which melts away
> or a still-born child which never sees the sun!
> All unawares, may they be rooted up like a thorn-bush,
> like weeds which a man angrily clears away (Ps. 58.6ff.).

The vindictive nature of the divine justice is obviously a great deal of its attraction:

> O Lord, thou God of vengeance,
> thou God of vengeance, show thyself.
> Rise up, judge of the earth;
> punish the arrogant as they deserve (Ps. 94.1f.).

Reading such language it is well to remember the sage comment of the seventeenth-century theologian Benjamin Whichcote on such religion:

> The insolent, usurper, self-assumer; such think the divine excellency to be self-will, because they themselves affect to be arbitrary, unaccountable, to do as they list, and to have their will for a law . . . The spiteful or revengeful: they think it God's privilege to be able to do harm, to crush, to oppress at pleasure, to keep under: for nothing gratifies bad natures more than to be revenged, or to have others at their pleasure.[2]

As long as such a God is thought to exist his worshippers can find in their picture of him the legitimation of their worst instincts. If God does not exist that alibi is at an end and we have to admit that the picture of God faithfully reflects the mentality of its authors.

Collective Providence: The Privileged People

The doctrine of providence was given powerful collective application in ancient Jewish religion. It was not in origin a cosmological claim; it articulated a particular view-point. God's providence was seen from three related positions in ancient Judaism, of which the basic one was tribal. Psalm 33 introduces many of its distinctive ideas. Fundamental is the notion of mutual possession:

> Happy is the nation whose God is the Lord,
>   the people he has chosen for his own possession (Ps. 33.12).

In its language it sounds self-deprecating, as if the tribe is merely the chattel of its God, but the advantage of such a position is that God can be trusted to look after his own:

The Lord brings the plans of nations to nothing;
    he frustrates the counsel of the peoples.
But the Lord's plans shall stand for ever,
    and his counsel endure for all generations (Ps. 33.10f.).

The possession of such a divine ally means that his people can scoff at all the usual signs of military might:

A king is not saved by a great army,
nor a warrior delivered by great strength.
A man cannot trust his horse to save him,
    nor can it deliver him for all its strength (Ps. 33.16f.).

The mutual relationship creates reciprocal obligations:

Let thy unfailing love, O Lord, rest upon us,
    as we have put our hope in thee (Ps. 33.22).

The people assure their ally of devotion and trust, and he in turn rewards them with his protection.

The corrollary of this belief is that the enemies of God's people must be God's enemies. The endangered plight of God's people is a wicked insult to the Almighty:

Rest not, O God;
O God, be neither silent nor still,
for thy enemies are making a tumult,
and those that hate thee carry their heads high.
They devise cunning schemes against thy people
and conspire against those thou hast made thy treasure:
'Come, away with them', they cry,
    'let them be a nation no longer,
    let Israel's name be remembered no more' (Ps. 83.1–4).

To leave the matter in no doubt the enemies are listed with care:

With one mind they have agreed together
to make a league against thee:
    the families of Edom, the Ishmaelites,
    Moabites and Hagarenes,
Gebal, Ammon and Amalek,
    Philistia and the citizens of Tyre,

Asshur too their ally,
all of them lending aid to the descendants of Lot (Ps. 83.5–8).

The previous history of God's intervention on behalf of his people is
then rehearsed; it provides a sublime confidence in the effects of
God's protection:

> Scatter them, O God, like thistledown,
>   like chaff before the wind.
> Like fire raging through the forest
> or flames which blaze across the hills,
> hunt them down with thy tempest,
>   and dismay them with thy storm-wind.
> Heap shame upon their heads, O Lord,
>   until they confess the greatness of thy name.
> Let them be abashed, and live in perpetual dismay;
> let them feel their shame and perish.
> So let them learn that thou alone art Lord,
>   God Most High over all the earth (Ps. 83. 13–18).

This represents a very specific form of religious education.

In keeping with this tribal understanding of God's providence is
the constant rehearsal of tribal history. For that history creates its
own obligations. Indeed the benefits which the people have enjoyed
in the past are cited as the basis of their continuing service. History is
not told as good fortune or as heroic achievement: the achievement is
entirely that of God. He requires it to be remembered, and gratitude
is expressed in the form of obedience:

> From their sons we will not hide
> the praises of the Lord and his might
> nor the wonderful acts he has performed;
> then they shall repeat them to the next generation.
> He laid on Jacob a solemn charge
> and established a law in Israel,
> which he commanded our fathers
>   to teach their sons,
> that it might be known to a future generation,
>   to children yet unborn,
> and these would repeat it to their sons in turn.

He charged them to put their trust in God,
to hold his great acts ever in mind
        and to keep all his commandments (Ps. 78.4–7; cf.81.1–5;
105 and 106).

The human contribution to this history of the people is merely a cautionary example. The fathers may have passed on the story but it does not place them in a flattering light. From them they could only learn:

not to do as their fathers did,
a disobedient and rebellious race,
a generation with no firm purpose,
with hearts not fixed steadfastly on God (Ps. 78.8; cf. 95.8–11).

Many of the features of this tribal providence, and the understanding of history which it created are brought together in Psalm 44. It begins with a rehearsal of God's feats in the past, which explicitly disclaims any creative role for the human beings involved:

O God, we have heard for ourselves,
        our fathers have told us
all the deeds which thou didst in their days,
all the work of thy hand in days of old.
Thou didst plant them in the land and drive the nations out,
thou didst make them strike root, breaking up the peoples;
    it was not our fathers' swords won them the land,
    nor their arm that gave them the victory,
        but thy right hand and thy arm
        and the light of thy presence; such was thy favour to them.
Thou art my king and my God;
    at thy bidding Jacob is victorious (Ps. 44.1–4).

In the crisis which the psalmist envisages in the present, he therefore disclaims any power to resolve the situation, instead he exalts the power of God:

By thy help we will throw back our enemies,
in thy name we will trample down our adversaries.
I will not trust in my bow,
    nor will my sword win me the victory;

for thou dost deliver us from our foes
and put all our enemies to shame.
In God have we gloried all the day long,
and we will praise thy name for ever (Ps. 44.5–8; cf.115.1).

God is not only the agent of victory, he also inflicts defeat: the
disasters which his people meet are also to be attributed to him:

But now thou hast rejected and humbled us
and dost no longer lead our armies into battle.
Thou hast hurled us back before the enemy,
and our foes plunder us as they will.
Thou hast given us up to be butchered like sheep
and hast scattered us among the nations
(Ps. 44.9–11; cf.60.1–4).

In this instance the psalmist makes no attempt to explain such
apparent treachery by any failing on the part of the people; instead he
contrasts the steadfast loyalty of the people with the divine
inconsistency:

All this has befallen us, but we do not forget thee
and have not betrayed thy covenant;
we have not gone back on our purpose,
nor have our feet strayed from thy path (Ps. 44.17f.).

Instead of indulging in recrimination, the psalmist does not dwell on
the unfairness of the situation. He simply presents it without
comment in a desperate invocation of divine aid:

Bestir thyself, Lord; why dost thou sleep?
Awake, do not reject us for ever.
Why dost thou hide thy face,
heedless of our misery and our sufferings?
For we sink down to the dust
and lie prone on the earth.
Arise and come to our help,
for thy love's sake set us free (Ps. 44.23–26).

The apparent indifference of God is most easily understood as sleep.
Such a belief in divine providence is obviously not a mature,

unbiased assessment of experience, let alone of speculation. It is not designed to explain evil, but to overcome it.

Collective Providence: The Privileged Place

Tribal providence expounded an account of history, which exalted the control of God and at the same time made the people the beneficiaries of his power over events. The story of God's providence was the story of a privileged people. Inter-related with that story were the claims of a privileged place – Zion, the city of Jerusalem. God's patronage ensured that the city was the source of a variety of blessings:

You shall eat the fruit of your own labours,
    you shall be happy and you shall prosper.
Your wife shall be like a fruitful vine
    in the heart of your house;
your sons shall be like olive-shoots
    round about your table.
This is the blessing in store for the man
    who fears the Lord.
May the Lord bless you from Zion;
    may you share the prosperity of Jerusalem
all the days of your life,
    and live to see your children's children! (Ps. 128.2–6)

Pilgrims to the holy city could be sure of God's protection even on their journey:

Happy the men whose refuge is in thee,
    whose hearts are set on the pilgrim ways!
    As they pass through the thirsty valley
    they find water from a spring;
and the Lord provides even men who lose their way
    with pools to quench their thirst.
So they pass on from outer walls to inner,
and the God of gods shows himself in Zion (Ps. 84.5–7).

As the people of Israel was God's possession, so Zion was his dwelling place, and gained considerable advantages from his residence:

> There is a river whose streams gladden the city of God,
>   which the Most High has made his holy dwelling;
> God is in that city; she shall not be overthrown,
> and he will be her help at the break of the day (Ps. 46.4f.).

The celebration of God and the celebration of the inviolable city go hand in hand:

> The Lord is great and worthy of our praise
>   in the city of our God, upon his holy hill.
> Fair and lofty, the joy of the whole earth
>   is Zion's hill, like the farthest reaches of the north,
>   the hill of the great King's city.
> In her palaces God is known for a tower of strength.
>   See how the kings all gather round her,
>   marching on in company.
> They are struck with amazement when they see her,
>   they are filled with alarm and panic;
> they are seized with trembling,
>   they toss in pain like a woman in labour,
>   like the ships of Tarshish
> when an east wind wrecks them.
> All we had heard we saw with our own eyes
>   in the city of the Lord of hosts,
>   in the city of our God,
>   the city which God plants firm for evermore
>   (Ps. 48.1–8; cf.125.1f.).

These claims of pride and confidence, became utterances of defiance and obstinacy, when the city was sacked and its temple destroyed. Experience did not lead to any abandonment or modification of the claims. Instead their reiteration only deepens the sacrilegious character of such havoc:

> O God, the heathen have set foot in thy domain,
>   defiled thy holy temple
>   and laid Jerusalem in ruins.
> They have thrown out the dead bodies of thy servants
>   to feed the birds of the air;
>   they have made thy loyal servants carrion for wild beasts.

Their blood is spilled all round Jerusalem like water,
and there they lie unburied (Ps. 79.1–3; cf.74.1–8).

Such atrocious behaviour does not in any way undermine the claims
made for Zion; it simply ensures the enmity of God towards the
ignorant heathen who presume to act in such a manner:

How long, O Lord, wilt thou be roused to such fury?
Must thy jealousy rage like a fire?
Pour out thy wrath over nations which do not know thee
and over kingdoms which do not invoke thee by name;
see how they have devoured Jacob and laid waste his homesteads.
Do not remember against us the guilt of past generations
but let compassion come swiftly to meet us,
we have been brought so low (Ps. 79.5–8).

The human and divine residents of the city share a common interest;
the compassion which they solicit is a compassion towards themselves. It is quite consistent with the most blood-thirsty retribution
directed elsewhere:

O Babylon, Babylon the destroyer
happy the man who repays you
for all that you did to us!
Happy is he who shall seize your children
and dash them against the rock (Ps. 137.8f.).

In a more tranquil mood later generations were satisfied to dwell
on the reconstruction of Jerusalem, as a sign of God's mercy and
power. His prestige and that of the city are one:

But thou, Lord, art enthroned for ever
and thy fame shall be known to all generations.
Thou wilt arise and have mercy on Zion;
for the time is come to pity her.
Her very stones are dear to thy servants,
and even her dust moves them with pity.
Then shall the nations revere thy name, O Lord,
and all the kings of the earth thy glory,
When the Lord builds up Zion again
and shows himself in his glory (Ps. 102.12–16).

Significantly this is also a vindication of the power of prayer:

> He turns to hear the prayer of the destitute
>> and does not scorn them when they pray (Ps. 102.17).

The doctrine of prayer is as ambiguous as the doctrine of providence with which it is associated. While proclaiming the power of God, it actually promises that that power is more immediately available.

Collective Providence: The Privileged Ruler

Jerusalem was the centre of an earthly kingdom as well as a heavenly one, and the two thrones were complementary:

> The Lord swore to David
>> an oath which he will not break:
> 'A prince of your own line
>> will I set upon your throne . . .'
> For the Lord has chosen Zion
>> and desired it for his home:
> 'This is my resting-place for ever;
>> here will I make my home, for such is my desire'
> (Ps. 132.11–14).

Just as Jerusalem was God's special home, so the Davidic line was his chosen agency. This is the third privileged focus of God's providence. Just as the kingship of God was associated with control of the natural world, so the king was associated with the fertility of the land. Dreams of international tribute and enduring fame stand side by side with prayers for plenty:

> May there be abundance of corn in the land,
>> growing in plenty to the tops of the hills;
> may the crops flourish like Lebanon,
>> and the sheaves be numberless as blades of grass (Ps. 72.16).

It is not simply modern governments which have sought to benefit from claiming responsibility for economic improvements outside their control. Kings like their modern successors were popular in times of prosperity, and would certainly attract discontent in times of scarcity.

At the heart of the relationship between God and the king was an exchange which is well exemplified in Psalm 21. On the one hand the king ascribes all power and success to God, on the other hand God rewards such loyalty by sharing his attributes with his servant:

> The king rejoices in thy might, O Lord:
>> well may he exult in thy victory,
>> for thou hast given him his heart's desire
>>> and hast not refused him what he asked.
>> Thou dost welcome him with blessings and prosperity
>> and set a crown of fine gold upon his head.
> He asked of thee life, and thou didst give it him,
>> length of days for ever and ever.
> Thy salvation has brought him great glory;
> thou dost invest him with majesty and honour,
>> for thou dost make him glad with joy in thy presence
> (Ps. 21.1–6).

In all respects this God is the answer to a king's prayer – victory (Ps. 2.8–12; 72.8–15), prosperity, legitimation (Ps. 2.1–7), a long reign (Ps. 21.4; 61.6f.), prestige (Ps. 72.17), not to say happiness. All these the king receives at God's hand. In other contexts one might speak of cupboard love. It is not surprising that,

> The king puts his trust in the Lord;
>> the loving care of the Most High holds him unshaken
> (Ps. 21.7).

Many of the royal psalms reflect a quite untroubled relationship between the king and his God (Ps. 18.1–3; 2.8–12; 72.8–15; 144). The praise of God is exuberant, and the benefits which the king derives from him are unequivocal. The psalmist is clear that the king's conspicuous service of God creates obligations which can be appealed to in time of need:

> The name of Jacob's God be your tower of strength,
> give you help from the sanctuary
>> and send you support from Zion!
>> May he remember all your offerings
>> and look with favour on your rich sacrifices,
> give you your heart's desire
>> and grant success to all your plans! (Ps. 20.1–4)

Yet not all kings were so satisfactory from the divine point of view. The privileged position of the Davidic line was conditional. After the glowing endorsement of David in Psalm 89, God adopts a more cautious attitude towards his successors, tempering the promise of his constant support with a reminder that disobedience would certainly be punished:

> I will establish his posterity for ever
>> and his throne as long as the heavens endure.
> If his sons forsake my law
>> and do not conform to my judgments,
>> if they renounce my statutes
>> and do not observe my commands,
> I will punish their disobedience with the rod
>> and their iniquity with lashes.
> Yet I will not deprive him of my true love
>> nor let my faithfulness prove false;
>> I will not renounce my covenant
>> nor change my promised purpose (Ps. 89.29–34).

In these terms any royal disaster could be satisfactorily placed in the scheme of God's providence. The king was disobedient, or the successor of a disobedient king, or had connived at disobedience among his subjects. The religious royal histories used all these devices to reconcile the religious claims with political realities.

A prudent king therefore could not be too careful. He had every inducement to rule justly, as his throne depended upon it. The claim to uphold justice which legitimated his power might always be turned against him. The ideal king does not enforce his own justice, he is merely the instrument of the divine king, from whom he seeks guidance:

> O God, endow the king with thy own justice,
>> and give thy righteousness to a king's son,
> that he may judge thy people rightly
>> and deal out justice to the poor and suffering.
> May hills and mountains afford thy people
>> peace and prosperity in righteousness.

> He shall give judgement for the suffering
> and help those of the people that are needy;
> he shall crush the oppressor (Ps. 72.1–4).

The king's sovereignty was therefore by no means absolute. It had to bow to defeat, which might be understood as God's repudiation. It was also vulnerable to orchestrated criticism. Long before disaster overtook him internal criticism might be anticipating God's verdict: in many of the prophets we see this process at work. The qualifications of the godly prince might be disputed, but ruled and ruler alike had every interest in not criticizing the notion of divine rule and providence. The ruler found in it a vehicle for his claims, his subjects found in it a means of mitigating his excesses.

The psalter therefore reflects a highly developed understanding of God's providence determining collective life, at the level of the people, the city and the king. In origin it does not seem to have been a doctrine of universal control, though the pressure of its own rhetoric and the need to protect its particular claims pushed it constantly in a more universal direction. God needs to control the entire world in order to be a satisfactory guarantor of the safety of the particular objects of his attention and favour. The uniqueness of God, which this religion asserts, is far removed from the cosmological concerns of philosophical theology. The uniqueness of God is the corrollary of the unique people, the holy city, the anointed king. The uniqueness of their God is the pledge of their own privileged position. Later rationalizing theology, which tried to harmonize the bewildering variety of hellenistic religion, would see in this unique God the one God by which philosophers hoped to make sense of the confusion of local deities, when the pantheon was no longer plausible. This identification is understandable and was brilliantly exploited by Christian hellenistic theologians, but it was a mistake. The Hellenistic God was universal, making all men brothers, abolishing local differences and distinctions. The God of the Old Testament was passionately attached to a particular people, a definite place, one royal line, and all his dealings with mankind were understood as evidence of that attachment. Particularity may be the scandal of biblical religion; it was also its motive. The praise of God and the assertion of his people were complementary: in every sense he was the God of Israel.

Personal Providence: The Special Relationship

Much the greater part of the psalter is, however, devoted to the exposition of God's providence as it impinges on the individual. Throughout subsequent history, within the Jewish and Christian religions, it has functioned as a kind of religious grammar, in terms of which religious people have learnt to articulate their relationship with God. Of course this individual language takes for granted that the person concerned belongs to God's holy people, looks towards God's holy place, and reverences God's anointed king; nevertheless, it enables us to see from the inside, so to speak, the joys and anxieties of that privileged identity. In some ways it resembles the thinking behind the royal Psalms, which certainly provide the nearest analogy, but it reflects much more intimate concerns, not political ones. Fundamental to the relation between the person and God is the observance of a covenant which distinguishes the good from the wicked. A great deal of the literature reassures the righteous of the reward that is his due. On the one hand it exemplifies and projects an image of exuberant piety:

O Lord, it is good to give thee thanks,
to sing psalms to thy name, O Most High,
to declare thy love in the morning
    and thy constancy every night,
    to the music of a ten-stringed lute,
    to the sounding chords of the harp.
Thy acts, O Lord, fill me with exultation;
    I shout in triumph at thy mighty deeds.
How great are thy deeds, O Lord!
How fathomless thy thoughts (Ps. 92.1–5; cf. Ps. 1, and 5.12).

At the same time it holds out the manifest reward of such piety; often representing this as a matter of present enjoyment, rather than of anxious hope. The psalter was written before the consolations of a life after death had been conceived. Obedience issues in present delight:

I lift my head high, like a wild ox tossing its horn;
    I am anointed richly with oil.
    I gloat over all who speak ill of me,
I listen for the downfall of my cruel foes.

> The righteous flourish like a palm-tree,
> they grow tall as a cedar on Lebanon;
>> planted as they are in the house of the Lord,
>> they flourish in the courts of our God,
> vigorous in old age like trees full of sap,
>> luxuriant, wide-spreading,
> eager to declare that the Lord is just,
> the Lord my rock, in whom there is no unrighteousness
>> (Ps. 92.10–15; cf.34).

The righteousness of God is exemplified precisely in the reward of those who obey him. He keeps his side of the bargain. Learning to use such language initiates one into a world where it makes sense to be godly.

It is not now thought seemly that one of the delights of the Christian heaven should be a lively sense of the torments of hell, which the saints have escaped, and which others are suffering. The psalter is altogether less squeamish in representing the alternative to obedience: at the outset the contrast is stated with smug complacency:

> Happy is the man
>> who does not take the wicked for his guide
>> nor walk the road that sinners tread
>> nor take his seat among the scornful;
>> the law of the Lord is his delight,
> the law his meditation night and day.
>> He is like a tree
>> planted beside a watercourse,
>> which yields its fruit in season
>> and its leaf never withers:
>> in all that he does he prospers.
> Wicked men are not like this;
>> they are like chaff driven by the wind (Ps. 1.1–4).

It is likely that moral reality then as now was much more ambiguous. Even in asserting the contrary the psalmist is conscious that often the wicked have a better time of it than his notion of divine providence suggests they should:

He who does not know this is a brute,
a fool is he who does not understand this:
that though the wicked grow like grass
and every evildoer prospers,
    they will be destroyed for ever.
While thou, Lord, dost reign on high eternally,
    thy foes will surely perish,
    all evildoers will be scattered (Ps. 92.6–9).

A great deal of the vindictiveness of the Psalms is probably to be understood as a means of repressing doubt. It can never have been entirely easy or plausible to say:

I have been young and am now grown old,
and never have I seen a righteous man forsaken (Ps. 37.25).

Instead of questioning the justice or the reality of the relationship with God, relief was obtained from the resulting tensions by picturing the savagery of divine retribution:

    The wicked shall perish,
and their children beg their bread.
The enemies of the Lord, like fuel in a furnace,
    are consumed in smoke (Ps. 37.20).

Although all such language is directed towards the wicked, it also conveys a discreet warning to the reader not to become one of them. The menaces, which threaten the disobedient, discourage the righteous from reconsidering their position.

    The man who is the object of God's attention and care is subject to the most exacting scrutiny: only total obedience suffices. At no point can he take his favoured status for granted, the sense of dependence must be continuous. Psalm 30 provides a cautionary tale briefly told:

Carefree as I was, I had said,
    'I can never be shaken'.
But, Lord, it was thy will to shake my mountain refuge;
thou didst hide thy face, and I was struck with dismay.
    I called unto thee, O Lord,
        and I pleaded with thee, Lord, for mercy:

'What profit in my death if I go down into the pit?
Can the dust confess thee or proclaim thy truth?' (Ps. 30.6–9)

The tone is extremely sombre. It has little to do with the child-centred worship of the modern school assembly:

So we are brought to an end by thy anger
    and silenced by thy wrath.
Thou dost lay bare our iniquities before thee
    and our lusts in the full light of thy presence.
All our days go by under the shadow of thy wrath;
    our years die away like a murmur (Ps. 90.7ff.).

Isaac Watts only hinted at this passage in his metrical version, 'O God our help in ages past'. A relationship with God which necessarily interpreted personal misfortune as a symptom of sin issued in endless pleas for mercy:

Wash away all my guilt
    and cleanse me from my sin.
For well I know my misdeeds,
and my sins confront me all the day long.
Against thee, thee only, I have sinned
    and done what displeases thee,
so that thou mayest be proved right in thy charge
    and just in passing sentence (Ps. 51.2ff.).

It must be remembered that neither sin nor guilt were merely psychological states; the sick and the unfortunate had very tangible reminders of their condition before God, quite apart from the state of their consciences.

Personal Providence: The Benefits of the Covenant

The covenant established a pattern of reciprocal obligation. Whatever the disparity of power between God and man, each party to the covenant had claims on the other. This is neatly described in Psalm 41:

Happy the man who has a concern for the helpless!
The Lord will save him in time of trouble (Ps. 41.1).

By doing what he can for those who are in difficulties now, the righteous man gains the help of an omnipotent God for the future. The exchange is not unattractive. In Psalm 91 it is God himself who catalogues the benefits:

> Because his love is set on me, I will deliver him;
> I will lift him beyond danger, for he knows me by my name.
>   When he calls upon me, I will answer;
>   I will be with him in time of trouble;
>   I will rescue him and bring him to honour.
> I will satisfy him with long life
> to enjoy the fullness of salvation (Ps. 91.14ff.).

All these benefits are, however, entirely conditional: they demand the faithful love of the worshipper. It is easy for the modern Christian, reared on a soft, personalist religion which places a very high value on intimate relationships, to fail to see what is at issue here. The love of the Psalms is not a matter of feeling, but of obedience to God's law. It required the strictest conformity. Indeed some of the most lyrical passages of the entire psalter dwell in a quasi-sensual manner on the gratifications which the Law affords:

> The law of the Lord is perfect and revives the soul.
>   The Lord's instruction never fails,
>   and makes the simple wise.
> The precepts of the Lord are right and rejoice the heart.
>   The commandment of the Lord shines clear
>   and gives light to the eyes.
> The fear of the Lord is pure and abides for ever.
> The Lord's decrees are true and righteous every one,
>   more to be desired than gold, pure gold in plenty,
>   sweeter than syrup or honey from the comb (Ps. 19.7–10).

The benefits of the covenant are entirely dependent on the good behaviour of the beneficiary. Because a false step can deprive a person of so much good, the psalms echo with a plea for guidance:

> If there is any man who fears the Lord,
> he shall be shown the path that he should choose (Ps. 25.12).

Or:

> Guide me, O Lord,
> that I may be true to thee and follow thy path;
>> let me be one in heart
>> with those who revere thy name (Ps. 86.11).

Again God himself speaks to reassure:

> I will teach you, and guide you in the way you should go.
>> I will keep you under my eye.
> Do not behave like horse or mule, unreasoning creatures,
> whose course must be checked with bit and bridle (Ps. 32.8f.).

In this way the pious man appropriates to himself the obedience, which his religion demands, and celebrates its demands.

All the obligations of the Law can be accepted and indeed affirmed, because of the benefits which they convey. These are made the more compelling by a repeated denigration of human achievement and staying power. The exaltation of God and the disparagement of man seem to be complementary to each other:

> Man's days are like grass;
> he blossoms like the flowers of the field:
> a wind passes over them, and they cease to be,
> and their place knows them no more.
> But the Lord's love never fails those who fear him (Ps. 103.15ff.).

The appearance is, however, rather deceptive. Far from a mood of bleak pessimism, such a view of man can be affirmed because of what his God does for him. The care of God embraces the whole of life from the cradle to the grave:

> Thou art my hope, O Lord,
> my trust, O Lord, since boyhood.
> From birth I have leaned upon thee,
> my protector since I left my mother's womb.
> To many I seem a solemn warning;
> but I have thee for my strong refuge.
> My mouth shall be full of thy praises,
>> I shall tell of thy splendour all day long.
> Do not cast me off when old age comes,
>> nor forsake me when my strength fails (Ps. 71.5–9).

The range of benefits, which an individual can hope for from his God are extensively developed in the Psalms. Here they can only be indicated: the promise of protection (Ps. 91.1–13; 27.1–5) finds its most frequent form as relief from persecution (Ps. 5.6–10; 7.12–16; 13; 17; 35). God is the cure of misery (Ps. 6.1–5; 31.10–13; 42) and sickness (Ps. 38). God is the source of prosperity and descendants (Ps. 23; 25.13–15; 102.28), and of wisdom (Ps. 90). His intervention can be expected in social conflict (Ps. 12.1–5). Nowhere do the Psalms envisage the reversal of death, but they are content that death can at least be postponed (Ps. 88.10ff.; 102.23–28). The concerns of the psalmist may seem rather surprising. They are not those of today's comfortable, educated middle-class; they are much closer to the preoccupations of a modern slum-dweller: opportunities to be alone with his God are rare, instead he lives in a jostling, overcrowded, violent world, insecure, wracked by suspicion and anxiety, a prey to ill-health and misfortune. Such it would seem was everyday life in ancient Israel.

It would be unjust to portray all the love of God in the Psalms as interested; but the note of altruism is rare, and seldom sustained. The belief that God should be served without any reward belongs to a more sophisticated and later religious outlook. Even when the psalmist approaches such an outlook, he is not entirely convincing:

> There are many who say, 'If only we might be prosperous again!
> But the light of thy presence has fled from us, O Lord'.
>   Yet in my heart thou hast put more happiness
>   than they enjoyed when there was corn and wine in plenty.
> Now I will lie down in peace, and sleep;
>   for thou alone, O Lord, makest me live unafraid (Ps. 4.6ff.).

The psalmist has difficulty in not envying the prosperity of the wicked; he achieves some detachment, but his happiness still needs the consolation of the wrath that will come to the wicked. That presumably is the reference to living 'unafraid'. The same tensions are apparent in the only other passage from the Psalms to approximate to the love of God for his own sake:

> When my heart was embittered
> I felt the pangs of envy,

> I would not understand, so brutish was I,
> I was a mere beast in thy sight, O God.
>> Yet I am always with thee,
>> thou holdest my right hand;
>> thou dost guide me by thy counsel
>> and afterwards wilt receive me with glory.
> Whom have I in heaven but thee?
> And having thee, I desire nothing else on earth.
> Though heart and body fail,
> yet God is my possession for ever.
> They who are far from thee are lost;
> thou dost destroy all who wantonly forsake thee.
> But my chief good is to be near thee, O God;
> I have chosen thee, Lord God, to be my refuge (Ps. 73.21–28).

Even at its most sublime the religion of the psalter needs a vindictive God to make its demands tolerable. The reward of righteousness is unsatisfying without the gratification of the punishment of others. The envy remains to be exorcised.

I have deliberately tried to represent these ancient beliefs in God's providence in a relatively disembodied fashion; simply examining some of the texts and the assumptions they contain. These doctrines did not, however, drop from heaven. They were propagated and affirmed by people, and it is now time to face what are perhaps painful questions: What were they doing? How do assertions about God and his will, his care and his promises, relate to human wills, claims and hopes?

Providence and Propaganda

The doctrines of collective providence are very close to what today would be recognized as propaganda. They clearly served the interests of the leadership which propagated them. The leaders offered a privileged status for their group in return for obedience. The obedience was spoken of as being obedience to God, but was administered by human agents who also transmitted and celebrated those beliefs. The psalter seems to contain two rather distinct political traditions. On the one hand there is the history of the people of Israel, which I have referred to earlier as tribal. The group is defined by an interlocking history of God's deliverance, and obedience to God's law. Its exponents could threaten divine retribution against any who challenged their primacy: the whole community would suffer for the insubordination of a few. It conveyed a powerful message of conformity. Membership of the privileged people was defined by obedience: every member had the duty to avoid contamination. Much of the pre-exilic history of both kingdoms seems to have been marked by conflict between a traditional religious authority expounding the law and proclaimed by the prophets, and the prestige and administration of the king. If God's providence was understood as centring on Israel, that is because it is a theology produced to express Jewish interests. Even when, as in Amos, God's rule is extended to include the neighbouring countries the unique status of Israel is still reasserted in the very sentence of judgment:

> For you alone have I cared
> among all the nations of the world (Amos 3.2).

To dismiss such beliefs as simply primitive forms of a more general belief in God's ordering of world history is to put the cart before the horse. God is the God of Israel; Israel is represented as his possession precisely because he is Israel's construction. He serves their interests and distinguishes them from others; it is not unnatural that they should celebrate him. In doing so they are affirming their own identity.

The beliefs in God's special care of Jerusalem and the Davidic monarchy were both the creation of the Jerusalem priesthood. While monarch and prophet were usually at strife with each other, priest and king stood together. The king was represented as the builder of the temple; his palace and God's stood side by side. In the Psalms we see the priestly orchestration of both these beliefs. The people are encouraged to ascribe a particular value to Jerusalem; in return the priests promised blessings and received offerings. The role of the king was legitimated by the priesthood; royal rule was identified with that of God and could look to God for assistance. In return the kings respected the temple and its priesthood. In this exchange there was no deliberate deceit. The existence of the institutions themselves supplied sufficient evidence for their claims, evidence which must have convinced not only their subjects, but priest and king alike. For priest or king to have doubted its truth would have meant challenging their own position in society. That position would have made their beliefs as plausible as they were flattering. Monarchs have never been unhappy to believe that they reign by the grace of God; even the most radical bishops are not afraid to hold their sees by divine permission. Human beings are surprisingly ready to accommodate themselves to such claims.

It might be thought that the trauma of defeat and exile could only have meant the end of such beliefs, but as is often the case the courtiers survived their kings. In the hopes which Second Isaiah entertained about Cyrus there is a striking attempt to accommodate the old beliefs about the Davidic monarchy to a new political reality:

> Thus says the Lord to Cyrus his anointed,
>> Cyrus whom he has taken by the hand
>> to subdue nations before him
>> and undo the might of kings;
>> before whom gates shall be opened
>>> and no doors be shut:
>> I will go before you
>>> and level the swelling hills;
>> I will break down gates of bronze
>>> and hack through iron bars.
>> I will give you treasures from dark vaults,
>>> hoarded in secret places,
>> that you may know that I am the Lord,
>>> Israel's God who calls you by name.
> For the sake of Jacob my servant and Israel my chosen
>> I have called you by name
> and given you your title, though you have not known me
> (Isa. 45.1–4).

In the Daniel stories there is even an inconsistent attempt to accommodate Nebuchadnezzar to the same pattern, when the restored king confesses:

Now I, Nebuchadnezzar, praise and exalt and glorify the King of heaven; for all his acts are right and his ways are just and those whose conduct is arrogant he can bring low (Dan. 4.37).

A similar process took place in ancient Egypt where the Roman Emperors took on the attributes of the Pharaohs. This not only suited the susceptibilities of their Egyptian subjects; it preserved the credibility of the traditional Egyptian priesthoods. In Israel the Jerusalem temple was re-established. The hopes that once had been centred on an actual royal family with all its consequent disappointments and fragility, were transferred to a king whom God would send in the future. The priests could not afford the royal tradition to fall into total discredit. Deprived of their king, his courtiers found a very satisfactory substitute in the expectation of a king. They had the reward of being courtiers still. So satisfactory was this new arrangement that when once again kings ruled in the Jerusalem of the Herods, the priesthood preferred to honour the claims of the imagined Messiah of the future, rather than identify themselves too closely with a monarchy which while it might be actual was also new and compromised.

A more detached eye may think such beliefs absurd. The incoherences are startling. How is God's choice of Israel to be reconciled with his responsibility for the other nations of the earth? Is such a notion of gratuitous favour compatible with any rational concept of divine perfection? History itself seemed to mock the claims of the Davidic dynasty. At the consecration of the temple, the incompatibility between the claims of the temple and the God of creation are uttered in the prayer itself:

But can God indeed dwell on earth? Heaven itself, the highest heaven, cannot contain thee; how much less this house that I have built! Yet attend to the prayer and the supplication of thy servant, O Lord my God, listen to the cry and the prayer which thy servant utters this day, that thine eyes may ever be upon this house night and day, this place of which thou didst say, 'My Name shall be there'; so mayest thou hear thy servant when he prays towards this place. Hear the supplication of thy servant and of thy people Israel when they pray toward this place. Hear thou in heaven thy dwelling and, when thou hearest, forgive (I Kings 8.27–30).

If all these beliefs about God's providential care of his people, their temple and their king were simply explanatory, such inconsistencies must have been fatal. They were believed, not because they explained history, but because they promised to be effective in negotiating history. They were entirely plausible to those who propagated them because they saw in them either the pledge of their own privileged status or the means of their own rule.

In much of its subsequent history the psalter has been used to create in imagination not only a king, but a whole society which fulfils the promises which the society we know makes, but fails to honour. In this imagined world the king provides dependable security and reliable justice. The city is safe, labour secures its objective, the temple is a place of unity and peace. The people of Israel are united in the obedience to God and rest secure in his defence. In the psalter the individual enters a society which he can fully appreciate and affirm, and which secures for him the benefits he seeks in vain elsewhere. In origin this was the self-serving propaganda of ancient Jewish institutions – but the prayers have outlived all the institutions which originated them. In most Jewish and all Christian use, they have referred not to an actual, but an imagined world. Despite their political origins, they have therefore become progressively apolitical. Part of the genius of the psalter has been this creation of an alternative world to the actual one. It sustains by providing a context which fosters our confidence and our self-respect, which the actual world so often threatens. In this alternative world, conjured up in our imaginations, we possess the satisfactions which actual human society denies us. To dismiss this as pie in the sky, propagated by the oppressors to distract the oppressed, is only justified if we believe in the perfectibility of society; but judging by the evidence that is quite as much an illusion as any religious imagining, and often much more destructive. For if human society, however improved and ameliorated, will always be deeply unsatisfying to many of its members – denying them dignity and self-respect, if not security and prosperity – the creation of an imagined alternative in which we experience the satisfactions which now elude us is not to be despised.

The propaganda origins of the beliefs about God's collective providence and their subsequent transformation in imagination sheds some light on the elaboration of beliefs about individual providence, but here the phenomenon is rather more complicated. It may well be that many of the models were created by religious leaders to serve their interests. They created formulae which, when learnt by the ordinary believer, both promised a privileged status and promoted obedience. In learning them the believer was acquiring a predetermined identity, the object of blessing and the subject of scrutiny. In this way the religious control of society developed an intimacy far greater than the old collective beliefs could ever have fostered. We see here a counterpart to the notion of a transparent consciousness, which was examined as part of the doctrine of God's omniscience (above, pp. 29f., 41f.). This use of the Psalms has been appropriated by successive and quite different forms of religious discipline. Jews through the generations, Roman Catholic Christians and Protestant Christians have asked God:

> Wash away all my guilt
> and cleanse me from my sin (Ps. 51.2).

They have used a common literature of prayer, while having radically different notions of what constitutes sin, and the means by which they might be cleansed. The same texts have been used by conflicting systems of religious jurisdiction: the groups may be in competition, but rabbi, priest and minister have all found it beneficial for their people to learn such language.

Providence and Personal Gratification

It must, however, be doubted whether the Psalms could have retained their vitality as a vehicle of such diverse religious identity, if that was the whole story. The psalter is not simply an imposition, it is also a choice. Much of its use has always been self-administered. In using the Psalms of individual providence the self learns a variety of roles, takes on perhaps a new identity, is reassured and fortified by the sense of being part of a story. To stress the role of prayer in forming our identity does not equate prayer with a withdrawal from society. It is because the psalter is so concerned with the formation of our identity that it is preoccupied by society, and its tensions. To enter the world of the psalmist is to enter a world of vibrant social imagery and conflict. As has already been noted there is a preoccupation with persecution which verges on paranoia.

In this the psalmist reflects an unchanging conflict of human social experience. On the one hand we need other people, we depend on them in numberless ways, so that our life outside society is inconceivable. On the other hand no society has ever been devised which is equally satisfying to all its members. The oppressed are filled with bitterness and resentment which they are inhibited from expressing. The privileged are haunted by a sense of insecurity and the need to defend what they possess, and yet have to affect an air of confidence and benignity. Thus we are presented with the harsh fact that the others on whom we depend are a threat if they are unsatisfied, or an affront if they are successful. Both sides of the dilemma find expression in the Psalms. The social context may be menacing:

> Do not let them gloat over me.
> Do not let them say to themselves, 'Hurrah!
>   We have swallowed him up at one gulp'.
> Let them all be disgraced and dismayed
>   who rejoice at my fall;
> Let them be covered with shame and dishonour
>   who glory over me (Ps. 35.24ff.).

Equally it may be a source of moral outrage:

> Be angry no more, have done with wrath.
> Strive not to outdo in evildoing (Ps. 37.8).

Human society is never far away from the psalmist – unavoidable and disturbing. Generations of religious people have found that they could recognize their own experience in such words.

The Credibility of Providence

Such an approach to the Psalms is obviously quite inadequate for the traditional religious believer. Believing that there exists a God who answers prayer, the Psalms of personal providence subtly strengthen him in that belief. The rehearsal of God's interventions in the past give him, so to say, a credible record. The prayers themselves, passed through successive generations across the centuries, reassure that this is no isolated eccentricity or unsubstantiated hope. Their language seems to represent the voice of experience. The urgency of our present hopes and fears easily leads us to confuse our aspirations with reality. We then come to see the Psalms of individual providence as a record of man's relationship with an objective existing God who uses his power to intervene on our behalf. When our wishes are realized, we say that our prayers are answered. When our desires are frustrated, we say that God's will is not our will. If events continue to disappoint us, we compensate ourselves not by revising the belief, but by a reluctant acquiescence which makes our continuing prayers only more vehement. If we then experience a deliverance for which we had almost ceased to hope, that becomes a sign of God's mercy and miraculous power. If we die in bitterness and disappointment that both demonstrates the weakness of our faith and silences our doubts. In that way prayer triumphs over experience.

To the challenge, 'Why do people believe that God answers prayer?' if such a God does not exist, it would be too slick an answer simply to say that they believe because they want to. So much of the discussion of the difference which prayer makes has concentrated on the power of prayer to change situations by the direct or mediated intervention of God. Once again the conservative believer and the impatient atheist prefer to conduct the debate at that level – the atheist because it assures him of victory, the believer because it conceals the contribution of his own motivation. If such a God does not exist then the benefit, which generations of those who prayed have experienced, must be explained differently. Quite apart from any answer, prayer conveys a certain consolation in the utterance. I learn to see myself differently: the story I tell promises to rescue my life from the threat of confusion and meaninglessness. In speaking of God as the rescuer, I learn to see myself as the object of favour. The attention, which society refuses me, God gives me and, as was indicated in the Introduction, every prayer has strong narrative and dramatic implications.

In concentrating the debate about prayer on the power of God, the vital issue of religious morality has been obscured – and anyone who questions that power is swiftly discredited as a non-believer. Very simply, the power of God is the counterpart of the privilege of the person who prays. Many versions of that privilege would seem to be morally unacceptable. Whenever we seek in prayer immunity from the afflictions that trouble others or unequivocal vindication in our disputes with others, it is difficult to see how such prayers help us to grow either in charity or humility. That kind of privilege is vicious, but when we have firmly rejected it, we may still see a role for prayer in establishing the unique identity and worth of every human being, not in terms which discriminate and divide, but in terms which acknowledge our interdependence and solidarity. In such prayer we discover ourselves not by condescending to the afflicted, but in sharing their experience, acknowledging that, if we can help to sustain them, their courage often confounds our fears, and gives us a new confidence which we could not have discovered without them. As we learn to confess our sin, we are no longer concerned to vindicate our special rectitude, but to see more truly the extent of our responsibility. When we no longer flatter ourselves in our prayer, we are free to discover the self-respect which needs no extraneous power to sustain it.

3

The Creator of the World

O Almighty Lord God, who for the sin of man didst once drown all the world, except eight persons, and afterward of thy great mercy didst promise never to destroy it so again: We humbly beseech thee, that although we for our iniquities have worthily deserved a plague of rain and waters, yet upon our true repentance thou wilt send us such weather, as that we may receive the fruits of the earth in due season; and learn both by thy punishment to amend our lives, and for thy clemency to give thee praise and glory; through Jesus Christ our Lord.

Churches tend to be coy when they have changed their beliefs; like the Church of Rome they prefer to pretend that their new position is precisely what they have always believed and affirmed. So in the Prayer Books of this century the old prayers for fair weather and for rain have quietly disappeared. This is a loss because they are a wholesome reminder of what was traditionally implied by a belief in God's creation. The story of the flood and Noah's ark was not simply an ancient folk tale appended rather thoughtlessly to the rational account of God's creation in Genesis, it was its complement: the same God of absolute power was portrayed in both stories. Only the Almighty Creator can destroy: he declares his pleasure and his punishment in the accidents and the order of the natural world. It is our good fortune that he has promised never to obliterate his handiwork again, but our repentance and amendment are necessary if we are to enjoy 'the fruits of the earth in due season'. On such a view it was entirely consistent to see righteousness, and not chemicals, as the best fertilizer.

The two presuppositions of this book which will probably be most strange to the reader, are that the God of cosmology is quite secondary in the development of our religion, and that despite the later rationalizations of philosophers of religion the function of that belief was not primarily explanatory. I have argued that the images of Judge and King were the fundamental beliefs about God, legitimating as they did the control of human behaviour, and promising the most powerful sanctions of reward and punishment. In this chapter I will try to justify those presuppositions by looking more closely at the doctrine of creation as it appears in the Psalms. An examination of how the psalmist considered the natural world shows the way in which the belief in God the creator functioned, and once that function has been appreciated it is unnecessary to posit any other origin. Human beings did not believe in God in order to explain to themselves the origins of the world; instead they believed in a divine Judge, who was their particular King. In order to defend the social control of that God it was necessary to arm him with the most sweeping powers, and to ensure that there was no escape from his jurisdiction.

The Natural World and the Extent of Divine Jurisdiction

There are several suggestions in the Psalms that it was the need to ensure a universal jurisdiction, which first gave to the tribal God of Israel a universal dimension. We have already seen in the examination of Psalm 139 (above, pp. 30ff.) how the notion of God's omniscience demanded that God's scrutiny and power be cosmic:

Where can I escape from thy spirit?
    Where can I flee from thy presence?
If I climb up to heaven, thou art there;
    if I make my bed in Sheol, again I find thee.
If I take my flight to the frontiers of the morning
    or dwell at the limit of the western sea,
even there thy hand will meet me
    and thy right hand will hold me fast (Ps. 139.7–10).

It is striking that there is no mention of God the creator here, but in order to be an effective judge he has to be omnipresent. The whole universe is transformed into a giant cage. Similarly the Psalms contain frequent references to God's universal jurisdiction:

> Let all the ends of the earth remember and turn again to the
>   Lord;
> let all the families of the nations bow down before him
>   (Ps. 22.27).

God may be the God of Israel, but that only indicates those who benefit from his attention, it is not intended to limit his scope. This remarkable juxtaposition of universal claims with a quite specific focus is most clearly seen in the opening words of Psalm 50:

> God, the Lord God, has spoken
> and summoned the world from the rising to the setting sun.
> God shines out from Zion, perfect in beauty (Ps. 50.1f.).

The same cosmic imperialism is today most spectacularly maintained by the Roman Catholic Church, where the bishop of Rome still claims to speak *urbi et orbi*, to the city and the world. Historically universalism has been the rhetoric of imperialism; in the ancient world Greeks and Romans equated their citizenship with humanity. Today the interests of the USA and the Soviet Union are disguised respectively as those of 'the free world' and of the international working class. In speaking for such a God the religious man was transcending the constraint of any particular local audience:

> Hear this, all you nations;
> listen, all who inhabit this world,
> all mankind, every living man,
> rich and poor alike;
> for the words that I speak are wise,
>   and my thoughtful heart is full of understanding
>   (Ps. 49.1ff.).

Only a universal audience can satisfy the majesty of God and the vanity of man.

The Natural World and the Power of the Divine Judge

Today the universe is a puzzle to be explained, and once it has yielded its secrets it can be manipulated by technology. For ancient man the disparity between the power and permanence of the created world, and his own puny strength and brief life-span was overwhelming. At most he might associate himself with such power. So in the royal propaganda of Psalm 72 the king was associated with some of the qualities of the natural world:

> He shall live as long as the sun endures,
>> long as the moon, age after age.
> He shall be like rain falling on early crops,
>> like showers watering the earth (Ps. 72.5f.).

In the same way the natural world provided images of God's character:

> Thy true love is firm as the ancient earth,
> thy faithfulness fixed as the heavens (Ps. 89.2).

Here God is not represented directly as the creator of heaven and earth, rather he is associated with their permanence. So one of the ways in which God was related to the natural world was not as its transcendent creator, but as manifesting himself in some of its most terrifying phenomena. Storms in particular were experienced as vivid occasions of his presence:

> The waters saw thee, O God,
>> they saw thee and writhed in anguish;
>> the ocean was troubled to its depths.
> The clouds poured water, the skies thundered,
>> thy arrows flashed hither and thither.
> The sound of thy thunder was in the whirlwind,
>> thy lightnings lit up the world,
>> earth shook and quaked.
> Thy path was through the sea, thy way through mighty waters,
>> and no man marked thy footsteps (Ps. 77.16–19).

The directness of the identification is a little startling to those brought up in a more rational orthodoxy. To see this simply as an explanation of natural phenomena which would otherwise be inexplicable, is to parody the evidence. The psalmist is not concerned to explain the thunderstorm, but to exalt his God. All the manifestations of the storm establish the supremacy of God over man: as the psalmist reveals his intention in the last line quoted: 'no man marked thy footsteps'. It may well be that such a view of storms could only be held in a state of ignorance about the natural world; the psalmist, however, is not concerned to overcome such ignorance, but to exploit it. The storm God is then directly associated with the Exodus history of Israel:

> Thou didst guide thy people like a flock of sheep
>   under the hand of Moses and Aaron
>   (Ps. 77.20; cf. 78 and 114).

The brutal power of the storm, which seems quite beyond human direction, is nevertheless seen in the end as the ally of two privileged beings.

In Psalm 97 we can see how the power of the storm and of the judge are intertwined:

> Cloud and mist enfold him,
>   righteousness and justice
>   are the foundation of his throne.
> Fire goes before him
> and burns up his enemies all around.
> The world is lit up beneath his lightning-flash;
>   the earth sees it and writhes in pain (Ps. 97.2ff.).

Here the storm does not simply produce awe: it is conceived as the instrument of divine justice. Another phenomenon with which God was closely associated was the earthquake:

> When the earth rocks, with all who live on it,
> I make its pillars firm.
> To the boastful I say, 'Boast no more',
> and to the wicked, 'Do not toss your proud horns'
>   (Ps. 75.3f.; cf. Pss. 82.5, 68.8).

The association is almost always menacing. There is nothing like an earthquake for cutting man's pretensions down to size, and exposing the vulnerability of our achievements. To this day the prospect of another San Francisco earthquake exercises a macabre fascination. In the psalmist's eyes such disasters are only a matter of terror for the wicked: he can be quite fearless amid such havoc:

> God is our shelter and our refuge,
> a timely help in trouble;
> so we are not afraid when the earth heaves
> > and the mountains are hurled into the sea,
> > when its waters seethe in tumult
> > and the mountains quake before his majesty
> (Ps. 46.1ff.).

All this terrifying power is only evidence of God's glory. His control of the political world is as absolute as his control of the natural world:

> Nations are in tumult, kingdoms hurled down;
> > when he thunders, the earth surges like the sea (Ps. 46.6).

The psalmist can even gloat about the ensuing destruction, which makes a mockery of all military strength:

> > Come and see what the Lord has done,
> > the devastation he has brought upon the earth,
> > from end to end of the earth he stamps out war:
> he breaks the bow, he snaps the spear
> > and burns the shield in the fire (Ps. 46.8f.).

It is a very aggressive form of anti-militarism. The secret of such belief and its attraction is that while immense and destructive power is attributed to God, he is nevertheless 'our God':

> The Lord of Hosts is with us,
> > the God of Jacob is our stronghold (Ps. 46.7,11).

What appears at first sight simply to be a belief about God proves on examination to be a very specific and consoling belief about ourselves.

The Appropriation of Divine Power

This introduces one of the most consistent features of the psalmist's account of creation: the ascription of power to God is almost invariably balanced by the appropriation of that power by men. The exaltation of God indirectly benefits those who praise him. It is not accidental that this feature has attracted little attention. The whole literary structure artfully directs the attention of the worshipper away from himself towards God. At first sight the references to the natural world seem self-depreciatory; they underline the impermanence of man. This is done not by contrasting man's transience with an unchanging natural world, but by suggesting that before God both are equally fleeting. Psalm 102 provides a clear example of this process of thought. The psalmist articulates his mortality and in doing so our own:

> My strength is broken in mid course;
> the time allotted me is short.
>> Snatch me not away before half my days are done,
>> for thy years last through all generations (Ps. 102.23f.).

God's creation is then referred to as a pledge of his endurance:

> Long ago thou didst lay the foundations of the earth,
> and the heavens were thy handiwork (Ps. 102.25).

But that only introduces a more radical contrast between the transience of created things and the eternity of the Creator:

> They shall pass away, but thou endurest;
>> like clothes they shall all grow old;
>>> thou shalt cast them off like a cloak,
>>> and they shall vanish;
> but thou art the same and thy years shall have no end
> (Ps. 102.26f.).

However, just as the power which man declines to claim for himself and ascribes to God, he subsequently appropriates, so here the permanence of God assures the psalmist of posterity:

> thy servants' children shall continue,
> and their posterity shall be established in thy presence
> (Ps. 102.28).

The psalmist is not here seeking for an explanation of the world in his beliefs about the Creator; he is using that belief in a carefully measured approach to a God who can assure him of a future in his children.

On a more personal note the belief that man is God's creation out of the dust of the earth, functions in the same way. At first all seems self-depreciation:

> For he (God) knows how we were made,
> he knows full well that we are dust.
> Man's days are like the grass;
> he blossoms like the flowers of the field:
> a wind passes over them, and they cease to be,
> and their place knows them no more (Ps. 103.14ff.).

The tone of humiliation, however, gives way to one of confidence: the endurance which man himself does not possess, he receives from his God, providing that he obeys him:

> But the Lord's love never fails those who fear him;
> his righteousness never fails their sons
> and their grandsons
> who listen to his voice and keep his covenant,
> who remember his commandments and obey them
> (Ps. 103.17f.).

This process of veiled appropriation, where the benefit which the whole exchange envisages only appears as an afterthought can be seen in Psalm 29:

> The God of glory thunders:
> the voice of the Lord echoes over the waters,
> the Lord is over the mighty waters.
> The voice of the Lord is power.
> The voice of the Lord is majesty.
> The voice of the Lord breaks the cedars,
> the Lord splinters the cedars of Lebanon.

> He makes Lebanon skip like a calf,
> Sirion like a young wild ox.
> The voice of the Lord makes flames of fire burst forth,
> the voice of the Lord makes the wilderness writhe in travail;
> the Lord makes the wilderness of Kadesh writhe.
> The voice of the Lord makes the hinds calve
> and brings kids early to birth (Ps. 29.3–9).

Here God is associated with the sound of the thunder: there does not seem any notion of God as maker. He exercises his power through the perceived effects of thunder. Nevertheless after this impressive catalogue of divine power the psalmist then appropriates that power for the people of Israel:

> The Lord will give strength to his people;
> the Lord will bless his people with peace (Ps. 29.11).

In Psalm 29 the power ascribed to God turns out to be available to Israel, but even where a more reflective and universal note is struck, the same process of ascription and appropriation is equally present. Psalm 8 is perhaps as near as the psalter gets to the lofty abstraction of the philosophy of religion. Even here God is 'our God' and takes a lively interest in 'silencing enmity and vengeance to teach thy foes a lesson', and there is entire confidence that the foes of God and the psalmist are the same. Even so, the psalm is ostensibly not about Israel but about mankind:

> When I look up at thy heavens, the work of thy fingers,
> the moon and the stars set in their place by thee,
> what is man that thou shouldst remember him,
> mortal man that thou shouldst care for him?
> (Ps. 8.3f.)

Here the notion of creation is explicit; just as the heavens disparage the significance of man, so they in turn are diminished by being seen as the work of God's fingers. The verses of self-humiliation only prepare for the most sublime self-assertion:

> Yet thou hast made him little less than a god,
> crowning him with glory and honour.
> Thou makest him master over all thy creatures;

thou hast put everything under his feet:
all sheep and oxen, all the wild beasts,
    the birds in the air and the fish in the sea,
    and all that moves along the paths of ocean
        (Ps. 8.5–8).

The glory that was first projected on to God rebounds to magnify the worshipper, who participates in the same mastery over nature which he has first ascribed to God.

Similarly the apparent permanence of the natural world could be appropriated in the same way. Psalm 93 draws attention to the age and permanence of the world, which reflects qualities of its maker:

Thou hast fixed the earth immovable and firm,
    thy throne firm from of old;
    from all eternity thou art God.
O Lord, the ocean lifts up, the ocean lifts up its clamour;
    the ocean lifts up its pounding waves.
    The Lord on high is mightier far
    than the noise of great waters,
    mightier than the breakers of the sea
        (Ps. 93.2ff.).

These qualities of the natural world are then appropriated for far more human artefacts:

Thy law stands firm, and holiness is the beauty of thy temple,
    while time shall last, O Lord (Ps. 93.5).

In this way all the human arrangements of Jewish law, and the man-made temple in Jerusalem are associated with the unchanging power of the natural world. Despite the artistry of Constable we are reluctant to make any such claims for our cathedrals, but some Christians still like to associate their moral viewpoint with 'natural law'. The tendency is weaker today, but it has not quite disappeared. It has the advantage for those who promulgate such laws, that their rulings can no more be challenged than the force of the tides.

The Doctrines of Providence and Creation

While in later dogmatic theology the doctrines of creation and providence tended to be treated separately, in the Psalms they are combined. All the power inherent in the natural world is made available to the psalmist to deliver him in emergencies. When the psalmist calls to God the reply is spectacular:

The earth heaved and quaked,
the foundations of the mountains shook;
they heaved, because he was angry.
Smoke rose from his nostrils,
devouring fire came out of his mouth,
glowing coals and searing heat.
He swept the skies aside as he descended,
thick darkness lay under his feet.
He rode on a cherub, he flew through the air;
he swooped on the wings of the wind.
He made darkness around him his hiding-place
and dense vapour his canopy.
Thick clouds came out of the radiance before him,
hailstones and glowing coals.
The Lord thundered from the heavens
and the voice of the Most High spoke out.
He loosed his arrows, he sped them far and wide,
he shot forth lightning shafts and sent them echoing.
The channels of the sea-bed were revealed,
the foundations of earth laid bare
at the Lord's rebuke,
at the blast of the breath of his nostrils (Ps. 18.7–15;
    cf.II Sam. 22.8–16).

If the response to prayer was always like that, the power of prayer would not be in question. This rehearsal of divine strength is not, however, an explanation of a thunderstorm, it represents the promise of effective intervention and deliverance:

He reached down from the height and took me,
he drew me out of mighty waters,
he rescued me from my enemies, strong as they were,
from my foes when they grew too powerful for me (Ps. 18.16f.).

The cosmic strength of my God is the pledge of my safety. God's power over creation and my security are complementary beliefs.

This helps to make sense of a feature of the ancient understanding of creation which is otherwise inexplicable. Like many of the surrounding nations the ancient Israelites had a creation myth which saw the origin of the world in terms of a triumphant struggle between God and a sea-monster. While this is not the account which is given in Genesis, it is plainly present in Psalm 74:

> But thou, O God, thou king from of old,
>> thou mighty conqueror all the world over,
> by thy power thou didst cleave the sea-monster in two
>> and break the sea-serpent's heads above the waters;
>> thou didst crush Leviathan's many heads
>> and throw him to the sharks for food.
> Thou didst open channels for spring and torrent;
>> thou didst dry up rivers never known to fail.
> The day is thine, and the night is thine also,
> thou didst ordain the light of moon and sun;
>> thou hast fixed all the regions of the earth;
> summer and winter, thou didst create them both
> (Ps. 74.12–17; cf. Ps. 89.9f.).

Considered as an explanation of the origin of the world the story of a cosmic struggle is not at all satisfactory. It immediately prompts the question, who created the sea-monster? If, however, one considers the non-explanatory function of the belief, its attractions become clear. Those who are seeking divine intervention and victory in their own struggles will cheerfully see the created world as a pledge of the divine conqueror's power. It is not that they are trying to explain the world, it is rather that they want to see the world in such a way that it gives them confidence.

For the happy consequence of the ancient belief in the divine Creator was that he was sufficiently strong to vindicate the innocent and punish the wrong-doer. Human systems of justice are always fragile, and liable to be corrupted by powerful law breakers, as the psalmist was well aware:

> Put no faith in princes,
>> in any man, who has no power to save.

> He breathes his last breath,
> he returns to the dust;
> and in that same hour all his thinking ends (Ps. 146.3f.).

The disparagement of all competing human systems of control is deliberate, it serves to exalt the alternative. Divine justice had an impressive objective strength:

> Happy the man whose helper is the God of Jacob,
> whose hopes are in the Lord his God,
> maker of heaven and earth,
> the sea, and all that is in them;
> who serves wrongdoers as he has sworn
> and deals out justice to the oppressed (Ps. 146.5f.).

The greatest challenge to such beliefs could only be practical: the apparent triumph of the wicked. Natural disasters like famine and earthquakes in no way discredited it; they could always be seen as punishments. If they wiped out the innocent, that only proved that no one was as innocent as they thought, and in the nature of the case the dead cannot question such a verdict.

There was probably always a tension in the religion of ancient Israel between the traditions associated with the Lord of hosts who promised victory, and the more indigenous traditions which looked to God for the benefits of the natural world: food and fertility. The preoccupation with famine was in all ancient societies recurrent:

> All of them look expectantly to thee
> to give them their food at the proper time;
> what thou givest them they gather up;
> when thou openest thy hand, they eat their fill.
> Then thou hidest thy face, and they are restless and
>   troubled;
> when thou takest away their breath, they fail
> [and they return to the dust from which they came];
> but when thou breathest into them, they recover;
> thou givest new life to the earth
>   (Ps. 104. 27–30; cf. Pss. 105.16; 111.5).

Many of the ancient Israelites, like the authors of the Book of Common Prayer, had starkly physical expectations of their God. It is difficult to distinguish description from invocation:

> Thou dost visit the earth and give it abundance,
>   as often as thou dost enrich it
> with the waters of heaven, brimming in their channels,
>   providing rain for men.
> For this is thy provision for it,
> watering its furrows, levelling its ridges,
> softening it with showers and blessing its growth.
> Thou dost crown the year with thy good gifts
>   and the palm-trees drip with sweet juice;
>   the pastures in the wild are rich with blessing
>   and the hills wreathed in happiness,
>   the meadows are clothed with sheep
>   and the valleys mantled in corn,
>   so that they shout, they break into song
>   (Ps. 65.9–13).

These were the rewards of religious practice; just as famine was the penalty of disobedience. To suggest that these were simply consequences of a belief in God's creation is to ignore the strong motivation of starving people. They needed to believe that their God was in control of their world:

> Thou art girded with strength,
> and by thy might dost fix the mountains in their place,
> dost calm the rage of the seas and their raging waves.
>   The dwellers at the ends of the earth
>   hold thy signs in awe;
>   thou makest morning and evening sing aloud in triumph
>   (Ps. 65.6ff.).

Societies whose limited technology still made them very vulnerable had every reason to believe in a God, whose power would supply their weakness.

The Doctrine of Creation – a Rationale of Obligation

The doctrine of God's creation not only promised immense objective rewards and sanctions for the system of religious control, it also provided a rationale of religious obligation. In asserting the fact of God's creation, it was also asserting an obligation. At its simplest God's creation of the world made it his possession:

> The earth is the Lord's and all that is in it,
>   the world and those who dwell therein.
> For it was he who founded it upon the seas
>   and planted it firm upon the waters beneath (Ps. 24.1f.).

Modern clerical fund-raisers are particularly fond of this teaching. It enables them to make claims on the property of others which ignore the usual conventions which suggest that the person who owns something has it as his own disposal. The doctrine that God owns everything had its most successful implementation in the medieval arrangement of the tithe on all produce. The doctrine is developed rather differently in the Psalms: God's possession of the natural world is taken for granted and makes any material gift or sacrifice to God redundant:

> I need take no young bull from your house,
>   no he-goat from your folds;
> for all the beasts of the forest are mine
>   and the cattle in thousands on my hills.
> I know every bird on those hills,
>   the teeming life of the fields is my care.
> If I were hungry, I would not tell you,
>   for the world and all that is in it are mine (Ps. 50.9–12).

Although the clear-sightedness of such language sounds almost irreverent that was by no means the psalmist's intention. He disparages sacrifice, not to liberate men from an onerous obligation, but to supplant it with something far more conscious and intimate:

> Offer to God the sacrifice of thanksgiving
> and pay your vows to the Most High (Ps. 50.14).

A religion based on a material exchange of goods can leave the worshipper untouched and with the impression that he can manipulate God with gifts. A religion of thanks and conscious duty demands the entire submission of its devotees.

So the creation of the world by God established a sense of awe in those who perceived themselves as his creatures. First the power of God in creation is proclaimed:

> The Lord's word made the heavens,
> all the host of heaven was made at his command.
> He gathered the sea like water in a goatskin;
> he laid up the deep in his store-chambers (Ps. 33.6f.).

The immensity of the sea, which usually gives man a sense of insignificance, is here reduced to the contents of a goatskin in the exaltation of God. The psalmist then indicates the attitude which is appropriate to such power:

> Let the whole world fear the Lord
> and all men on earth stand in awe of him (Ps. 33.8).

Such a God can both require and also enforce a universal obedience:

> For he spoke, and it was;
> he commanded, and it stood firm.
> The Lord brings the plans of nations to nothing;
> he frustrates the counsel of the peoples.
> But the Lord's own plans shall stand for ever,
> and his counsel endure for all generations (Ps. 33.9ff.).

The Natural World and the Prestige of the Divine King

Apart from considerations of reward and punishment, prestige is an integral part of all human power. Every focus of power needs and creates its propagandists, who project its claims and effectiveness; indeed this was a major function of ancient courts: those who enjoyed patronage responded with flattery, and both protected and monopolized the source of benefit; proclaiming to outsiders its legitimacy and benignity, and carefully husbanding it for their own use. While we might see the ancient priesthoods fulfilling the same function, they gave God a far greater royal state. Consistently the natural world is personalized as a court which sings the praises of its divine king:

> The heavens tell out the glory of God,
>   the vault of heaven reveals his handiwork.
> One day speaks to another,
> night with night shares its knowledge,
>   and this without speech or language
>   or sound of any voice.
> Their music goes out through all the earth,
>   their words to the end of the world (Ps. 19.1–4).

The relationship between this personification of the natural world and the doctrine of creation is varied. In Psalm 19 it is exuberant rather than reflective. In Psalm 148 the praise of the natural world is portrayed as a conscious response of thanks to its maker:

> Praise him, sun and moon;
>   praise him, all you shining stars;
> Praise him, heaven of heavens,
>   and you waters above the heavens.
> Let them all praise the name of the Lord,
> for he spoke the word and they were created;
> he established them for ever and ever
> by an ordinance which shall never pass away (Ps. 148.3–6).

In Psalm 65 the thought is more confused:

> The dwellers at the ends of the earth
>   hold thy signs in awe;
> thou makest morning and evening sing aloud in triumph (Ps. 65.8).

In part the natural world is seen as evidence of God's power, so that the belief in God's power is some kind of rational deduction. On the other hand morning and evening are both personified and made the direct instruments of divine propaganda (cf. Ps. 69.34; 98.8; 103.22; 145.10ff.).

The Doctrine of Creation and the Supremacy of Israel's God

There is one more vital function of the doctrine of creation as it appears in the Psalms that requires examination: it served to distinguish the God of Israel from the idols of the surrounding nations, and also established his supremacy over them. The distinction is crisply stated in Psalm 96:

> Great is the Lord and worthy of all praise;
>> he is more to be feared than all gods.
> For the gods of the nations are idols every one;
>> but the Lord made the heavens
>> (Ps. 96.4f.; cf. 97.6–9; 115.2–8,15f.).

The contrast between the idols fabricated by men and the God who made the heavens had tremendous polemical possibilities, which will be explored later. Here it suffices to point out that the objectivity of the world gave to its maker a reality which the fabrications of men clearly lacked. The supremacy of the God of Israel over the gods of their neighbours was a belief to which the Israelites were understandably attached.

Psalm 95 provides an instructive example of the way in which the doctrine of creation enabled them to exalt their God at the expense of their neighbours. It begins with a rousing statement of the supremacy of their God:

> Come! Let us raise a joyful song to the Lord,
> a shout of triumph to the Rock of our salvation.
> Let us come into his presence with thanksgiving,
> and sing him psalms of triumph.
> For the Lord is a great God,
> a great king over all gods (Ps. 95.1ff.).

This supremacy is then justified by his power in creation:

> the farthest places of the earth are in his hands,
>> and the folds of the hills are his;
> the sea is his, he made it;
> the dry land fashioned by his hands is his (Ps. 95.3ff.).

The appropriate response is then indicated: a gesture of total self-abasement:

> Come! let us throw ourselves at his feet in homage,
> let us kneel before the Lord who made us (Ps. 95.6).

Such beliefs and good manners then receive their proper reward: the promise of care and protection:

> for he is our God,
> we are his people, we the flock he shepherds.
> You shall know his power today
> if you will listen to his voice (Ps. 95.7).

In this way a small and precariously placed people, constantly threatened by larger neighbours, sustained their morale and their identity. Egypt and Assyria might represent powerful empires, but their gods were simply human inventions. Israel, by contrast, could rely on the God who had the power of the world at his disposal. His supremacy was the pledge of Israel's very existence in an insecure and anxious world.

Assertion and Explanation in the Doctrine of Creation

The Psalms deserve this close attention because they are among the earliest and most influential texts of the Jewish and Christian religions, which are still in constant use. It is therefore difficult to represent them as merely the application of beliefs, which were already well grounded in a careful consideration of the natural world; or at least we have no evidence for making that assumption. The embarrassing truth seems to be that the assertions about God's power over the natural world were made first for powerful immediate motives, and only justified later. The functions of those beliefs show quite clearly the motivations which drove religious men to make such claims: the need to offer rewards and threaten punishments, to give an account of the all-embracing nature of religious obligation, and to assure the supremacy of their God over all competing claims. The Psalms show the gradual transition from associating God with powerful natural phenomena like storms and earthquakes, to a more sophisticated view which attributes glory to

God by his causal power as the Creator of all things. This belief is not an attempt to explain the world, though it is probably only really plausible in a state of ignorance about the world. Its purpose is rather to exalt the divine king. Christians have particular reason to be aware of this process as a very similar development took place in the early church in relation to Jesus. When Christians declare in the words of the Nicene Creed that 'through him all things were made', it is far from clear that they are intending to explain the natural world. Instead this represents the culmination of a process, which began with claims for Jesus' control of the storm and the waves, and ended by attributing to him the might and majesty of the entire world. The origin and the justification of such claims is not to be found in the natural world, but in the desire of the early church to arm their Messiah with the whole panoply of the Creator God.

It is not accidental that both in Judaism and in early Christianity the greatest stress on the doctrine of creation took place in contexts where one of the usual sources of religious propaganda and prestige was not available. With the destruction of the first temple in Jerusalem and the exile, Jews were deprived of a historic focus for their faith, and those who were dispersed had to live in physical environments dominated by the grandiose buildings of other gods. At first sight the Jews possessed nothing. By ascribing the whole created world to the handiwork of their God they created a comparatively indestructible temple which dwarfed the grandest constructions of men. In the same way the early Christians lived in a predominantly urban environment which was both imposing and hostile. Turning from the fragile and corrupt environment of the city, they found confidence in the belief that the world itself was theirs: for the God who made the world was their God. A reflection of the same process can be seen in modern times. The haunting spiritual, 'He's got the whole world in his hands', may represent the same defiant response to an experience of immediate deprivation.

The Existence of God and the Natural World

This transcendence of any physical location represented a most significant mutation of religious belief. The refusal to make physical representations of God and the eventual disconnection between

God and any holy place was interpreted by some ancient observers as atheism. That seems to have been one contemporary response at the destruction of the second temple, when the Holy of Holies was discovered to be empty. Judaism and those religions which derive from it, were able to dispense with human fabrications, because the world itself was the pledge of the objectivity of their God. Its existence spoke of his existence – indeed as we have seen they could happily envisage the destruction of the created order, because of their confidence in the reality of their God. In retrospect this appears an exaggerated act of imagination – first they used the existence of the world of nature to assure themselves of the reality of their God, and then looked forward to discarding that world in order to exalt their God yet more. In their more sublime moments they would say that God is, the world only exists.

On such a view the existence of the world demands that its maker also exists if such a word does not diminish him. Only a God who exists can intervene with power in the world of existing creatures. Before leaving this treatment of the power of God, it is only necessary to remind the reader that the power of God is also the privilege of men, or more precisely the advantage of some men over others. Only in denying the existence of such a God and refusing the blandishments of such power can we be certain that our religion is not a form of disguised domination, encouraging human beings to seek privilege and shun solidarity. The God of power can only use the language of love as a rhetoric to silence dissent and conceal aggression. The radical denial of such a God is necessary if the language of love is ever to be credible on the lips of religious people.

Part Two

THE REVERSAL OF
RELIGIOUS PRIVILEGE

4

The Man of God in a Predatory World

You know that in the world the recognized rulers lord it over their subjects, and their great men make them feel the weight of authority. That is not the way with you; among you, whoever wants to be great must be your servant, and whoever wants to be first must be the willing slave of all (Mark 10.42ff.).

The Refusal of Privilege

For nearly two millennia the Christian church has continued to offer its prayers to God in the language of the psalter. It is the most powerful statement of continuity between the Old Testament and the New. The language of judgment was transferred to the return of Jesus at his second coming. The privileged people were no longer defined by circumcision, but by baptism. Jesus' kingship was proclaimed in the ancient royal Psalms. The hopes which had once centred on Jerusalem were transferred to a heavenly city. The Christian soul appropriated the language of personal providence – seeing enemies first as demons and more recently as sins. The Creator of the world was envisaged in yet more sovereign terms – he no longer struggled with the sea-monster, he created all things out of nothing: in this way the Jewish belief in creation became the pledge of the resurrection hope. In that Christian reading the Psalms continued to celebrate a God of power; the delay of his triumph only made such prayers more urgent. This life was, however, no longer an adequate theatre for his victory. While Jews had looked to their God to establish his power in the context of lives terminated by death,

Christians proclaimed a God whose power reversed death itself. Any affliction was only a temporary trial: nothing could prevent the glorious outcome.

This Christian adaptation of the religion of power, which owed much to the cult of martyrdom developed during the Maccabean period of Jewish history, had the immense strength of being impossible to discredit, once it had been accepted. No longer promising any temporary success, no failure could conceivably discredit it. Such experiences only aroused more desperate expect-ations. The resurrection of Jesus – understood as the reversal of his death – was its only basis. Historians might dispute the adequacy of its evidence, but that inevitably appeared to most Christians as merely academic and far more remote than the alleged event itself. For armed with the conviction that Christ had reversed death, no future experience could shake them in their hope. It was a faith which gave to its adherents a unique confidence: they discovered in the language of the Psalms a new note of triumph. For in this Christian reading the psalter became the most impressive of prophecies. The religion of power which the Jews had created for themselves – only to experience its disappointment – became in Christian terms an anticipation which found its fulfilment solely in themselves. Such startling arrogance could lead them to draw this conclusion from the whole history of Jewish faith:

> These also, one and all, are commemorated for their faith; and yet they did not enter upon the promised inheritance, because, with us in mind, God had made a better plan, that only in company with us should they reach their perfection (Heb. 11.39f.).

In modern times atheist and rationalist critics of Christianity have seized on the inadequacy of the evidence for the reversal of Jesus' death: for both the critic and the exponent of the triumphalist version of Christianity the reality of that reversal of death is as fundamental as the objective reality of God, which is its precondition. Unlike many Christians I am prepared to accept that the evidence for those claims is inadequate: in that form they cannot be made. I believe, however, that Christians must repudiate their triumphalist past, not simply because of the force of external criticism, but because of a much more compelling voice at the very heart of their religion. The

Christian, who reads the Psalms with his attention on the cross, will find in the figure of the crucified the most radical and consistent critic of the religions of power. The life and death of Jesus represent a refusal of privilege, a deliberate vulnerability, which subverts the triumphalist versions of both Christianity and Judaism. I have argued that the desire for privilege and the exercise of privilege are at the heart of all religions of power. We attribute strength to God because we trust that he will exercise it on our behalf. Much of Christianity has been marked by exactly that process: the only difference between that version of Christianity and other religions of power is the more extravagant nature of its promises; for no earthly happiness can compare with an eternity of bliss. God, however, is still their God who secures for them a special destiny. So through most of Christian history the expectation of heaven has required a lively sense of the possibility of hell. The nature of the Christian privilege was portrayed with savage detail in the doom paintings of medieval art.

It is the conviction that God looks after his own, that he protects them from the ills which afflict other men, that the crucified man of God so powerfully repudiates. The language of victory, of security and deliverance, with which the Psalms abound, cannot be placed on his lips without being questioned. This is no mere embarrassment that the God of power has deserted him: he condemns the hopes and desires that create such a God. Every Christian prayer, which honestly approaches God 'through our Lord Jesus Christ' has to recognize that the man of God is not distinguished by avoiding trouble, but by the manner of his bearing it. The crucified Jesus defines the man of God in a way which excludes every form of privilege, apart from the consciousness of God. Religion ceases to be a matter of overcoming our weakness by invoking the power of God to preserve us from the suffering of others. Instead the man of God forgets his weakness and dares to encounter human destructiveness: he does not seek privilege either in flight or protection. He meets destructiveness. He suffers destruction. In that meeting with his fellow men, he is sustained only by his God. The crucified Jesus defines the man of God in a way which does not fulfil the stereotypes of the psalter, but rebukes them.

The Absence of Protection

Betrayed into the hands of his enemies, in the grip of cruel physical pain, reviled and isolated, Jesus in his death had become a figure of utter misery. The early church liked to discover in the crucified Messiah an example of all those afflictions which the psalmist had both dreaded and prayed to be spared. The sense that the horror had been anticipated served to mitigate its impact. It is from this source that the writers of the first three Gospels allow Jesus' enemies to supply their own commentary as he dies on the cross:

> The passers-by hurled abuse at him: they wagged their heads and cried, 'You would pull the temple down, would you, and build it in three days? Come down from the cross and save yourself, if you are the Son of God'. So too the chief priests with the lawyers and elders mocked at him: 'He saved others', they said, 'but he cannot save himself. King of Israel, indeed! Let him come down now from the cross, and then we will believe him. Did he trust in God? Let God rescue him, if he wants him – for he said he was God's Son' (Matt. 27.39–43).

This mockery is presented with conscious irony, for Jesus' foes utter the same taunts with which the wicked torment the righteous man in the psalter (Ps. 22.7f.). The reference is, however, more disturbing than the evangelists realize. The righteous man of the psalter is certainly no stranger to mockery (Pss. 12.2; 31.11 and 18; 35.15–25; 55.3–15), but equally he expects it to be silenced by God's intervention (Ps. 52.1–7). The same has ultimately to be said of the evangelists. They may place the doubting words of the wicked on the lips of Jesus' enemies, but in fact they themselves share the same point of view. The miraculous reversal of Jesus' death in his subsequent resurrection demonstrated in their eyes that Jesus' enemies were short-sighted, not that their expectations were mistaken. As the evangelists tell Jesus' story, on the third day God did indeed rescue him and show that he wanted him.

We do not know when the Wisdom of Solomon was written, but at the latest it must have been composed within a few years of Jesus' death. Like the Christian evangelists the writer of Wisdom also has the taunts of the wicked in the psalter ringing in his ears, and he envisages a scene which curiously echoes their portrayal of Calvary. As the Old Testament Apocrypha is not always well known even to Christians, it is worth quoting at some length:

> The wicked say: 'For us let might be right! Weakness is proved to be good for nothing. Let us lay a trap for the just man; he stands in our way, a check to us at every turn; he girds at us as law-breakers, and calls us traitors to our upbringing. He knows God, so he says; he styles himself "the servant of the Lord". He is a living condemnation of all our ideas. The very sight of him is an affliction to us, because his life is not like other people's, and his ways are different. He rejects us like base coin, and avoids us and our ways as if we were filth; he says that the just die happy, and boasts that God is his father. Let us test the truth of his words, let us see what will happen to him in the end; for if the just man is God's son, God will stretch out a hand to him and save him from the clutches of his enemies. Outrage and torment are the means to try him with, to measure his forbearance and learn how long his patience lasts. Let us condemn him to a shameful death, for on his own showing he will have a protector' (Wisd. 2.11–20).

I shall not speculate on the historical relationship of this passage to the Christian texts: suffice it to say that the scoffing words of Psalm 22 are common to them all. They introduce a significantly different set of interests from either the story of Job or the figure of the Suffering Servant in Isaiah. Job is afflicted by cruel accident, envisaged as sent from God, however indirectly. His wife and comforters may irritate him, and make a bad situation worse, but his conflict is fundamentally not with them, but with God. He doubts the justice of God, he does not question his power. His conclusion – overawed by the sheer strength of the Almighty – is strangely similar to that of the wicked in Wisdom. 'For us let might be right' (Wisd. 2.11). The wicked may refer that might to themselves, while Job ascribes it to God, but both endow power with moral worth. This the author of Wisdom refuses to do, and the story of Jesus' suffering also rebukes that identification.

Like Job the Suffering Servant of Isaiah is afflicted by God:

> He grew up before the Lord like a young plant
> whose roots are in parched ground;
> he had no beauty, no majesty to draw our eyes,
> no grace to make us delight in him;
> his form, disfigured, lost all the likeness of a man,
> his beauty changed beyond human semblance
> (Isa. 53.2).

He suffers shame and humiliation, but that seems to be only the human response to the disease and deformity which God has inflicted on him:

> He was despised, he shrank from the sight of men,
> tormented and humbled by suffering;
> we despised him, we held him of no account,
> a thing from which men turn away their eyes.
> Yet on himself he bore our sufferings,
> our torments he endured,
> while we counted him smitten by God,
> struck down by disease and misery (Isa. 53.3f.).

Because God is conceived as the author of affliction, it is his justice which is vindicated by the notion of vicarious suffering. So like Job the Servant is amply compensated for his injuries:

> Yet the Lord took thought for his tortured servant
> and healed him who had made himself a sacrifice for sin;
> so shall he enjoy long life and see his children's children,
> and in his hand the Lord's cause shall prosper.
> After all his pains he shall be bathed in light
> after his disgrace he shall be fully vindicated;
> so shall he, my servant, vindicate many,
> himself bearing the penalty of their guilt.
> Therefore I will allot him a portion with the great,
> and he shall share the spoil with the mighty,
> because he exposed himself to face death
> and was reckoned among transgressors,
> because he bore the sin of many
> and interceded for their transgressions (Isa. 53.10ff.).

There is a discrepancy in this picture of the servant which begins by representing his sufferings as the affliction of God and ends by regarding them as something which he has voluntarily undertaken. The change of focus and responsibility is necessary to obscure a subtle shift in the subject of vindication. It makes possible the rehabilitation of the servant rather than of God. In this way the suffering which might have discredited God's justice acquires an unsuspected merit. This both assures the servant's future reward and benefits his sinful contemporaries:

> He was pierced for our transgressions,
> tortured for our iniquities;
> the chastisement he bore is health for us
> and by his scourging we are healed.
> We had all strayed like sheep,
> each of us had gone his own way;
> but the Lord laid upon him
> the guilt of us all (Isa. 53.5f.).

His peers, however, are only indifferent to his plight, they are not represented as themselves its cause.

Wisdom and the Gospels envisage a quite different situation and are preoccupied by another problem. The suffering here is social. It takes place not as the sentence of God, but in the course of human conflict about God. It is evil men who destroy the man of God and their ability to do so is not questioned. The cruel pattern of secular experience is not challenged. Evil is not explained as divine visitation, it is the outcome of human destructiveness. For this reason both stories have deeply subversive implications, for the weakness of the man of God impugns the power of his Master. It is the achievement of both stories that they allow themselves such honesty in facing the death of the good at the hands of the wicked; but it proves to be a vision they are unable to sustain. They cannot refrain from trying to rehabilitate the God of power in fantasy, by a sublime and defiant act of imagination. The disciples of Jesus stubbornly proclaimed that the man whom men had killed, God had raised. The author of Wisdom is driven to make equally arbitrary claims:

But the souls of the just are in God's hand, and torment shall not touch them. In the eyes of foolish men they seemed to be dead; their departure was reckoned as defeat, and their going from us as disaster. But they are at peace, for though in the sight of men they may be punished, they have a sure hope of immortality; and after a little chastisement they will receive great blessings, because God has tested them and found them worthy to be his. Like gold in a crucible he put them to the proof, and found them acceptable like an offering burnt whole upon the altar. In the moment of God's coming to them they will kindle into flame, like sparks that sweep through stubble; they will be judges and rulers over the nations of the world, and the Lord shall be their king for ever and ever (Wisd. 3.1–8).

We should not allow the beauty of such language to hide the perplexity of its thought. The reality of death is only equivocally acknowledged – it is the mere semblance of defeat and disaster: a mistake which only the foolish can make. What appears to man as punishment is the pledge of peace and immortality, but the grounds which the writer has for claiming this, other than the desire that it be true, are left unspoken. Equally the purpose of the test is quite obscure, unless God is thought to be ignorant. The first part of this book will have well prepared the reader to understand the triumphant reversal with which the passage ends: a promise that the power of the divine king will be vindicated, and that he will reward the godly by sharing it with them – 'They will be judges and rulers over the nations of the world' (cf. I Cor. 6.1–3). This represents a final desperate tribute to the God of power, in the hope that his servants will, despite all appearances, participate in his victory. The failure of God to intervene decisively in present experience is not a failure but a test. The glorious dénoument is only postponed. It is an evasion with which the successive disappointments of Adventists and Jehovah's Witnesses have made us entirely familiar.

The Distinction of Goodness from Greatness

The story told in the Book of Wisdom is structurally identical to that of the New Testament Gospels. Apart from their historical reference, the only difference between the two is that the fictional character in Wisdom is unambiguously righteous, while Jesus' righteousness is the point at issue in his suffering. It is what his followers affirm and what his enemies deny and indeed intend the ignominy of his death finally to discredit. No evangelist could say of Jesus that he girded at his enemies 'as law-breakers'. He may have been a 'living condemnation of all their ideas', but he conspicuously did not shun the company of sinners. Interestingly he refrained from boasting that God is his Father, and surprisingly in view of the convictions of his followers, he was far from unmoved by the prospect of his death. The belief that 'the just die happy' is not found in his teaching, nor does he himself exemplify it. I would suggest that in these differences lies the distinction between Judaism and Christianity; be that as it may, Jewish sage and Christian evangelist are in every other respect telling the same story and wrestling with the same problem. They share the same ambivalence towards it. For both of them the man of God is a figure of real goodness. Nevertheless he suffers at the hand of wicked men. The man of God thus combines two characteristics which they would prefer to separate – goodness and weakness. The story of vulnerable goodness suggests that even if virtue is not its own reward in the superficial sense of guaranteeing happiness, it nevertheless deserves respect regardless of its fate. It is the affirmation of the centurion at the crucifixion who recognizes Jesus' worth without benefit of resurrection.

The ambivalence lies in the fact that those who tell the story cannot accept its implications. They cling to the God of power whose very existence is called in question by the experience which underlies their tale. At issue is the nature of moral integrity. If goodness was necessarily accompanied by happiness and success there would be no difficulty. But it would be a very different kind of goodness from the one which our world of violence and conflict demands. As we have seen in the religions of power righteousness was valued as the condition of the prosperity with which it was in theory rewarded. The story of the Gospels and of Wisdom reminds us that if we only value human goodness for the power to which it gives us access, it is power and not goodness that we really worship. The vulnerable figure of the good but powerless man of God questions what it is we seek to gain in our worship of God. We long for power and goodness to be combined because that saves us from painful choice. Against all such easy compromise, the crucified man of God insists that power and goodness are different, and invites us to make our choice. All my satire in the first part of this book, which may have seemed too relentless in its exposure of the way in which men appropriate to themselves the power they ascribe to God, is only an attempt to express the message of the crucified. For all its appearance of orthodoxy and objectivity the worship of the God of power is a form of devious and aggressive self-assertion. That is no discovery of glib, modern atheism – it is the subversive word from the man of God on the cross.

The transformation of religion which he represents is the new testament. The new religion has a different understanding of the misery of man from that of the religions of power which preceded it. This becomes plain once we strip the story of the crucified man of God of its fanciful additions. Wisdom's postponed resurrection and the Christians' anticipated resurrection change the emphasis of the story and distract us from its meaning. Religion is safely once again a matter of happy endings. The suffering and death of Jesus become mere incidents which are gloriously reversed. Belief in God is an invitation to believe that we will live happily ever after. The gospel of the cross becomes a fairy tale. If we resist such cheap consolations, we can begin to see an alternative to the religions of power.

Unlike the death of Socrates, who went to his end without any thought that divine or human intervention might save him, the hope against hope that God's cavalry might arrive at the last minute haunts the synoptic accounts of Golgotha. Nor is the possibility of human rescue entirely absent. The Gospels contain conflicting views as to whether Jesus himself entertained a hope of divine deliverance. In Mark's Gospel it seems to be the clear implication of Jesus' reply to the High Priest's interrogation, when he confesses that he is the Messiah, and adds: 'and you will see the Son of Man seated at the right hand of power and coming with the clouds of heaven' (Mark. 14.62). Nowhere in Mark does Jesus disclaim that hope until his last despairing words. The horror of the scene is heightened by a macabre comedy of misunderstanding. The words in which Jesus gives up all hope of intervention are misheard by the crowd, and create a final scene of cruel cross-purposes:

> At midday a darkness fell over the whole land, which lasted till three in the afternoon; and at three Jesus cried aloud, '*Eli, Eli, lema sabachthani?*', which means, 'My God, my God, why hast thou forsaken me?' Some of the bystanders, on hearing this, said, 'Hark, he is calling Elijah'. A man ran and soaked a sponge in sour wine and held it to his lips on the end of a cane. 'Let us see', he said, 'if Elijah will come to take him down'. Then Jesus gave a loud cry and died (Mark 15.33–37).

The brooding darkness which might have promised divine attention signifies nothing. The outstretched hand of God proves to be only the taste of sour wine on a sponge.

It is not perhaps surprising that none of the other evangelists chooses to imitate the stark brutality of Mark's account. Matthew prefers to rule out the possibility of divine deliverance at the outset of the Passion. During the struggle that accompanied Jesus' arrest in the garden of Gethsemane Jesus forbids violent opposition, claiming the availability of divine intervention, while declining to invoke it:

> 'Put up your sword. All who take the sword die by the sword. Do you suppose that I cannot appeal to my Father, who would at once send to my aid more than twelve legions of angels? But how then could the scriptures be fulfilled, which say that this must be' (Matt. 26.52ff.).

Here the powerlessness of Jesus is represented as a deliberate, studied obedience to his scriptural destiny. In that way the appearance of weakness is reconciled with the hankering for divine power. It may not be used, but it is nevertheless in the background.

Only in John has the wistful longing for divine intervention entirely disappeared. Instead the only possibility envisaged is that of human rescue which is mentioned in the examination before Pilate:

> Jesus replied, 'My kingdom does not belong to this world. If it did, my followers would be fighting to save me from arrest by the Jews. My kingly authority comes from elsewhere'. 'You are a king, then?' said Pilate. Jesus answered, '"King" is your word. My task

is to bear witness to the truth. For this was I born; for this I came into the world, and all who are not deaf to truth listen to my voice' (John 18.36f.).

The strong sense of the futility of earthly power that is present in Matthew is here taken further. The attitude is uncompromisingly dismissive. Even the title of King with its inevitable connotations is only most grudgingly admitted. The rationale is, however, quite different from Matthew's – the mysterious unspecified scriptural destiny has been replaced by a role which plausibly makes power redundant. The witness to the truth only destroys his credibility if he seeks to compel.

I would argue that John has seen the true logic of the tale he tells. Extraneous power might have rescued Jesus or repressed the evil that he suffered. It could, however, only have compromised his goodness, it could have added nothing to it. The disconcerting feature of his goodness is precisely that it has discarded all claim to power, human or divine; it does not need them. The man of God needs neither the violent defence of men nor the privileged intervention of an Almighty God – his goodness is quite independent of such support and alone sustains him in his weakness. To a humanity preoccupied by its sense of weakness and seeing in that weakness its misery, Jesus presents himself as victim not as victor, a lamb rather than a lion. The utter vulnerability of goodness is displayed without equivocation, in a way which makes it possible to realize that our wretchedness comes not from the pain we suffer but from the damage we inflict. Instead of feeling threatened and looking for protection, the victim directs our attention towards our own destructiveness. Instead of presenting happiness as the natural reward of virtue, the new testament presents the best of men being destroyed by his fellows, and dares to believe that precisely that destiny is both worthy of the best of men, and is one which only the best of men can sustain. In a world where every man is either a predator or a victim, only the man of God, sustained not by power but by goodness, can take the decision to be a victim. For him alone that is not defeat.

The Preoccupations of Weakness: Self-Pity and Violence

The power of God reflected a preoccupation with the weakness of man. I have spoken repeatedly of the ancient religions – Jewish and pagan – as religions of power, looking to the claims they made for their gods, and the benefits which they sought from them. It might have been less misleading to speak of them as religions of weakness, in which the whole purpose of religious observance was to overcome the fears which that perception of weakness engendered. Part of the attraction of such religion came from the success with which it articulated recurrent anxieties. From the horrors of pillage (Ps. 74.4–8) to the wretchedness of illness (Ps. 22.14f.) and unspecified personal misery (Ps. 6.6f.) the note of lamentation is seldom distant from the psalter. It provides the necessary counterpoint to the praise of the Almighty – it ensures that his 'Almightiness' is appreciated. Successive generations have found solace and relief in suffering by giving utterance to their desolation in beautiful language which yet suggests that no case is hopeless. The words which console are also a threatening reminder in more prosperous times. For no experience of success and security can banish anxiety; they only heighten it. We dread the loss of what we presently possess, and are terrified of the afflictions which our good fortune has preserved us from experiencing.

At the heart of such religion is the urge to self-pity which relieves us of all responsibility for our condition. We place the blame for our unhappiness elsewhere: God or society, illness or accident, the quirks of fortune or the temperament of other people. We only suffer the consequences of their deficiencies. In self-pity we no longer need to persuade other people that we are injured – it is sufficient to luxuriate in the consciousness of our oppressed condition. In much of Christian history the crucified Jesus has been easily appropriated by that vision. For millions Jesus has become the man of sorrows, on to whom they can project the whole weight of their misery and disappointment. The figure on the cross comes to symbolize every kind of human affliction. In mourning for him we mourn for ourselves, as anyone who has sung of 'the Sacred Head sore-wounded' to the music of Bach must be aware. As the suffering of the saviour mingles with the tears of the penitent, it is difficult to distinguish the object of grief. This is not a confusion in which we are encouraged to linger:

> Great numbers of people followed, many women among them, who mourned and lamented over him. Jesus turned to them and said, 'Daughters of Jerusalem, do not weep for me; no, weep for yourselves and your children (Luke 23.27f.).

Most Christians have, however, found no difficulty in combining their pity for Jesus with their compassion for themselves. Nowhere is this more movingly expressed than in those masterpieces of late medieval art – the great sculpted entombments of Christ, which adorn so many French churches. A people living with the horror of endemic plague, portrayed their own grief around the grave that they shared with their Saviour. Even so while compassion can inspire heroic action, self-pity is usually paralysing. Once we have succumbed to it no one can pity us as much as we pity ourselves. The understanding of others is then always inadequate, it never appreciates the true nature of our condition. Only an all-knowing God can do justice to our pain. Jesus becomes the pledge that God understands.

The response which the religions of power elicited from their devotees was one of deep inertia – a ready acceptance that initiative like responsibility reside elsewhere. Yet powerlessness, the consciousness of being unable to act in a way which would change our situation, fosters a sense of injury which both resents the inability to act and yet clings to it. The result is that lethargy is punctuated by spasmodic violence. Ostensibly such violence removes those who endanger that privileged identity which the religions of power articulate; it also serves to relieve the internal tensions which the associated human structures of dominance inevitably create. From the persecutions of the Roman Emperors to the pogroms of Czarist Russia lethargy has been punctuated by violence. Fear and self-pity both inhibit our compassion; so the violence of those who have come to see themselves as weak and threatened has an especially merciless character. Those who have come to believe that they are in peril seldom act with magnanimity.

The violence, which Jesus suffers, is an integral part of the religions of power. This is confirmed by all the accounts of his death in the Gospels, for they are largely free of the atonement theories of later

Christianity. Instead of expounding notions of vicarious suffering or dwelling on the all-embracing sinfulness of the event, they portray the religious dynamics which brought about his death, with refreshing precision. Not for them the pietist sentimentality of Mrs Alexander and 'There is a green hill far away'; both the Jewish and the Roman authorities are shown to be defending their prestige, and acting out of fear for their position. In all the Gospels Jesus' death is the outcome of a strategy of self-preservation. His life discredited the prevailing sections of his society (Mark 1.21–3.5). The priests needed to silence him because of the danger of disorder and their fear of Roman reprisals:

> 'If we leave him alone like this the whole populace will believe in him. Then the Romans will come and sweep away our temple and our nation' (John 11.48).

Pilate is not represented as the grand impassive representative of imperial power, but as the timid victim of blackmail, anxiously looking over his shoulder lest he be denounced to the Emperor:

> 'If you let this man go, you are no friend to Caesar; any man who claims to be a king is defying Caesar' (John 19.12).

All are shown to act in fear of a mob, which with cunning they may manipulate, but which they cannot with certainty control. The brutality with which Jesus is treated is portrayed as the result not of strength but of desperation. Faced with such a threat to themselves, Caiaphas and Pilate discover that they have no alternative.

The Subversive Sacraments

We are now in a position to appreciate the deeply subversive possibilities in the Christian sacraments. In so far as Christianity has been only another religion of power, the sacraments have been accommodated to its demands. In that form of Christianity they confer a privileged identity and promise to their participants divine aid. The believer receives the pledge of a special immortality, freed from the threat of hell. While in this life the Christian can expect supernatural power to live free from lust, a faithful and obedient member of the redeemed community. Access to such sacraments was a privilege, to be excluded from them a means of discipline. Through their sacramental monopoly the hierarchy came to exert an increasingly firm control of behaviour. The claims made for such rituals became steadily more extravagant: to question that development was to incur the suspicion of heresy. In exalting the sacraments the priesthood was exalting itself, so modesty was not perhaps to be looked for.

In that way the sacraments became a superior form of magic. It was the heroic achievement of the Protestant reformers to perceive those claims as superstitious, though only the Baptists had the audacity to be entirely consistent. Their critical courage deserves the highest admiration, but they involved themselves in formidable difficulties. How could they give a convincing rationale for a separate priestly class, once they had denied the sacramental religion which it had created? If justification before God was by faith alone, why were sacraments necessary and what benefits did they confer – or were they merely an expression of the believer's faith? If faith was essential in the sacramental transaction between God and man, how could the baptism of infants be defended? The dilemma of the reformers was that although they questioned many of the supernatural claims made for the Mass, they still wanted the religion of power of which in its Christian form the Mass had been an integral part. Moreover, they shared with the old priesthood a desire to control society. In Milton's wry comment: new presbyter is but old priest writ large. Thus they needed the universal obligation which infant baptism imposed on every member of society. Only the Baptists were prepared to limit their jurisdiction to a gathered church, and compensated themselves for such restraint by the rigour of their internal discipline.

The sacraments are, however, only two of many public celebrations in which we acquire and reinforce our fragile identity. The celebrations may be religious or secular in character, but they have in common the enjoyment of triumphant power and conspicuous success. The victory parades of military might, the sumptuous pageants of coronation or inauguration, sporting contests and trophies, the sexual display of dance and dress, the sleek satisfactions of prosperity seductively purveyed by advertising copy, all invite us to identify ourselves with power and success. In them we align ourselves with life's winners. Wherever Christianity has become a religion of power, the sacraments are associated with such celebrations, often becoming a part of them. The victory march ends in the cathedral, the eucharist becomes an integral part of the marriage ceremony.

Wherever the sacraments have not been entirely absorbed in their secular context they cannot help but introduce a discordant threatening note. Baptism with its connotations of being immersed and overwhelmed, the eucharist with its reminiscence of the passion, both are essentially symbols of the crucified. They are reminders of just those dimensions of experience, which secular celebrations are designed to repress. Behind every victory there is the bitterness of defeat, hereditary pomp goes hand in hand with hereditary poverty, the domestic complacency which some enjoy exacerbates the loneliness of the unattractive and the frustration of the barren. The man on the cross reminds the soldier not of his victory, but of his victim. He introduces into the splendour of courts a nakedness which mocks all pretension. He disrupts the dreams of love with the unlovely face of misery. Everything that power and success seek to evade, to distance, to consign to other people, the crucified exemplifies.

All secular celebrations imply that success is deserved: that in this life power and goodness walk together. Victory is not simply the triumph of might, but the vindication of justice. Hereditary privilege is not mere accident of birth, but the source of legitimacy. Sexual attraction becomes the recognition of personal worth. Prosperity is the reward not of luck but of labour and prudence. The privileged and the powerful are never content simply to enjoy their advantage, they always seek the acclaim and applause, which only the disadvantaged can supply. The affirmation of the crucified threatens every comfortable equation of merit with success. He exposes the violence latent in power, the shame which is the corrollary of honour, the deprivation which luxury only accentuates. Naked and vulnerable he dares us to identify ourselves with a goodness that needs no power to defend it, no honour to proclaim it, no wealth to reward it. In baptism that is the identity we acquire, and every eucharist is only a reminder of that destiny.

Provocation and Peace

This is to suggest a radically different understanding of Christ's death from that offered by the traditional theories of atonement. While suffering and failure tend to destroy a leader, the followers of Jesus were eager to claim that his death was a source of blessing, his apparent failure a God-given destiny. Stubbornly they refused to allow his death to discredit him, and their own experience of persecution intermingled with his (viz. Philippians, II Corinthians and Colossians). The effect of this development was to separate Jesus' death and its consequences from its causes. Present sufferings and fear made them concentrate on the suffering of their Lord. In proclaiming the triumphant reversal of his resurrection they were asserting their own hopes about themselves. The pattern of death and resurrection came to dominate their understanding of the faith and of the sacraments. This abstraction of the death of Jesus from its context made it possible to become quite careless in identifying subsequent suffering and death with his. To speak of arthritis as a cross is only to succumb to misleading self-pity; to equate the death of a fighting man in battle with Jesus' sacrifice is a more serious mistake: it totally distorts its meaning. Anyone wishing to understand the betrayal of modern Christendom to the pressures of militaristic nationalism has only to read the words of 'The Supreme Sacrifice':

> Proudly you gathered, rank on rank to war,
> As who had heard God's message from afar;
> All you had hoped for, all you had, you gave
> To save Mankind – yourselves you scorned to save.
>
> Splendid you passed, the great surrender made,
> Into the light that nevermore shall fade;
> Deep your contentment in that blessed abode,
> Who wait the last clear trumpet-call of God.
>
> Long years ago, as earth lay dark and still,
> Rose a loud cry upon a lonely hill,
> While in the frailty of our human clay
> Christ our Redeemer passed the self-same way.

Still stands his cross from that dread hour to this
Like some bright star above the dark abyss;
Still, through the veil, the Victor's pitying eyes
Look down to bless our lesser Calvaries.

These were his servants, in his steps they trod,
Following through death the martyr'd Son of God.
Victor he rose; victorious too shall rise
They who have drunk his cup of sacrifice.

One cannot but admire the skill with which self-pity is here mingled with self-deceit. Reading such language one might imagine that Jesus also went to his death rifle in hand. After the heat of battle there has been a revulsion against such sentiment, but it shows how easily every painful experience becomes a pledge of resurrection. The attractions of such a doctrine are obvious, but it is a cheap travesty of the Gospels. They insist that Jesus' death be understood in terms of the life which led to it.

I have already indicated that the portrayal of Jesus' life sharply differentiates him from the fictional character in Wisdom. The protagonist of the Wisdom story is unequivocally righteous, his persecutors are firmly designated as wicked. He submits himself to the Law and suffers for its sake – even in persecution therefore he can be sustained by the consensus of his religious culture. We may suspect that the same authorities, which found it necessary to crucify Jesus, would have been quite happy to support or at least to patronize the righteous man of Wisdom – he would have been no threat to them. The tensions and contradictions in Jesus' story are far more disturbing. Jesus speaks of God and prays to God; he is a man of God – not only did his followers identify him with God, his intimacy with God was such that he identified himself with his God, as a son identifies himself with his father. Yet this man, so preoccupied with the love of God, is killed in the name of God. His life and teaching so challenged the Law of God and the Temple of God that their protectors were provoked into savage reprisal. The man of God suffers at the hands of God's guardians.

In our minds weakness is often confused with cowardice. When we speak of good people being weak we usually mean that they are timid. In representing the weakness and vulnerability of goodness on the cross, Jesus is not exemplifying cautious compromise or judicious submission. His weakness only demonstrates his courage. While the Benedictus dreams of a world where it is safe to be good, where free from fear we can worship God, Jesus dares to be good in a world which offers no such comforting security. In the name of God he dares to provoke those who claim to be God's representatives, without any other defence or protection than his faith in God. As a man of God he is not silenced by his lack of power, or overawed by his lack of prestige. He is perceived therefore as being destructive and disruptive.

So at the heart of this conflict there is a controversy about the nature of peace. In the words of the Johannine Christ:

'Peace is my parting gift to you, my own peace, such as the world cannot give' (John 14.27).

All the protagonists – the Jewish religious leaders, the Roman imperial administration, as well as Jesus – proffer peace, but they envisage it in terms which are diametrically opposed. Jesus died excluded from Jerusalem, the privileged city of holy peace. His crucifixion was the work of the Pax Romana, order established by consistent military might. Jewish priest and Roman official both equated peace with strength, and insisted that power and justice are at one. That shared confidence, however differently expressed, enabled them to demand submission and inflict punishment without self-question.

Jesus conspicuously refuses to submit. He does not humble himself before the High Priest, his insolent silence before Pilate defies the significance of that jurisdiction. He breaks the Sabbath, he associates with the renegade, he ignores the proscribed fasts. When he goes to the Temple it is to call in question its management. He is not therefore afraid either to draw attention to himself or to make a fuss. He is no example of self-effacing good manners. Equally he does not demand submission: in a way which has often embarrassed his followers his teaching is remarkably free of commands. Even the Johannine Christ, who repeatedly asks for obedience, is curiously reticent about its content. Instead of submission, he invites imitation, demanding of others no more than he asks of himself:

Anyone who wishes to be a follower of mine must leave self behind; he must take up his cross, and come with me (Mark 8.34).

His peace is not therefore a matter of enforced obedience. It needs neither police nor protection. It asks instead only to be practised. It demands that we cross the barriers which surround and confirm our own identity. In Jesus' case that meant a ready association with those publicly branded as sinners. For the early Jewish church it demanded that they welcome Gentiles, rather than discriminate against them. The price of such peace is a readiness to forgive and be forgiven, a refusal to nurse recrimination and revenge. No external power could enforce such demands, and all the assumptions behind the use and justification of force are undermined by them.

God and the Self-Respect of the Victim

A conspicuous feature of the death of Jesus is his deliberate and public humiliation:

> Then the soldiers took him inside the courtyard (the Governor's headquarters) and called together the whole company. They dressed him in purple, and plaiting a crown of thorns, placed it on his head. Then they began to salute him with, 'Hail, King of the Jews!' They beat him about the head with a cane and spat upon him, and then knelt and paid mock homage to him. When they had finished their mockery, they stripped him of the purple and dressed him in his own clothes (Mark 15.16–20).

Socrates went to his death with the company and support of his friends. His self-esteem was sustained by their affection and understanding to the end: it was never seriously threatened. Whereas the philosopher's disciples ministered to his last needs, Jesus is isolated and ridiculed. In the accounts of Socrates' end there is an underlying harmony and confidence, so that to the last he is able to behave with self-conscious decorum. He calmly rebukes the sorrow of his disciples:

> Really, my friends, what a way to behave! Why, that was my main reason for sending away the women, to prevent this sort of

disturbance; because I am told that one should make one's end in
a tranquil frame of mind. Calm yourselves and try to be brave.[1]

The process of Jesus' death is altogether more savage. It is not
enough that he is killed, he must be shamed. Self-composure is
hardly to be reconciled with crucifixion: the women standing at the
cross are not sent away lest their tears disturb the scene. The
dereliction is too unmitigated to consider appearances.

The orchestration of prestige and denigration remains one of the
most powerful forces in society. The process which was once the
preserve of the clergy from the pulpit has been eagerly taken over by
journalists, often safely anonymous. The change may have benefited
the church, but it seems only to have substituted one form of
hypocrisy for another which is even more impenetrable. The leaders
of any society attract resentment, which easily finds expression in
ridicule. The public humiliation is a means of manipulating the
destructive forces involved in a way which strengthens the structure
of power rather than endanger it. It results in a conspiracy between
the leaders and their underlings. The leaders connive at a degree of
unseemly disorder. The underlings take the opportunity to vent their
spite and resentment, not on their leaders, but on those who are even
weaker than they are. All the disruptive tensions within a society are
thus given expression, but in a way which actually discourages
dissent. It is the school teacher's trick of establishing discipline by
picking on the least offensive or popular child in the class.

The story of Jesus' trial and humiliation gives no comfort to the
platitudes of democracy, nor does it in any way exalt public opinion.
Throughout the Gospels Jesus is portrayed as indifferent to the
response of the crowd, free from any control by his audience,
unimpressed by its praise and finally undeterred by its abuse. The
mob is shown to belong to the highest bidder – it may not be bribed
by the priests, but it is still manipulated by their cunning. The
implications are disconcerting to the complacency of common sense.
Any person who derives self-esteem from such a fickle source is
doomed to a path of moral cowardice. The denial of Peter, currying
the favour of a serving-girl, is a well-judged contrast to the integrity
of his master. In the moment of testing Peter seeks the company of
other people, and when they turn on him, he dissociates himself

from the relationship which would compromise him. He answers Jesus' gaze with tears and remorse.

Peter's betrayal stems from the same weakness that earlier in the Gospel leads him to dissociate the Messiah from the possibility of repudiation, 'You think as men think, not as God thinks' (Mark 8.33); in this rebuke Jesus indicates the source of his own confidence, and the conflict in which this necessarily involves him. Just as his goodness is quite independent of protecting power, so his integrity and confidence need no human applause or prestige to sustain them. His sense of God, his ability to pray to God and in that prayer to discover his true self, sustains him when every form of human prestige has been removed. He can suffer ridicule and abuse; he can be stripped of all his clothing, but his nakedness only shows what cannot be taken from him. Men make their heroes and destroy them: the man of God is differently placed. He lives in his prayer to his God; it is that prayer which makes him who he is. He has passed beyond the flattery of human fame or the shame of human censure.

The perpetrators of the crucifixion did not act as godless men – on the contrary they acted as men who believed that God was the property of the powerful and successful, that God was their God. Their position and prestige were the best – perhaps the only – argument for the existence of such a God. They were not therefore afraid to become God's executioners. In that way they played out the recurring drama of God's sovereignty: silencing dissent and manifesting yet again the dreadful power of his kingdom. In speaking of such a God they concealed themselves and their interests. The power of God cloaked the violence of men, the glory of God hid the self-regard of his agents. They wanted the power and the honour of this world, the power and honour which they actually possessed. They proclaimed and reverenced a God who gave it to them. Such were the predators who seized on Jesus, but the prey refused to submit. The lamb yielded himself to the lions, but would not equate their appetite with God's will. Instead the victim appropriated God as his sole resource. He was content to be deprived of all human power and stripped of all human prestige, because only in that way could the integrity of the man of God be demonstrated. The true God is inseparable from the man who invokes him. The true God provides no hiding place for the self-interest of those who proclaim him. The man of God is totally exposed to the scrutiny and ridicule of men. Only the man on the cross without power or prestige can speak to us of a God which our suspicion cannot sully. He shatters all our illusions about God and the world. The only benefit which such a God confers is the love and knowledge of himself, and once we have come to know him, which means becoming the kind of people who can love him, we realize that it is the world which deceives – that power is empty, that fame is hollow, that every other joy disappoints.

Living without Vindication

The triumphant faith of the church can easily distort and mitigate the depth of Jesus' affliction. Christians have always spoken of him as risen, ascended, glorified, but this creates a danger that we read back such language of acclamation, and forget that Jesus died without hearing it. More inisidiously still, when Jesus is thought to share the divine omniscience, he enters into his suffering and death, not as the end of his story, but knowing that it is only a disagreeable incident in his confident divine career. He then resembles an earnest young clergyman serving his time in some deprived parish, secure in the knowledge that his bishop will reward him with a suburban heaven. There may be a real measure of self-sacrifice in such a life: but the assurance of compensation safely interprets its frustrations as temporary – they are the means to a quite different end. The real horror of Jesus' death – misunderstood, betrayed, repudiated – depends on its finality. Otherwise it is merely a charade of condescension. Those who only gain a posthumous vindication live the whole of their lives without recognition or acclaim. Nothing in the attitude of human beings could have comforted Jesus in his agony. All refused to confer significance on his life and achievements. As Jesus died, he can only have thought that his gospel was dying with him. It is that failure which gives his death its particular bitterness: it also indicates the nature of its glory. Jesus dies sustained only by his God – the dreams of a human future are over – its compensations cannot be looked to. His God is not a God of tomorrow's fantasies. He is the God of his daily bread, the God who nourishes him and sustains him today and no further. For Jesus the last today was the day of Calvary. Only the bread of heaven fed him on his cross.

Perhaps the most searching theological problem which the churches now face concerns the account that Christians give of Jesus' vindication. The ancient creeds supplied an uncompromising and apparently uncomplicated answer: 'The third day he rose again from the dead; He ascended into heaven, and sitteth on the right hand of God the Father Almighty; from thence he shall come to judge the quick and the dead.' I shall not explore the philosophical difficulties which surround such miraculous claims, nor shall I do more than indicate that their historical basis is hard to establish. I would simply say that the objections of David Hume are far from new, and have never been satisfactorily answered.[2] Moreover, I sometimes wish that the self-proclaimed defenders of orthodoxy would be a little more candid about the nature of their task. In terms of that orthodoxy it is not simply a matter of a physical resurrection or an empty tomb. However improbable, one can at least envisage the kind of evidence on which such claims might be based. To speak of ascension into heaven and Jesus sitting at God's right hand, is an integral part of the traditional account – and I am mystified as to what might count as evidence for such claims – apart from the fact that Jesus' corpse, like the Mormons' golden tablets, does not appear to be available.

I do not, however, wish to dwell on the philosophical and historical difficulties of such claims: I am much more appalled by their religious implications. It is not just that they have often effectively robbed Jesus' death of its seriousness (though I regard that as a grave religious objection). The fundamental inadequacy lies in the notion of God, which such claims reflect and rehabilitate. What such doctrines reintroduce is an even more evasive version of the God of power. No experience can now falsify its claims. However much God's final intervention may be delayed, on such an account his decisive intervention has already taken place. Despite all appearances God is the fount of power and glory. He does not cure men of that hunger, he merely demands that we satisfy it by obtaining such benefits from him. It is the religion of Handel's *Messiah*. Its deeply secular assumptions do much to explain its enduring popularity.

However meagre it may appear in comparison with the lofty metaphysical dimensions of credal orthodoxy, I believe that Jesus was vindicated retrospectively, not by a miraculous intervention of divine power, but by the stubborn acclamation of his followers. His achievement was so to educate his disciples, that however falteringly and inconsistently, despite mistake and fantasy, they were able to recognize the figure on the cross as truly the man of God. Their proclamation was at times confused, self-serving, and even vindictive. Nevertheless they justified Jesus' vision of God and came to share it as they affirmed and celebrated the memory of his death. They neither mourned nor forgot him. However much they may have delighted in the prospect of his vengeance, they never repressed the memory of the death which their Redeemer underwent. Far from trying to re-write history to obliterate his ignominy, their Judge retained the marks of his passion. It was Jesus' achievement that he created followers who refused to let him die. Taught by him to despise the power of men, they ensured that judicial murder would not silence him. Learning from him a confidence which comes from God alone, they refused to allow shame and failure to discredit him. If I deplore and question some of their claims as extravagant and fantastic, I must recognize in their faith their finest tribute to their Master. Only by such a Master could their eyes have been opened to see that the man whom others crucified was nevertheless the man of God.

The Republic of Plato contains a strange and ultimately cynical anticipation of the story of Jesus' death. It is only an incident in Plato's wider argument, but I am aware nevertheless that much of my understanding of Jesus' death is probably derived from it:

> Consider the just man, simple and generous, and desiring, as Aeschylus said, not the appearance but the reality of justice. So we must take away from him the appearance . . . He must be stripped naked of everything except justice. Without ever committing an injustice, he must have a reputation for the greatest injustice, so that his justice may be proved by the fact that he will not be influenced by his evil fame and its effects but will continue unflinchingly until death, going through life in the appearance of injustice but in the reality of justice.[3]

Plato even imagined a destiny, which strikingly resembles that of Jesus in its details:

The just man so disposed will be scourged, tortured, enchained, his eyes will be burnt out, and at the end of all his sufferings he will be crucified.

This startling convergence only highlights the moral gulf between the viewpoint of *The Republic* and of the Gospels:

Then he will know that what is desirable is not the reality but the appearance of justice.[4]

The Greek philosopher could not envisage a desire for goodness, which might overcome such ignominy. It is the achievement of Jesus both to exemplify such a desire and even to arouse it in his followers.

As we come to share their vision our expectations of God and our understanding of what is good are also changed. Jesus' death gives no comfort to the wistful hope of sentimental liberalism that if you are nice to other people they will necessarily be nice to you. Human reality is far more destructive and contrary than such a view allows, and Christianity cannot be reduced to that kind of prudential moralism. We have to learn to be sustained by the goodness of God – we only court disappointment if we find our satisfaction in the applause of other people. Our delight in God ensures us neither welcome nor agreement. Even when we have learnt to love God and to become the kind of people who can find their joy in prayer, we cannot coerce the response of others. We have no excuse to refuse our love, we must always be hopeful and positive towards others, but we should be under no illusion that the response for which we yearn will necessarily be forthcoming. The person who has learnt to depend upon God may be repudiated for just that reason. That is one of the disconcerting implications of Jesus' story:

Remember what I said: 'A servant is not greater than his master'. As they persecuted me, they will persecute you; they will follow your teaching as little as they have followed mine (John 15.20).

That is not only the death knell of defensive and manipulative sentimentality, it is also a warning against the hunger for a guru. There remains a longing for the spiritual master, who will take responsibility for our religious destiny. The religious desire to be relieved of responsibility continually creates such figures, and there is never a lack of those willing to fill the role:

> Clement of Alexandria's *gnostic*, the spiritual fathers of the Eastern tradition, and especially of the desert tradition, the *startsi* of the Russian tradition. Here what is important is the relation of the disciple to his master, the voice of his master . . . The living voice of the master, the one who through prayer and self-discipline has come to know, that is, come to communion with the heart of the faith, has immediacy and directness, and incarnates the fundamental experience of encounter with the living Lord.[5]

It is a beguiling vision of immediacy and assurance, but both the teaching and the story of Jesus speak of a different reality, in which the would-be disciple betrays his master, and the true master reconciles himself to being neither understood nor obeyed.

Part Three

THE USE OF GOD IN A RELIGION OF PEACE

5

The Credibility of God and the Responsibility of Man

The essence of religion, thus hidden from the religious, is evident to the thinker, by whom religion is viewed objectively, which it cannot be by its votaries. And it is our task to show that the antithesis of divine and human is altogether illusory, that it is nothing else than the antithesis between the human nature in general and the human individual; that consequently, the object and contents of the Christian religion are altogether human.

Feuerbach

Can Religion Survive the Consciousness of its Human Origins?

It is unfortunate that the most brilliant account of the human origins of religion in general and of Christianity in particular was written by a man who saw his work as not only the elucidation of religion but its end. Ludwig Feuerbach's *The Essence of Christianity* appeared in 1841. Its immediate influence on the development of Christian theology was limited, but its indirect influence through the work of Marx and Freud has been immense. Neglected in his own lifetime, he came to set the agenda of modern theology. It is instructive to compare his work with that of the Oxford Movement in England of which he is the exact contemporary. While Newman was encouraging a relatively uncritical return to medieval religious ideas, Feuerbach was also recognizing the role of monasticism and virginity within the Christian tradition. English high churchmen would have been puzzled and appalled to see their priorities so faithfully reflected and so mercilessly explained. It is a mark of the deliberate archaism and unconscious insularity of the Tractarian revival that despite the translation of Feuerbach by George Eliot in 1854 none of its leaders found it necessary to take account of his chapter on 'The Significance of Voluntary Celibacy and Monachism'. More generally Feuerbach's account of religious projection had a seminal influence on the subsequent understanding of religion.

For all Feuerbach's imaginative sympathy his conclusions about religion are quite uncompromising:

> When religion – consciousness of God – is designated as the self-consciousness of man, this is not to be understood as affirming that the religious man is directly aware of this identity; for on the contrary, ignorance of it is fundamental to the peculiar nature of religion. To preclude this misconception, it is better to say, religion is man's earliest and also indirect form of self-knowledge. Hence, religion everywhere precedes philosophy, as in the human race, so also in that of the individual. Man first of all sees his nature as if *out of* himself, before he finds it in himself.[1]

Most of Feuerbach's readers, whether believing or unbelieving, have agreed with him that if he is correct in relating the consciousness of God to the self-consciousness of man, then he is also correct in seeing the proper culmination of religion in philosophy. At the heart of his conception of religion there lies a failure of 'direct awareness'. He can only have been fortified in that conviction by the defensive hostility with which the religious authorities regarded his work.

Feuerbach's enthusiasm for the abstractions of nineteenth-century German idealism and his taste for biological terminology to enhance the scientific quality of his conclusions does not wear well:

> Where there arises the consciousness of the species as a species, the idea of humanity as a whole, Christ disappears, without, however, his true nature disappearing; for he was the substitute

for the consciousness of the species, the image under which it was made present to the people, and became the law of popular life.[2]

Nevertheless I endorse Feuerbach's insight that self-consciousness and religion are intimately related:

Such as are a man's thoughts and dispositions, such is his God; so much worth as a man has, so much and no more has his God. Consciousness of God is self-consciousness, knowledge of God is self-knowledge. By his God thou knowest the man, and by the man his God; the two are identical. Whatever is God to a man, that is his heart and soul; and conversely, God is the manifested inward nature, the expressed self of a man.[3]

Feuerbach assumes that once the religious person has become aware of this that is the end of his religion. It is that assumption that I wish to challenge. The evasion of responsibility is a strategy which lies at the heart of a great deal of religious credibility, and Feuerbach's critique of that is just and devastating. Nevertheless he was mistaken in assuming that all religious credibility was secured in that way, and hasty in his confidence that the language of religion could be reduced to the terms he offered, when he wrote:

We have reduced the supermundane, supernatural, and super-human nature of God to the elements of human nature as its fundamental elements. Our process of analysis has brought us again to the position with which we set out. The beginning, middle and end of religion is man.[4]

Instead I shall argue that it is possible for the religious person to recognize his responsibility for his God and yet to continue to believe in God; to insist that belief in God is identical with the evasion of human responsibility is to beg the question. I may believe in God in order to practice such evasion; but I might fully recognize my responsibility for my God and yet believe that only in the use of such language, in which I address God and discover myself in speaking to him, can I approach a self-knowledge which is both honest and sustainable. That, however, is to anticipate.

Theological Criticism within the Religious Tradition

Superb arrogance is natural to youth, in middle-age – aware of failing powers – we cultivate the kindliness we hope to meet. Much the same is true of Christianity. Its recent conversion to being nice, while in itself commendable, is also an aspect of its defensiveness, the anxious smile of insecurity. Ecumenical politeness and denominational weakness grow together. Faced by an irreligious culture and a secularized society there is a strong temptation for Christians to look with favour on any sign of faith or reverence. The attractions of forming a religious front are obvious, and the inhibition of rational criticism seems a small price to pay. For Christians are painfully aware that reason is double-edged and can easily be turned against those who employ it. So the distinctively modern Christian outlook is to see religion as simply a matter of faith. In religious terms it might be said that ours is *par excellence* the age of faith: by contrast medieval Christendom with its universities and debates, the carefully constructed architecture of both its cathedrals and its theology, deserves to be seen as the age of reason.

We have chosen to forget that the triumph of Christianity in the ancient world was not simply a triumph of faith. It represented the victory of a radical and destructive critique of traditional religious belief and practice, from which Christians had ostentatiously dissociated themselves. Their conspicuous lack of reverence lay at the root of the persecution they suffered. Their non-conformity was noticed and feared: it threatened to undermine the public decencies on which depended, so it was believed, the security and prosperity of society. Tactfulness towards other religious traditions is no part of the Christian inheritance. Instead they displayed an aggressive confidence. At the earliest opportunity they began to pillage the holy places of antiquity. Egyptian shrines, which were already old before the call of Abraham, were destroyed. Not even the politically sensitive statue of Victory in the Roman senate house was spared. Early in the fourth century Athanasius could survey the devastation inspired by the new religion with undisguised triumph:

> In old times the whole world and every place in it was led astray by the worship of idols, and men thought the idols were the only

gods that were. But now all over the world men are forsaking the
fear of idols and taking refuge with Christ.[5]

The bishop exults in a glorious enlightenment.

The furious polemic with which Christians ridiculed the idols of
antiquity was not their own invention. Christianity like Islam inherits
from Judaism a strain of robust rational criticism. The prohibition of
images may be presented as a positive revelation of the divine will at
Sinai; but Jews were not slow to perceive the absurdity of idolatry –
the more so as it belonged to other people. It suggested to them
(above, pp. 107ff.) a flattering distinction which reinforced their
viewpoint and provided a basis for remorseless satire: we worship the
living God, they worship idols, which are their own handiwork:

> Why do the nations ask,
> > 'Where then is their God?'
> Our God is in high heaven;
> > he does whatever pleases him.
> Their idols are silver and gold,
> > made by the hands of men.
> They have mouths that cannot speak,
> > and eyes that cannot see;
> they have ears that cannot hear,
> > nostrils, and cannot smell;
> with their hands they cannot feel,
> > with their feet they cannot walk,
> > and no sound comes from their throats.
> Their makers grow to be like them,
> > and so do all who trust in them (Ps. 115.2–8).

The distinction between 'our God' and 'their idols' reflected and
strengthened obstinate social divisions. For Jews it was a part of their
refusal to be assimilated by surrounding and often victorious aliens.
For Christians, as later for Muslims, it ruled out the possibility of any
accommodation with existing religious institutions. To 'our God' is
attributed the power of the natural world, which he transcends and
which guarantees his total freedom of action. The words, 'He does
whatever pleases him', not only elevate the deity, they also function
as an implicit but gratifying promise to his worshippers. By contrast

the idols are powerless; and the psalmist revels in the human consequences of their futility. The impotence of the idols marks both their makers and their worshippers – a view which conveys its own discreet menace.

There is an unmistakably aggressive quality in this polemic, an ill-concealed self-assertion. In reflective prose image-making was subjected to a more searching examination. The powerful glamour of the cult object was stripped away by a scrupulous account of its human origin, and a refusal to dissociate the image-maker from the image-user. The prophet's art is to insist that the worshipper must not forget the craftsman, instead of the customary collusion, which hides the artist behind his art:

A man plants a cedar and the rain makes it grow, so that later on he will have cedars to cut down; or he chooses an ilex or an oak to raise a stout tree for himself in the forest. It becomes fuel for his fire: some of it he takes and warms himself, some he kindles and bakes bread on it, and some he makes into a god and prostrates himself, shaping it into an idol and bowing down before it. The one half of it he burns in the fire and on this he roasts meat, so that he may eat his roast and be satisfied; he also warms himself at it and he says, 'Good! I can feel the heat, I am growing warm'. Then what is left of the wood he makes into a god by carving it into shape; he bows down to it and prostrates himself and prays to it, saying, 'Save me; for thou art my god'. Such people neither know nor understand, their eyes made too blind to see, their minds too narrow to discern. Such a man will not use his reason, he has neither the wit nor sense to say, 'Half of it I have burnt, yes, and used its embers to bake bread; I have roasted meat on them too and eaten it; but the rest of it I turned into this abominable thing and so I am worshipping a log of wood'. He feeds on ashes indeed! His own deluded mind has misled him, he cannot recollect himself so far as to say, 'Why! this thing in my hand is a sham' (Isa. 44.14–20).

The tone throughout is one of clear-eyed observation; there is no appeal to the knowledge or the sanctions of revelation. It is enough to describe the human process of fabrication to point the inescapable conclusion: idolatry necessarily involves an act of self-deception.

What is particularly impressive is that there is no attempt to evade the human being's responsibility for his religious action. While the early Christians often associated the idols with demons, the prophet acknowledges the entirely human origin of idolatry: 'his own deluded mind misled him'. Throughout there is of course an unspoken contrast with the living God, who even provides the rain and the wood which are the preconditions for such folly, but the primary appeal is to human reason. We are being invited to repudiate behaviour, which is inconsistent and demeaning; for the maker of the image is so clearly superior to the object he has made.

Christianity and Islam were both heirs of this Jewish rationalism, and their triumph was at least in part one of reasoned criticism. It is also important, if embarrassing, to recognize that much of the plausibility of their belief in the one invisible creator was dependent on what that belief enabled them to deny. As we have seen the belief in such a God was not primarily an explanation of the world – that is an illusion propagated by modern philosophers of religion – rather the belief developed as the product of polemic against idolatry. Its negative, prohibiting function was fundamental. It is not accidental that the model of fabrication, derived from the human action involved in idol manufacture, is seized upon by its opponents, and imaginatively reversed in the doctrine of divine creation. It produced a rhetoric of contrast between the false gods made by men, and the one God who, far from being man's creation, was the creator of the whole world of which man was but a small part. So long as the multiplicity of idols survived to be opposed, the vitality of monotheism was assured. Its strongest rationale was not provided by any inferences drawn from the existence of the world, but by the manifest absurdities of the polytheism it attacked. Indeed the refusal to make reassuring and concrete images of God gave the invisible God a credibility his competitors lacked. Their shrines might be despoiled, their very existence discredited by the destruction of their images. The invisible God, who far transcended his handiwork, seemed to be invulnerable.

The distinction between the living God and false gods, plainly made by men and discredited by the very fact of their human fabrication, did not simply represent a conflict of differing beliefs. It was articulated in competing social groupings and organizations which were mutually exclusive. The people of Israel, the Christian church, and the followers of the Prophet, each in turn focussed their identity in this way. Their struggle for survival or dominance inevitably raised questions of power. The weakness of the purely human productions of idolatry was that they could not be expected to transcend the power of their manufacturers: they were unable to answer prayer. On the other hand it seemed quite plausible that the creator of the world might be able to guide and order what he had made. The debate about the power of prayer, while overtly concerned with the power of God, was always conducted with one eye to its human beneficiaries.

Nevertheless it is possible to look at the ancient polemic against idolatry with a certain sympathy. The close connection between palace and temple in so many ancient societies indicates the political function of such religion. The priesthood conferred legitimacy on the holders of political power. The monarchical political structure lent plausibility to the imaginative constructions of the religious leaders. Courts, human and divine, reinforced each other, and both were supported by landholding and taxation. For both indulged in prestige building, which overawed those who paid for it by the splendour that their own sacrifices had provided. Gratuitous building and embellishment celebrated the power to compel such expenditure. The attack upon idolatry was therefore resistance to forms of religion which were economically exploitative and politically repressive. The violence which Jewish and Christian non-conformity suffered is an indication of the coercion which was implicit in the ancient religious structures. Moreover, the local god promised to his or her adherents privileges, which distinguished them from other people: they were therefore intrinsically divisive – and once they became amalgamated in the hellenistic pantheon they inevitably lost their vitality. Where all have prizes there is no longer excitement. The fundamental weakness of ancient idolatry was, however, its inability to give an honest account of itself. Long before the attacks of Jews and Christians, its adherents had already begun to question its propriety. The literal stories, beliefs and practices were seen to be intellectually indefensible. The moral and spiritual understanding of them threatened to make their physical accompaniment redundant. Idolatry therefore was unable to foster honesty, because that proved self-destructive. Instead it was driven to abdicate responsibility and resort to an increasingly unreflective liturgical conformity. There is a disconcerting anticipation of the modern emphasis on the eucharist in the preoccupation with prescribed sacrifices which marked decadent paganism. The Roman exploitation of the hellenistic religious inheritance did nothing to resolve those tensions, rather it accentuated them. Roman ruthlessness about the political implications of religion had therefore deeply contradictory and ultimately destructive consequences. On the one hand it fostered the hellenistic cults as a deliberate instrument of statecraft. On the other hand the attempt to use religion in this way destroyed its credibility and therefore its ultimate usefulness. It remains to be seen whether Christianity, which benefited so spectacularly from the bankruptcy of hellenistic religion, can escape the same fate. Indeed at one level this has already overtaken it, for the politicial catholicism of early nineteenth-century France, the throne and altar attitudes of Wilhelmine Germany or Czarist Russia, or the conservative Anglicanism which built churches to contain social unrest, have proved as barren as the calculated piety of Caesar Augustus.

The Dilemmas of a Self-Critical Theology

Christianity cannot therefore disown rigorous theological criticism without repudiating its own history, and today this places it in a dilemma. For the rational criticism of idolatry voiced by the prophets appears to have its most convincing modern exponents among those atheists and agnostics outside the church. It is true that apart from Marxism modern atheism is as yet amorphous and disorganized. It is, however, pervasive, and if religious practice is to have a future the arguments of disbelief require careful attention. We have already seen that Judaism and its heirs prided themselves on not being man-made – a distinction which was fundamental to their identity and self-understanding. Today the same rational criticism, which once exposed the absurdity of idolatry, now questions the existence of the invisible creator, the all-knowing God of providence. The living God of Judaism would seem to be as much a human creation as the images of Baal and Diana.

Two considerations lead inescapably to this conclusion. It is disturbing to admit how much of the polemic against idolatry rested on a very simple mistake. It consistently refused to recognize that images could be constructed with words, as well as with wood and precious metal. The Old Testament therefore presents us with the paradox that the same texts which ridicule the manufacture of idols do not hesitate to speak of God in frankly anthropomorphic terms. The early hellenistic theologians of the Christian church were already uneasy about this aspect of the Jewish scriptures, but were confident of a solution. In their eyes such imagery was a concession to the simple, which prepared for a more spiritual, abstract understanding of God, expressed most appropriately in negative terms. This development has always been criticized as threatening to rob religious beliefs of any real content – indeed it seems the most orthodox and ancient precursor of that process so aptly designated by Professor Flew as 'death from a thousand qualifications'. Nevertheless, however different the rich personal imagery of scripture may be from the bloodless abstractions of later theologians, both are human imaginative constructions. They are alike human productions, albeit of a literary culture rather than an artist's workshop. Yahweh may be the work of the pen rather than the chisel, but human responsibility for his creation is as obvious as for any more physical work of the imagination. The rich web of stories, laws, poetry and proverbs, which express the Jewish conception of God, are no less man-made than the statues of the pagan gods; though until recently they may have proved less destructible.

In origin the distinction between the living God and the idols seems to have been ill founded, and this has been confirmed by more recent intellectual developments. The traditional arguments for the existence of such a God have never recovered from the criticisms of Hume and Kant, and subsequent emphasis on religious experience seems an inadequate substitute. The strength of the atheist's case is well stated in J. L. Mackie's *The Miracle of Theism*. The collapse of the arguments for the existence of God has opened the way for an account of belief in terms of its human origins – social and psychological. It was the achievement of Feuerbach to realize that the personal character of the invisible God of Christian doctrine was man's signature on his own creative enterprise. The orthodox doctrine that man was made in the image of God has thus been reversed. Man creates God in his own image, so that any family resemblance is hardly surprising. The immediate Christian response was to reaffirm the objectivity, the otherness, the initiative of God. From the neo-orthodoxy of Barth in the 1920s through the stress on revelation and the historical character of Christianity to more recent defences of an interventionist notion of God, the conservative reassertion has been strident. Its arguments, however, have been less convincing, for these restatements have all tended to engage and repudiate liberal theologies of accommodation rather than address themselves to the stark arguments of atheism and disbelief. Karl Barth's fulminations against natural theology in the 1930s or David Brown's entertaining satire of the modern deists in *The Divine Trinity*[6] are alike misleading about the nature of the intellectual and social challenge confronting the Christian religion. The massive indifference of Western Europe is not the result of uncertain and belated attempts to modernize Christian doctrine – it is the consequence of a much more wide-ranging and negative verdict on the whole religious quest.

Christians should not hide from themselves the gravity of their situation. The malaise of contemporary Christendom echoes the end of hellenistic religion. As the ancients were embarrassed by the fables and not infrequent immorality of the gods, so the Christian theologian confronts the miracles of the New Testament and endeavours to accommodate traditional political and sexual attitudes to a new moral sensitivity. It is not impossible, however, to conceive of a successful accommodation combining the sympathetic elimination of the fanciful and an unconscious assimilation of the old and new moralities. Equally there seems no intrinsic reason why Christianity need be either domineering or divisive. The crucial question today is whether it can give an account of itself which is not self-destructive. At first sight the prospect is not encouraging: for Christianity cannot avoid the question of God, and must begin by making the damaging admission that the God of power and privilege, with which it has always been closely associated, does not exist. Belief in the existence of such a God is at best mistaken and at worst deceit. The implications of such an admission are obviously far reaching.

The Displacement of Responsibility: In Ancient Prophecy

The authority of the prophets was inevitably problematic; only in retrospect when proved right by events could the prophet be acclaimed with certainty. Both the prophet and his audience were therefore in a position of anxiety. The prophet's status at least at the outset of his career was unproven, his audience was unsure of his credentials. In such circumstances the prophet was only able to command attention and obedience, because his audience was convinced that a God existed who had an interest in their actions and that the prophet had a special relationship to him. The prominence of the call of the prophet in the surviving literature is symptomatic, for the role of the prophet is unintelligible unless he enjoys a privileged access to God, which distinguishes him from those whom he addresses. Equally his message is interesting to his hearers because they believe that the God whom he represents has the power to punish and protect. Indeed a great deal of the prophetic message is devoted to fondling the anticipated sanctions and rewards – invasion, earthquake, famine and pestilence – victory, fertility, prosperity, and peace. At least in theory the prophet himself had no power to bring down punishment or reward virtue, though in practice his audience was often ambivalent in this respect, and the prophets themselves were not always averse to magnifying the extent of their influence with their Lord. Thus the bringer of evil tidings might not only be feared but blamed – while the prophets sometimes represented themselves as at least endeavouring to intercede to avert threatened evil.

Once the objective existence of the God of power is denied the prophet's position is transformed. In the first place he loses all access to external power. He is immediately reduced to the position of one more harmless commentator, competing for attention on the basis of his insight. At best his wisdom may command respect, but it will have to establish itself. It invites analysis before it has any claim to our obedience. This is why the political pundits of modern Christendom make so little impression. The most that they dare claim is an understanding of the forces inherent in a situation, and because their convictions are unmitigated by responsibility their awareness is often defective. They may like to portray themselves in a prophetic mantle, but they seldom have the courage to tell us of their divine commission. The heroic witness of Archbishop Tutu in South Africa is a telling example: he gains his credibility not from any story that God has chosen him, but because he represents an interest which otherwise lacks articulate political expression. One has only to examine the sanctions invoked by the modern Christian spokesmen to discern how far they have travelled from their prophetic forebears. Confronted by economic or political oppression or religious indifference they can no longer resort to threats of famine or invasion, but point instead to social unrest and disintegration. They therefore place themselves in the unseemly position of appearing to orchestrate the violence they deplore. The modern political churchmen still hanker for the coercive social power that religion once exercised, without appreciating the sanctions on which that power depended. Only in the revival of fundamentalism – Roman, Protestant or Islamic – does something of the old religious aggression survive. Such reactions to the new powerlessness of religion are entirely understandable – they represent a last stubborn refusal to recognize that God has been disarmed.

The impact of prophetic religion was undeniable, but in one respect all the prophets were mistaken. They insisted on disclaiming responsibility for their utterance. Only false prophets were credited with responsibility for their lying messages. Indeed the possibility of such falsehood was essential to the plausibility of the prophetic institution. It meant that prophecy itself was never discredited by the errors of individual prophets. It might be very difficult to distinguish the true from the false, but God in his own time would make the matter plain. We may smile at such retrospective legitimation, but we should hesitate to dismiss all prophets as deceivers, although false prophet and true must have been equally the authors of their messages. Some may have been cynical manipulators of a superstitious audience or tame panders to a very demanding one – others may have been quite genuinely mistaken. The existing pattern of thought and behaviour, which they inherited, may have predisposed them to understand their thoughts as God-given. The urgency of their sympathy or indignation combined with the expectations of their audience may well have created situations where the prophet was quite unconscious of any element of deception. The prophet who claimed to speak for God may not therefore have been a deceiver, but we must say that his understanding of his relation to God was mistaken. He believed that he was not the author of his message, but that there existed a God who was its author. He could thus disclaim responsibility and attribute it to God. If such a God does not exist then the prophet was indeed the author of his message; in that respect the prophet was mistaken in attributing his words to God, and thereby misled his audience. We may excuse the prophet's error, but we are not free to imitate it. Today we cannot escape taking responsibility for what we say. Others may affirm what they hear by ascribing it to God, but we should not be misled by the apparent implications of such language. The speaker will instead eschew any divine preface to his words.

It is therefore impossible to take at face value the frequent stories of the prophet's call. It was clearly their function to relieve the prophet of any further responsibility for his message – all that is asked of him is the faithful repetition of God's words. The art of the stories carefully separates the identity of the prophet from that of his divine authority by anticipating, and thus disarming, opposition. Moses asks, 'Who am I that I should go to Pharaoh, and that I should bring the Israelites out of Egypt?' (Ex. 3.11). Jeremiah declines his international mission with words of exemplary modesty: 'Ah! Lord God,' I answered, 'I do not know how to speak; I am only a child' (Jer. 1.6). The repeated self-pity of Jeremiah in which he laments the burden placed upon him further dissociates him from his destructive message. Isaiah responds with dread to the vision of God in majesty:

> Woe is me! I am lost,
>   for I am a man of unclean lips
> and I dwell among a people of unclean lips;
>   yet with these eyes I have seen the King, the Lord of hosts.

Only when his lips have been seared by coals from the heavenly altar is he ready to receive his call: 'Then I heard the Lord saying, "Whom shall I send? Who will go for me?" And I answered, Here am I; send me'. (Isa. 6.5ff.) The reluctance of the prophet is a commonplace of prophetic religion and receives its final expression in the satire of Jonah. Like the reluctance of the Speaker of the House of Commons it is always overcome.

The Displacement of Responsibility: In Early Christianity

It would be misleading to give the impression that historical Christianity has freed itself from the problems inherent in the prophetic religion of ancient Israel. Indeed the charismatic phenomenon of the early church and modern times merely reproduced them. The early Christian prophets may have been less ambitious in their political impact – though the Book of Revelation is a reminder that they were far from apolitical – but like the Old Testament prophets they repudiated any responsibility for their message. Confronted by the vision of the risen Christ, John of Patmos renounces any power of initiative or authorship:

> When I saw him, I fell at his feet as though dead. But he laid his right hand upon me and said, 'Do not be afraid. I am the first and the last, and I am the living one; for I was dead and now I am alive for evermore, and I hold the keys of Death and Death's domain. Write down therefore what you have seen, what is now, and what will be hereafter (Rev. 1.17ff.).

John's identity is overwhelmed and submerged in that of his Lord, and the letters to the seven churches are written in a style which deliberately represses any awareness of their human author. The 'I' of the letters is not that of John but of Christ. Any coincidence of view or information is purely accidental. The only responsibility which John acknowledges is one of faithful repetition, he is a secretary taking divine dictation. The distinctively Christian nature of John's utterance is not that he has learnt to take responsibility for it, but that he now attributes his words to Christ and the Spirit rather than Yahweh. It is a confusion of identity given classic expression by Paul: 'The life I now live is not my life, but the life which Christ lives in me' (Gal. 2.20). As with the stories of the prophet's call, John's account of his vision of Christ sets the terms which make possible his repudiation of responsibility. Equally his credibility depends on the reality and honesty of that repudiation. It is that claim which ensured the attention and obedience of his original audience. Once John's responsibility for his revelation is acknowledged, his original credibility is destroyed.

The decline of prophecy in the early church was not accompanied by any greater honesty in religious utterance. While responsibility was no longer disclaimed by the direct simplicity of vision, a much more complicated reference to infallible scriptures and an infallible hierarchy took its place. Augustine's *Confessions* provides a mature example of this. The bishop writes from a confidence in the viability of metaphysical theology. He is sure that his God exists, the Creator of the world out of nothing, the Guide who anticipates every step of his painful pilgrimage. Not for nothing is the *Confessions* interlaced with reminiscences of the psalter. In the words of one of his biographers, Augustine

> had undergone experiences which he could only express in the language of the Psalms. It was the language of a man who addressed a jealous God, a God Whose 'hand' was always ready to 'stretch out' over the destinies of men. Like any gentleman of feeling in the ancient world, the Psalmist had a 'heart'; but he also had 'bones' – that is, a part of himself that was not just a repository of feeling, but was the 'core of the soul', with which God dealt directly, in His rough way, 'exalting' and 'crushing'.[7]

While the God of power, outlined in the first part of this book, is ever present to Augustine, no previous writer has taken his readers so generously into the working of his religious imagination, giving us the sense that we are with him in his prayers. Peter Brown conveys a vivid impression of this:

> Just as a dialogue builds up a lasting impression of the speakers, so Augustine and his God emerge vividly in the prayers of the *Confessions*: God, in the little phrases with which He is approached – *Deus cordis mei*, 'God of my heart', *Deus dulcedo meo*, 'God, my sweetness', *O tardum gaudium meum*, 'O my late joy'; Augustine, as the eager listener, breathless, fussy, an impenitent poser of awkward questions, above all, gloriously egocentric.[8]

So while much of Augustine's conviction was drawn from confidence in his arguments, his persuasiveness is the fruit of his rhetorical training: it owes as much to the power of his imagination as of his reasoning.

The way in which at the beginning of the *Confessions* Augustine separates himself from his God is a fascinating example of this. It is a work of the highest art. He begins with two quotations from the Psalms:

Great art thou O Lord, and greatly to be praised; great is thy power, and thy wisdom infinite.

The direct address to God in the second person immediately implies his presence and distinctness. In marked contrast, man is introduced in a generalized third person, which is then discreetly modified by the more incisive first person plural.

Man is one of your creatures, Lord, and his instinct is to praise you. He bears about him the mark of death, the sign of his own sin, to remind him that you *thwart the proud*. But still, since he is a part of your creation, he wishes to praise you. The thought of you stirs him so deeply that he cannot be content unless he praises you, because you made us for yourself and our hearts find no peace until they rest in you.

Only then does Augustine begin to speak in the first person singular, and significantly his first explicit presence takes the form of a questioning prayer:

Grant me, Lord, to know and understand whether a man is first to pray to you for help or to praise you, and whether he must know you before he can call you to his aid. If he does not know you, how can he pray to you?

By the end of the first chapter Augustine has both created the style which makes possible the *Confessions*, and introduced us to its two protagonists – himself and God:

I shall look for you, Lord, by praying to you and as I pray I shall believe in you, because we have had preachers to tell us about you. It is my faith that calls to you, Lord, the faith which you gave me and made to live in me through the merits of your Son, who became man, and through the ministry of your preacher.[9]

The moment that Augustine begins to sense his own contribution to his prayer and his faith he quickly disclaims it. His faith is something that is God-given; it comes to him immediately from the preacher and ultimately from the incarnation.

At one level the whole of the *Confessions* is an attempt by Augustine to impose upon God the responsibility for his life. In a manner with which the Psalms have made us familiar, petitions to God intermingle with descriptions of God:

> O Lord our God, let *the shelter of your wings* give us hope. Protect us and uphold us. You will be the Support that upholds us from childhood till the hair on our heads is grey. When you are our strength we are strong, but when our strength is our own we are weak.[10]

The only contribution which Augustine makes in his own person is as one of 'the proud' who has to be thwarted by God. This pride expresses itself characteristically in his sexuality, so that the story of his conversion to God is renunciation of his sexual identity:

> You were my true Joy while I was subject to you, and you had made subject to me all the things that you had created inferior to me. This was the right mean, the middle path that led to my salvation, if only I remained true to your likeness and, by serving you, became the master of my own body. But when I rose in pride against you and made onslaught against my Lord, proud of my strong sinews, even those lower things became my masters and oppressed me, and nowhere could I find respite or time to draw my breath . . . All this had grown from my wound, for the proud lie wounded at your feet, and I was separated from you by the swelling of my pride, as though my cheeks were so puffed with conceit that they masked the sight of my eyes.[11]

The overtones of sexual tumescence which mark the metaphors by which he describes pride in this passage are probably significant.

By dramatizing himself in this manner Augustine made credible the separate identity and initiative of God. The fleeting vision at Ostia is only a foretaste of the heavenly reward – a sign that Monica and Augustine have become the kind of people who might see God. It is not that vision that motivates them and decisively changes them. The crucial interventions of God come in external things: in the example of the saints and the words of scripture, which answer the condition of the reader, in the words of a child's game,[12] or a servant's rebuke:

> My mother used to go to the cellar with a servant-girl. One day when they were alone, this girl quarrelled with her young mistress, as servants do, and intending it as a most bitter insult, called my mother a drunkard. The word struck home. My mother realized how despicable her fault had been and at once condemned it and renounced it. Our enemies can often correct our faults by their disparagement, just as the flattery of our friends can corrupt us. But you, O Lord, reward them, not according to the ends which you achieve by using them, but according to the purpose which they have in mind. For the girl had lost her temper and wanted to provoke her young mistress, not to correct her . . . But you, O Lord, Ruler of all things in heaven and earth, who make the deep rivers serve your purposes and govern the raging tide of time as it sweeps on, you even used the anger of one soul to cure the folly of another.[13]

The unconsciousness of God's instruments or even their contrary intention only underlines the sense of his utter sovereignty. It is therefore quite consistent that so much of the *Confessions* is devoted to the praise of God, as the Creator of the world. Augustine's interest is not in explaining the origin of the natural world, but by seeing himself as only a part of God's handiwork, he is able to attribute everything that is good in himself to God:

> And yet, Lord, even if you had willed that I should not survive my childhood, I should have owed you gratitude, because you are our God, the supreme God, the Creator and Ruler of the universe. For even as a child I existed, I was alive, I had the power of feeling; I had an instinct to keep myself safe and sound, to preserve my own being, which was a trace of the single unseen Being from whom it was derived; I had an inner sense which watched over my bodily senses and kept them in full vigour; and even in the small things which occupied my thoughts I found pleasure in the truth . . . Should I not be grateful that so small a creature possessed such wonderful qualities? But they were all gifts from God, for I did not give them to myself. His gifts are good and the

sum of them all is my own self. Therefore the God who made me must be good and all the good in me is his.[14]

So Augustine's doctrine of creation ensures that all positive responsibility for his life reposes in God.

Moreover, God subtly acquires responsibility for the text of the *Confessions* itself, not by dictation on the prophetic model, but by a process of continuous suggestion. For despite the repeated presence of Augustine's 'I' it is no mere work of memory and reflection. Augustine's memory is not a solitary exercise in which the self conducts its own unaided search. Through the language of prayer Augustine tells the story of his past to a God who knows it better than he does himself. Such a God is not simply the audience of the *Confessions*, he is portrayed as actually facilitating the task of remembering:

> O Lord, the depths of man's conscience lie bare before your eyes. Could anything of mine remain hidden from you, even if I refused to confess it? I should only be shielding my eyes from seeing you, not hiding myself from you . . . So my confession is made both silently in your sight, my God, and aloud as well, because even though my tongue utters no sound, my heart cries to you. For whatever good I may speak to men you have heard it before in my heart, and whatever good you hear in my heart, you have first spoken to me yourself.[15]

Augustine continually addresses his questions to God. He does not directly attribute answers to God, but he supplies them indirectly, either by asking the question in a form which expects a particular answer, or by passing on to a new question, or by reflecting on a text of scripture. This turning to God to answer his perplexities is justified by the theological notion of truth which he expounds within the *Confessions*:

> Truth! Truth! How the very marrow of my soul within me yearned for it as they dinned it in my ears over and over again! . . . But my hunger and thirst were not even for the greatest of your works, but for you, my God, because you are Truth itself with whom there can be no change, no swerving from your course.[16]

So the whole work is conceived as incomplete without the contribution that only God can give:

> What man can teach another to understand this truth? What angel can teach it to an angel? What angel can teach it to a man? We must ask it of you, seek it in you; we must knock at your door. Only then shall we receive what we ask and find what we seek; only then will the door be opened to us.[17]

So Augustine's last word as the author of the *Confessions* is to stand aside and ask God himself to speak.

Within the Augustinian tradition an even more radical renunciation of authorship can be found in the Preface to Anselm's *Proslogion*. Not only does he hesitate to attach his name to the little book, he gives a careful account of the origin of its distinctive argument which disclaims any responsibility for it:

> I began to ask myself if it would be possible to find one single argument, needing no other proof than itself, to prove that God really exists, that he is the highest good, needing nothing, that it is he whom all things need for their being and their well-being, and to prove whatever else we believe about the nature of God. I turned this over in my mind often and carefully; sometimes it seemed to me that what I was seeking was almost within my grasp; sometimes it eluded the keenness of my thought completely; so at last in desperation I was going to give up looking for something that it was impossible to find. But when I wanted to put the idea entirely out of my mind, lest it occupy me in vain and so keep out other ideas in which I could make some progress, then it began to force itself upon me with increasing urgency, however much I refused and resisted it. So one day, when I was tired out with resisting its importunity, that which I had despaired of finding came to me, in the conflict of my thoughts, and I welcomed eagerly the very thought which I had been so anxious to reject.[18]

Although Anselm does not here explicitly attribute his argument to God, he clearly believes that it is more credible because it is not his own creation. It is striking that he is searching for an argument, which will do justice to the divine attributes by sharing them. It must be 'one', 'needing no other proof than itself', with entire consistency therefore the argument exercises its own initiative. 'It began to force itself upon me with increasing urgency, however much I refused and resisted it.' The terminology is very different from that of the prophets, but the displacement of responsibility is quite as deliberate. It prepares the reader for one of the hall-marks of the *Proslogion*, which indeed justifies its title – the appeal to God to take the initiative:

> How long, Lord, will you turn your face from us?
> When will you look upon us and hear us?
> When will you enlighten our eyes and show us your face?
> When will you give yourself to us again.
> Look, upon us, Lord, and hear us,
> enlighten us and show yourself to us.[19]

The Displacement of Responsibility: In a Wider Perspective

This deep-seated and continuous tendency to displace responsibility can only be fairly understood in terms of its social context and the religions of power of which it formed a part. It may help to put this in perspective by pointing out that Westminster has more in common with Babylon and Karnak than with Washington. Until very recently most human societies were dominated by an alliance of throne and altar, exemplified archaeologically in the interrelated complexes of temple and palace. Queen Elizabeth II may now appear a little isolated as the only surviving ecclesiastical heir of the Emperor Constantine, but the close relationship of religious and secular power which she still represents would have marked most human societies before the successful rebellion of the American colonies. The republican form of government is not, of course, new, but the secular republic is the peculiar and relatively recent creation of the USA. In most human societies the rule of God and the earthly monarch resembled each other. Though both kings were unseen by all but a tiny monority of their subjects, every part of their domain had a local representative. Often that representative was weak, venal and unimpressive. His credibility, however, was sustained by his known access to superior external power. The king's justice might be enforced by troops; the divine will made plain by famine, plague and invasion. An element of coercion was understood to be intrinsic to their power. Rebellions against temporal or spiritual power might prosper for a while, but in the end the sovereign had the ability to compel obedience. His kingdom would be apparent in the discomfiture of his enemies.

Such hierarchy depended on successful delegation. The direct exercise of power is time-consuming and exhausting. The distant king depended on royal officials, nobles or magistrates, just as the absentee landlord depended on his stewards. Religious delegation and human delegation were interrelated. Rulers did not conceive themselves as simply acting on their own initiative or merely protecting their own status and privilege. The Roman imperial administration, as truly as any Jewish prophet, saw itself as merely the agent of the gods. The hierarchy of human society, where clients looked to powerful patrons who rewarded their followers and took responsibility for the careers of their protegés, found its counterpart in the religious understanding. The whole of social experience was marked by conveniently displaced responsibility. The ruthless exactions of land agent and tax gatherer were represented as the demands of distant masters: the absence of the landlord could easily give opportunities to disguise and conceal the greed and self-interest of his bailiffs. The gods were also absentees. In proclaiming his accountability to them a ruler could ignore the more immediate scrutiny of his subjects.

The relation between social experience and religious belief is best represented as a subtle interchange. On the one hand the social experience gave plausibility to the constructions of the religious imagination. Men who so often encountered representatives of distant powers, which required them to act at least ostensibly on the orders of another, could readily understand the position of the religious man. On the lowest view he represented yet another external power, which had to be negotiated. In his own view, he represented the supreme external power. Moreover, those who exercised power in society easily understood the religious man as one of themselves. The terms in which the centurion envisaged Jesus are typical of this:

> You need only say the word and the boy will be cured. I know, for I am myself under orders, with soldiers under me. I say to one, 'Go',

and he goes; to another, 'Come here', and he comes; and to my servant, 'Do this', and he does it (Matt. 8.8f.).

This mutual respect and understanding between religious and secular leaders gave additional credibility to the claims of the religious. The fact that they were recognized by those who enjoyed secular power was a weighty testimonial to the reality of their claims. On the other hand by constructing the religious world and its relationships on human models, those human arrangements were strengthened and sanctified. So the Catechism of the Prayer Book expressed duty towards the neighbour in terms which echoed duty towards God:

> To love, honour and succour my father and mother: to honour and obey the Queen, and all that are put in authority under her: to submit myself to all my governors, teachers, spiritual pastors and masters: to order myself lowly and reverently to all my betters.

Religious deference and social deference went hand in hand.

Concealment as a Strategy of Credibility

The displacement of responsibility was not therefore confined to the religious world – it was a feature of a much wider range of social relationships. Wherever it occurred it demanded a complicated process of concealment. It is easy to parody and misunderstand this as one of mere deceit. On that account the displacement of responsibility is a cynical device by which rulers, religious or secular, deceived their subjects. The concealment serves to evade a proper accountability and often to disguise the weakness of their actual position. For the exercise of power always demands self-confidence and depends upon the perceptions of others. Obedience, which has to be continually enforced is ultimately exhausting and unsustainable. Power is therefore never a matter of clearly existing realities; it rests on much more elusive perceptions of what is possible and probable. The credibility of power has therefore always depended on concealing moments of weakness and vulnerability. What is less often admitted is that subjects as well as rulers have an interest in such concealment: for it removes the shame of compliance. The more that those who are subject can see themselves in terms of a common bondage, the less humiliating is their obedience. If I obey someone who speaks and acts simply in his own person, I cannot disguise from myself my weakness and subordination. If we are both only obeying orders, his position is fundamentally no different from mine. Paradoxically resentment at obedience impels those who are subject to connive at those illusions which facilitate their domination.

The crucial device in this process was the careful creation of distance. That is seen most obviously in architecture – the elaborate separation of the people from God in the Holy of Holies, the shrine which contains the cult object, the high altar approached by screens and steps, are its religious manifestation. In palaces the ante-chambers of the throne-room, the elaborate structures of walls and courtyards which exclude the public, the balcony or distant window for the carefully rationed public appearance. Architecture forms our experience and quickly conceals from us its human origin. The temple and the palace become a part of the urban landscape – apparently given and unchanging like the hills. The Queen waving at the crowds from Buckingham Palace, the distant face of the Pope speaking from an upper window, the impassive members of the *Politburo* taking the salute in Red Square – all occupy elevated positions, ceremonially recurring like the seasons. For such distance is created only to enhance the drama, the privilege, the excitement of its momentary removal. The crowds which rejoice in that experience choose to forget that they have both acquiesced in and contributed to these arrangements. In the excitement which surrounds pop stars the price of the tickets is forgotten – no television commentator precisely costs a papal kiss, or links a royal marriage with the income tax. The consumption of resources is silent.

Literature also plays its part in this process of distancing. The children's stories of princes and princesses first introduce us to the structures of domination in a form that delights. The honorific language which surrounds so much secular power serves to distinguish the transactions of government and its agents. Particularly in the Judaeo-Christian tradition literary devices are used to distinguish the human self from God. The continuous disparagement of the one and the elevation of the other is the most obvious lesson in all traditional religious language and, once we have learned to use it, we are as little aware of what we are doing and contributing to our experience, as when we enter a church building. Language and literature like architecture largely pre-date us. They are an inheritance rather than our creation. Having learned to use them, we forget the puzzled questions we once asked. Indeed learning is here equated with quiet acquiescence. We seem to have entered a world which exists, once we have forgotten that we had to learn how to frame it.

The credibility of the God of power was secured by the careful projection of his image, and significantly it used many of the means of secular power. Credibility was not primarily a matter of argued conviction, but of immemorial prestige. Building, public ceremonial decked out in lavish clothing and accompanied by expensive and enthralling music, the sacrifice of the mass and the appearance of a monarch were in most respects indistinguishable. Using the same contrivances of conspicuous expenditure to compel attention and enforce respect, both were equally dependent on effective taxation and policing.

The displacement of responsibility required the cultivation of illusion – the deliberate creation of social distance between human beings found its counterpart in the imagined gulf between God and man. While religious and secular leaders gained political and economic advantages from these arrangements, it is a mistake to see them as clear-sighted deceivers. It is probably fairer to say that they had learnt the art of flattering their public, and were both surprised and gratified when that public confirmed them in their privilege. In this interchange there was collusion between sovereign and subject, and both resented interference. There was therefore in all these arrangements the possibility of violence. Peace depended on the acquiescence in illusion – challenge and exposure met rigorous and often brutal repression. Such persecution was seldom unpopular. Anticlerical and egalitarian commentators may like to present Jesus' death as the work of Pilate and Caiaphas, but the most cursory reading of the Gospels makes it plain that they did not act alone.

The Challenge of Exposure

It is central to the argument of this book that the significance of Jesus is to be found in his confrontation with the religions of power, his repudiation of the means by which they were enforced, and his exposure of the violence and deceit which they harboured. Whatever may have happened after Jesus' death, and whatever crimes may subsequently have been committed in his name, his life was spent in challenging and subverting such religion, and he died as its victim, not its inaugurator. The precise circumstances of his death are obscure, and it is now probably impossible to judge whether the Jewish religious authorities or the imperial administration had the decisive hand in his crucifixion. From the religious perspective I have argued that there was much less difference between them than they imagined. The Jerusalem priesthood and the Roman governor may have represented competing religions, but they were fundamentally similar in their structure. The subversion of the distinction between the righteous and the sinner; the refusal to be preoccupied by the exercise of power; the suffering of evil rather than the attempt to control or repress it; the substitution of a forgiving disposition for conformity to the Law – all represented a rebuke to the existing religious structures and the gods of power they proclaimed. Characteristically they responded to the offence with violence.

Long before the criticism of modern atheists, Jesus in his life and death had challenged the religions of power and the God to whom they appealed. Jesus' very existence was an intolerable provocation, which had to be removed. The violence, which he attracted, is a tribute both to the power of his message and the destructiveness of its implications. He made his challenge not as an atheist, but in the name of his God. The response he encountered rules out the notion that it was therefore less radical than that of the modern atheist. Indeed despite its negative critique of metaphysical theology, modern atheism remains trapped in the categories of the religions of power which it purports to attack. I have already suggested that its preoccupation with the existence and objectivity of God is a perverse acknowledgment of the religious tradition it wishes to overthrow. Moreover, from the atheists of the Enlightenment and the French Revolution to those of the Soviet Union, there has been a tendency not to repudiate the religions of power, merely to secularize them. They still wish to have a privileged identity as the sole exponents of reason or the only representatives of the international proletariat. In practice they have proved as ruthlessly concerned with power as any of their overtly religious predecessors. The fires of the Holy Inquisition have been quenched. In the twentieth century deliberate torture and mass extermination have been practised by the militantly anti-Christian regimes of Hitler's Germany and his Soviet ally. The abstractions of race, the nation, the international working class, have provided men who disdain to believe in God with ready alibis for their cruelty and self-assertion. The crucified Christ is as subversive of the secularized religions of power as he was of their theistic predecessors.

It is for that reason that I believe that the Christian has nothing ultimately to fear from the rise of modern atheism. Many of its arguments must be frankly acknowledged and appropriated. The adjustment may be painful and difficult, but it is no serious challenge to the identity of the Christian religion. For that identity is not found in visions of a triumphant hierarchy, but in the isolated and despised victim of such illusions. I am therefore confident that the Christian tradition can respond to the most searching atheist critique. Accepting much of the atheists' argument does not threaten the heart of Christianity, rather it impels religious people to rediscover it. A critique, which returns Christians to the foot of the cross can hardly be regretted, however far-reaching the adjustment it demands. It means the end of the long equivocal accommodation between the ancient religions of power and the subversive religion of Christ.

Although Jesus is represented in continuity with the ancient prophets, an astonishing degree of responsibility for his message is attributed to him. The story of his baptism has obvious affinities with the stories of the prophets' call, but the divine voice confirms his status as God's Son among those who witnessed it; it does not dissociate Jesus from his words. Even in the story of the transfiguration, the divine voice admonishes the disciples to 'Hear him' (Mark 9.7), there is no sense that it is addressed to Jesus. Indeed the Gospels contain no story which represents his personal discovery and response to the call of God. Perhaps the closest approximation is the story of Gethsemane, but there it is Jesus who speaks and God who remains silent. In John's Gospel the dependence of the words of the Son on the Father is expressed in a way that is reminiscent of the prophets:

> I do not speak on my own authority, but the Father who sent me has himself commanded me what to say and how to speak. I know that his commands are eternal life. What the Father has said to me, therefore – that is what I speak (John 12.49f.).

Yet even in this Gospel Jesus speaks directly, in his own person, without divine preface or reference. While the prophets always made their listeners conscious of the chasm which separated the speaker of the words from the author of the message, in John's Gospel the speaker has himself become the divine Word.

At one level we must understand the directness of Jesus' speech in the New Testament as a means of expressing the early church's doctrine of the incarnation. The Son is differently placed from the servants, who went before him (Mark 12.1–9). It was doubtless intended to elevate Jesus above his prophetic predecessors and distinguish him from them. At the hands of the orthodox the doctrine of the incarnation became the pledge of Jesus' uniqueness and their own special significance. The identity between a living man and the living God was a mystery of condescension to arouse wonder and gratitude. As an example to be followed it impelled the rich and powerful to similar acts of self-abnegation. It did not provide a warrant for the poor and oppressed to get above themselves. The letter to the Hebrews may identify the Son with his brothers (Heb. 2.17), but there is obvious surprise that 'the Son does not shrink from calling men his brothers' (Heb. 2.11). The divinization of man may have been the corollary of the doctrine of the incarnation,[20] but it was envisaged as an eventual reward, not a present fact. Nevertheless the consequent portrayal of Jesus does elide the identity of God and man in a way which is more revealing than was intended. The traditional understanding of the incarnation gained its excitement and attraction from the vigour of its paradoxes. In exalting the majesty of God, it made possible the most astonishing reversals:

Our God, heaven cannot hold him
    Nor earth sustain;
Heaven and earth shall flee away
    When he comes to reign;
In the bleak mid-winter
    A stable-place sufficed
The Lord God Almighty
    Jesus Christ.

Enough for him, whom Cherubim
    Worship night and day,
A breastful of milk,
    And a mangerful of hay;
Enough for him, whom Angels
    Fall down before,
The ox and ass and camel
    Which adore.

The objective existence of the transcendent God was an integral part of the holy drama, but once that existence is questioned the identity of God and man in the portrayal of Jesus takes on a quite different character.

Subsequent doctrine and devotion dwelt on the distance between God and man to celebrate the excitement of the story of the incarnation. It is the disappearance of the divine presupposition that has made the modern Christmas so sentimental. There is no longer the sense of a great gulf crossed – instead most people are only really aware of the child in the manger. Wonder at the graciousness of God has become reduced to the platitude – O what a lovely baby. In the Gospels, however, it is not the distance between God and man which is stressed, but the intimacy of their relationship in Jesus. This is developed most consistently in John's Gospel. The astounding claim, 'My Father and I are one' (John 10.30), is not an isolated text. To Philip's request to see the Father comes the equally startling reply:

Have I been all this time with you, Philip, and you still do not know me? Anyone who has seen me has seen the Father. Then how can you say, 'Show us the Father'? I am not myself the source of the words I speak to you: it is the Father who dwells in me doing his own work. Believe me when I say that I am in the Father and the Father in me (John 14.9ff.).

Elsewhere the Father is conceived as the source and the goal of the Son:

I came from the Father and have come into the world. Now I am leaving the world again and going to the Father (John 16.28).

It issues in a defiant, triumphant confidence:

Look, the hour is coming, has indeed already come, when you are all to be scattered, each to his home, leaving me alone. Yet I am not alone, because the Father is with me (John 16.32).

For John, to draw attention to the distinction between God and man and suggest that Jesus does not or could not transcend it, is disbelief.

John is only the most thoroughgoing exponent of this intimacy. In a very different style the same claim recurs in the Synoptic Gospels, when Jesus appropriates to himself the specifically divine activity of forgiveness, so that praise of God and astonishment at Jesus are difficult to disentangle (Mark 2.2–12). Perhaps even more remarkable is Jesus' teaching about the Sabbath:

The Sabbath was made for the sake of man and not man for the Sabbath: therefore the Son of Man is sovereign even over the Sabbath (Mark 2.27f.).

Christians are so familiar with these words that they fail to recognize the theological reversal that they contain. The Book of Maccabees shows that Jews had been prepared to die without defending themselves if they were attacked on the Sabbath, rather than profane it (I Macc. 2.34–38). It is a precedent that Mattathias and his friends refuse to follow, but their argument is only one of desperation (I Macc. 2.40). They do not question the notion that Sabbath breaking was profane, an infringement of God's Law. What Jesus has challenged is the specifically divine sanction of the Sabbath. We have only to compare his words with those of Isaiah to realize the gravity of the provocation:

If you cease to tread the sabbath underfoot,
and keep my holy day free from your own affairs,
if you call the sabbath a day of joy
and the Lord's holy day a day to be honoured,
if you honour it by not plying your trade,
not seeking your own interest
or attending to your own affairs,
then you shall find your joy in the Lord (Isa. 58.13f.).

Jesus has dared to transform the badge of obedience to God into a custom from which man not only benefits, but which he also controls.

From Obedience to Involvement: the Father and the Son

Jesus inherited the belief of his society in an objective, existing God. In speaking of God as his Father, and seeing himself as God's son, he uses and appears to endorse an ancient pattern of religious subordination and obedience, given classic expression in the promise of Jeremiah:

I said, How gladly would I treat you as a son,
     giving you a pleasant land,
          a patrimony fairer than that of any nation!
I said, You shall call me Father
     and never cease to follow me (Jer. 3.19).

The will of man is to be aligned with the different, guiding will of God. So Jesus is portrayed as a model of filial obedience: in the Lord's Prayer it is God's will that is to be done – in Gethsemane the disparity between the will of the son and the will of the Father is clearly revealed and sternly overcome:

Abba, Father, all things are possible to thee; take this cup away from me. Yet not what I will, but what thou wilt (Mark 14.36).

In the Synoptic Gospels Jesus disclaims the greeting of 'Good Master', replying with studied orthodoxy, 'No one is good except God alone' (Mark 10.18). In John's Gospel the language of mutual indwelling does not infringe the Father's supremacy. Jesus can acknowledge that 'The Father is greater than I' (John 14.28). Paul sees the whole of human history culminating in the submission of the Son to the Father:

> Then the Son himself will also be made subordinate to God who made all things subject to him, and thus God will be all in all (I Cor. 15.28).

Such texts were favourites of Arius and those ancient theologians who saw Jesus as the model of subordination to the Father. Their account of Jesus reflected a strand of thought in the New Testament, which is undeniably present, and yet their orthodox opponents read the texts more perceptively. It is not my intention to rehabilitate Nicene dogma, but the holy fathers were correct to hear, despite the conventional language of obedience and subordination, a much more astonishing, almost subversive counterpoint: the divine identity of Christ. Their metaphysical assumptions about the existence and nature of God involved them in insoluble contradictions as they wrestled to assimilate this disruptive claim. It is a mark of their integrity that they did not allow their metaphysical assumptions to determine their reading of the scriptures. They were prepared to utter absurdity rather than compromise the divinity of Christ:

> So, then, the Son of God enters upon this lower world, descending from His heavenly seat without retiring from the Father's glory, generated in a new order by a novel kind of birth. In a new order, because He who is invisible in what belongs to Himself was made visible in what belongs to us, the Incomprehensible willed to be comprehended, He who continued to exist before time began to exist in time, the Lord of the universe took upon Him a servant's form shrouding the immensity of His majesty, the impassible God did not disdain to be passible man, nor the Immortal to be subject to the laws of death.[21]

Such confused thought and language cannot be unequivocally endorsed, but its tensions and paradoxes are eloquent witness both to the conviction of Christ's divinity and the impossibility of giving it adequate expression in terms of the categories available.

If we question the existence of the God of power, which the Fathers took for granted, the divine identity of Christ takes on a different, but equally important meaning. While the prophets had repeatedly repressed any awareness that they were responsible for their portrayal of God, it is the unique achievement of Jesus that while continuing to speak of God and to speak to God, he does not entirely conceal his responsibility for his God. For all the appearance of subordination, the relationship between the Father and the Son has an unparallelled degree of reciprocity. The orthodox doctrine of co-inherence or mutual indwelling, however unsatisfactory as an attempt to reconcile traditional metaphysical theology with the divine identity of Christ, is sensitive to a surprising quality in the relation of the Father and the Son as it emerges in the New Testament.

As we have seen, the origins of that language in the Old Testament were concerned with obedience. In learning to see himself as the Son of a heavenly Father, the religious man was creating an identity of dependence and irresponsibility for himself. He looked to his divine Father for earthly benefits, but he would have found the notion of appropriating anything of that Father's divinity blasphemous. To do so would have conflicted with the displacement of responsibility, which was one of the basic functions of such language. In the New Testament we enter a quite different world. Jesus understands himself as the Son of the divine Father, so that his identity as Son and God's identity as Father define each other. He gains his knowledge of himself as the Son in turning to his Father. Moreover, it is from the lips of the Son that we learn of the Father and come to recognize Jesus as the Son. So to everyone's astonishment the Son shares something of the divine identity. It becomes possible to see that God is his God in a way that the prophets never allowed. This Son is not simply responsible to his Father, he acquires some responsibility for Him. The relationship of the Son to the Father no longer distances man from God in obedience, it enables him to participate in God in love.

This involvement and participation in the divine identity are not portrayed as the unique distinction of Christ, they are altogether more inclusive. Indeed in affirming Christ's participation in the divine, his followers were also staking their own claim: they were achieving a new identity for themselves. The unity between Jesus and God is one which embraces all men who come to acknowledge it:

> It is not for these alone that I pray, but for those also who through their words put their faith in me; may they all be one: as thou, Father, art in me, and I in thee, so also may they be in us, that the world may believe that thou didst send me. The glory which thou gavest me I have given to them, that they may be one, as we are one; I in them and thou in me, may they be perfectly one (John 17.20ff.).

The modern Christian, who dares to acknowledge his responsibility for his God, is not weakly succumbing to the hostile pressures of atheist criticism. Instead he can use the arguments of atheists in ways of which they never dreamt. Learning to take responsibility for our God means learning to recognize and acknowledge that my identity and that of my God are not separate and heterogeneous, but intimately related. The identity which Jesus shared with his God is one which he invites us also to achieve. We must I think speak here of achievement rather than discovery, for that is a more accurate indication of our creativity. The atheist assumes that in once revealing our creativity in our religion, he has destroyed it; but the Christian has no reason to be surprised or abashed that he is responsible for his God. Instead he has only to learn to say with confidence and humility, 'My Father and I are one' (John 10.30).

At the heart of a responsible religion is the recognition that my portrayal of God represents choices that I have made. We choose whether to portray God as an inexorable judge, the stern guardian of our moral code, or the generous and forgiving father. We choose whether to portray him in terms of privilege and power, or of solidarity and peace. The choices we have made in the past will influence the choices that we make in the future. The person who has chosen to exalt the judge has prepared to become his executioner. More fundamentally the choice to be religious at all is mine. It may have been influenced by all kinds of experience for which I am not responsible: church services which were boring or inspiring, sermons which convinced or appalled, religious people who impressed or disillusioned. Nevertheless it is we, with the help of our notion of God, who make sense of that experience, and define our attitude towards it, and with our attitude ourselves. There is no compelling God who exists to impose such choices upon us. If I am religious it is because I want to be. It is a way of life and an attitude to life which attracts and fascinates me. I sense within it unique opportunities. Often the benefits I seek represent advantages over other people – the naive hope that if there is to be suffering, it will fall to other people; but it also offers other kinds of advantages. Instead of separating me from those around me, it may enable me to become a different kind of person. We seek rebirth not because we are jealous of other people, but because we are dissatisfied and discontented with ourselves.

The Discipline of Responsibility

In my laying such stress on the role of human choice in religion, some readers will detect a quite unsatisfactory subjectivism. Traditionally the objectivity of theology has been derived by reference to the objective reality of God; it has been my contention that that reference was in its nature evasive – that the reference to God enabled men to elude any honest engagement with their fellows. I do not believe that learning to acknowledge our creative contribution to our religion opens the way to fanciful extravagance or dishonest compensation – rather it provides the only defence against the possibility of self-deception. Such a view of religion refuses to provide any concealment for the self and its actions. In this sense I see it as providing a necessary discipline. Accountability to others is much more difficult to manipulate than accountability to the unseen God – our outraged peers can laugh and kick.

In the opening chapters of this book I argued that the God of power provided his self-proclaimed instruments with a convenient disguise. The objective existence of such a God relieved human beings of responsibility for many of their most controversial actions – in that way the unpalatable functions of religion were hidden. Throughout this book I am concerned with the way in which doctrines about God function in the lives of those who hold them. I began by drawing attention to those functions, and in the first part suggested that they explained the origin of the doctrines. I shall now argue that just as many beliefs about God are discredited once their function is exposed, the only way that belief in God can be defended is in terms of those functions which can be both acknowledged and approved.

An effective apologetic demands therefore that our own religious intentions are transparent to ourselves and each other; and that without mystification they commend themselves to other people. We have therefore both to acknowledge an element of creativity in our religion, i.e. that *we* are doing something. We also have to be honest about *what* it is that we are trying to do. Only when religion achieves that kind of candour is it really subject to scrutiny and criticism. Acknowledging the strong subjective contribution to all religion is not a warrant for unbridled eccentricity, it is the essential precondition for achieving honesty. I may say that God alone is my judge while intending to be both judge and jury in my own case. Only the jury of my peers can relieve me of the danger of self-deception.

Religion does not represent a continent awaiting discovery, it is rather an opportunity to be realized, and which like human art lives by being realized ever anew. We inevitably are recent creatures, but our God is no more our own invention than is our music. We learn our religion as we learn music by listening carefully to the achievements of the past. Our listening to the religion of the past has to be truthful. As we learn to delight in the nobility and beauty of the saints, we have also to face the horrors of our religious history. In scrupulous attention to our religious tradition, we learn to discriminate, in much the same way that we learn to discriminate between trivial and satisfying music. We are exposed to variety and find ourselves presented with choice. The rich denominational diversity is probably essential for the vitality of the Christian religion.

In this way mature responsible religion is very different in its demands from the self-consciously orthodox notion of vocation. There are many who still prefer to envisage a religious tradition primarily as a matter of repetition – and then are both hurt and surprised that they have made it boring. All such views of the religious vocation go back to the prophet who told himself and his audience that he was merely repeating the message of his master, and I have dwelt at length on the difficulties and self-deception inherent in such a stance. Instead we must learn to see the religious vocation, not in terms of punctilious repetition, but as the decision to take responsibility for a religious tradition. A clergyman is not paid to say things; that only robs his speech of all significance. He is paid to listen carefully to the complex faith of the past and to exercise discrimination in transmitting it. That process necessarily exposes his judgment and demands sometimes painful decisions. Only if he continually exercises that critical creativity is he distinct from a tape-recorded message – though some congregations may well prefer the safely standardized and well presented product.

6

The Lover of God in Search
of the True Self

I desire to have knowledge of God and the soul. Of nothing else?
No, of nothing else whatsoever . . . O God, always one and always
the same, if I know myself, I shall know thee.

Augustine, *Soliloquies*

The Self as the Agent and Agenda of Religion

In the previous chapter I argued that wherever we encounter talk
of God we must remember that man is at work. God is not an
external reality who imposes himself upon me; instead he is the
construction of my imagination and his character reflects my
choices. In understanding God in this way I am following a line of
thought suggested by Feuerbach, who was fascinated by the process
in which the self divested itself of many of its qualities, only to
reappropriate them more fully in God:

> To enrich God, man must become poor; that God may be all, man
> must be nothing. But he desires to be nothing in himself, because
> what he takes from himself is not lost to him, since it is preserved
> in God . . . What man withdraws from himself, what he renounces
> in himself, he only enjoys in an incomparably higher and fuller
> measure in God.[1]

For Feuerbach this is seen most conclusively in the way in which the initiative of the self is equivocally repudiated. His description of this is so striking that it deserves to be quoted in full:

> God is the highest subjectivity of man abstracted from himself; hence man can do nothing of himself, all goodness comes from God. The more subjective God is, the more completely does man divest himself of his subjectivity, because God is, *per se*, his relinquished self, the possession of which he however vindicates to himself. As the action of the arteries drives the blood into the extremities, and the action of the veins brings it back again, as life in general consists in a perpetual systole and diastole; so it is in religion. In the religious systole man propels his own nature from himself, he throws himself outward; in the religious diastole he receives the rejected nature into his heart again. God alone is the being who acts of himself – this is the force of repulsion in religion; God is the being who acts in me, with me, through me, upon me, for me, is the principle of my salvation, of my good dispositions and actions, consequently my own good principle and nature – this is the force of attraction in religion.[2]

In so far as Feuerbach is analysing what I have called the religions of power he is entirely correct. The self may be frequently disparaged in relation to God, but it is not itself problematic. Equally it conceals from itself precisely how much it contributes to its God. It is this kind of identity to which the Psalms give expression – once again they display the basic assumptions of the religions of power. As we have seen the psalms of personal providence elaborate a special relationship between God and the soul. The resulting dramas of the soul are thrilling, but the threats are all external – accidents and enemies. In affliction the soul may lament and express its misery, but its integrity is never breached. Sustained by the consciousness of belonging to a privileged, clearly defined people, the individual may be vulnerable to the machinations of his enemies, but he is not at war with himself. He may sin against his God and be punished; but there is no doubt about the agent of the sin, or the object of the punishment. Confident that his God can obtain the benefit he seeks, he has no need either to re-examine the benefit, or to question the beneficiary. All attention is focussed on the success of the prayer.

The identity of the person who prays is taken for granted, it is unproblematic.

In this respect the psalter shares many of the assumptions of the ordinary, unreflective secular outlook. This common sense view is enshrined and continually reinforced by the apparent clarity and simplicity of our personal pronouns – I, mine, you and yours etc. The very brevity of the sounds communicates a sensation of simple identity. Their adequacy seems sufficient – we have no undue problems arranging our possessions. The whole complicated law of property is based on notions of identity which are as unproblematic as our language. Moreover, the continuous satisfaction of material appetite provides its parody of Descartes – I swallow, therefore I am. This produces one of the comedies of modern secularism: people who have learnt to use the word 'I' with total unreflective confidence, and who turn away from the notion of God as confused and contradictory.

Feuerbach himself surprisingly shares this relatively uncomplicated view of personal identity. The only tension he envisages is between a partial individuality and the consciousness of the species. It is because he envisages the self in such a simplistic way that religion is on his account so easily resolved into philosophy. When the self as Feuerbach conceives it realizes that its consciousness of God is only an indirect form of its self-consciousness, that for Feuerbach is the end of the problem. Because he sees the self so naively, he can be astonishingly optimistic about the significance of the end of the religious illusion:

> Thus the work of the self-conscious reason in relation to religion is simply to destroy an illusion: – an illusion, however, which is by no means indifferent, but which on the contrary, is profoundly injurious in its effect on mankind; which deprives man as well of the power of real life as of the genuine sense of truth and virtue.[3]

He is able to believe in such a liberation because although he refers to self-consciousness and occasionally speaks in the first person, he is quite insensitive to the possibility that personal identity might be more complicated than he imagines. The reason for this is his highly rationalist account of the primacy of the understanding which he saw reflected in notions of God as a being of the understanding, and which he derived from Kant whom he quotes:

> In so far as we think, in the activity of the understanding as such, we are dependent on no other being. Activity of thought is spontaneous activity. 'When I think, I am conscious, therefore, that this thinking in me does not inhere in another outside of me, but in myself, consequently that I am a substance, i.e. that I exist by myself, without being a predicate of another being.'[4]

In the rest of the work the self receives little further attention. The nearest he gets to such a discussion is in his comment on the Christian doctrine of original sin. He complains that it assumes,

> that the individual by himself is a perfect being, is by himself the adequate presentation or existence of the species. Here is entirely wanting the objective perception, the consciousness, that the *thou* belongs to the perfection of the *I*, that *men* are required to constitute humanity, that only men taken together are what man should and can be.[5]

It is a most revealing passage, and indicates Feuerbach's awareness of the social dimensions of identity, but it is immediately lost in his lofty generalizations about 'man' and 'the species'.

By contrast it is a mark of the religion of peace that the self, far from being taken for granted as the suppliant of external goods, becomes itself the agenda of religion. While the religions of power controlled behaviour by demanding obedience and promising rewards, in the religion of peace the transformation of the self is not the condition of other benefits; the transformation of the self has become the goal of religion. From being a means to an end, it has itself become the end. Such a religion is necessarily self-conscious – it cannot afford to disguise from itself what it is doing. For where the religions of power were preoccupied by weakness and external danger, the religion of peace knows that the real enemy is within. The self is no longer an object of pity, but of careful scrutiny. I am not only destructive of others, often destroying those I love, I also have the possibility of behaving in ways which are self-destructive.

The distinctive question of the Christian religion, which decisively differentiates it from all the preceding religions of power is:

What does a man gain by winning the whole world at the cost of his true self? What can he give to buy that self back? (Mark 8.36f.)

Here the identity which might be secured in the possession of the whole world is disparaged by contrast with 'the true self'. The self is no longer simply one of the parties to the religious exchange, procuring from God strength, or health, or good fortune, while remaining unchanged. Instead the self participates as the substance of the transaction. His God transforms him. Thus in John's Gospel Jesus uses the uncompromising language of new birth: 'Unless a man has been born again he cannot see the kingdom of God' (John 3.3). In Pauline thought the transformation of the self is described in terms of the only process which approaches the violence of birth:

We know that the man we once were has been crucified with Christ, for the destruction of the sinful self, so that we may no longer be the slaves of sin, since a dead man is no longer answerable for his sin. But if we thus died with Christ, we believe that we shall also come to life with him (Rom. 6.6ff.).

The self now displays a complexity and a degree of discontinuity, which all the subtle changes of mood in the psalter never attain. The father of the demoniac can appeal to Jesus in words which contain a whole new religious sensibility: 'Lord, I believe. Help thou mine unbelief' (Mark 9.24). We see here the unlikely source of the thought and self-perception which culminates in the *Proslogion* of St Anselm. It is entirely right that Peter is the first of the Apostles, because he is the first exemplar of the distinctively Christian consciousness. His boasted loyalty is questioned by a Jesus who knows him better than he knows himself. Judas the betrayer of Christ is only a one dimensional character – the guilty agent of an unconscious destiny. Peter's betrayal gains its poignancy from the reader's awareness that Peter has betrayed himself. Tricked, taken by surprise, he does not realize what he has done until it is too late, and every Christian reader learns to shed the same tears, as the boastful self confronts the true. The turning point of the story of the prodigal, stripped of wealth and vanity, is when 'he comes to himself' (Luke 15.17).

The Distortions of an Imposed Identity

The religions of power articulated a dissatisfaction with human circumstances and sought to change them. It is no accident that the exponents of modern political religion, the theologians of liberation, often seem more at home with the texts of Judaism than with those of Christianity. The religion of peace is deeply sceptical of the capacity of changed circumstances to satisfy those who work for them. Instead it urges us to face our dissatisfaction with ourselves. This is not a device to sustain the status quo, for on this account the conservative, who dreams that happiness can be secured by preserving the structures of the past, is just as deeply mistaken as the revolutionary, who dreams that bliss will follow upheaval. Neither continuity nor change will satisfy us. Here we have no abiding city, and there is no reason to think that in that respect our future will be any more satisfactory than our past. Instead of turning attention to external circumstances the religion of peace invites us to discover our dissatisfaction with ourselves, and to try both to understand it and begin to overcome it.

I understand the origin of my dissatisfaction with myself in the tension between my social self, the identity which other people impose upon me, and the self, which struggles to make itself known in my immediate consciousness. The opening words of the Prayer Book Catechism are a sobering reminder of how much of our identity is imposed upon us:

Question. What is your Name?
Answer. N. or M.
Question. Who gave you this Name?
Answer. My Godfathers and Godmothers in my Baptism; wherein I was made a member of Christ, the child of God, and an inheritor of the kingdom of heaven.

We were given our names long before we learnt to use language. We did not choose the name we are known by; it was conferred upon us. Indeed according to the claims of infant baptism our eternal identity, the decisive orientation of a person's life, is not acquired at adolescence or maturity; the person becomes 'a member of Christ, the child of God, and an inheritor of the kingdom of heaven' when the only utterance of which we may be capable is a cry. As we learn to use the word 'I', we are not simply developing a role or a persona for ourselves. Instead our intimate needs and perceptions have to negotiate a complex world which has a past of which we have no memory, but to which we are horrifyingly vulnerable, and which surrounds us with expectations which are both loud and contradictory. We cannot understand our dissatisfaction as simply being a matter of our circumstances, but we cannot understand our dissatisfaction with ourselves apart from our relation to other people. Without other people we would not exist, but it is a co-existence, which is always confusing, often oppressive and threatening, and seldom free of conflict.

This tension between the social self and the conscious self is not something into which the individual 'falls' like a loss of innocence, or adolescent sexuality. It is integral to self-consciousness, from the earliest moments when the appetites and fears of the baby have to engage the inconsistent attention and nourishment of parents. By the time the child has begun to use language it has already acquired a history of which it has no memory. What the child means when it says 'I', and what its parents mean when they say 'you' are different. They already know and remember an infant of whom the child is unconscious, and their attitude to the self-conscious child will have been shaped by those experiences of which the child has no knowledge. The parents train their child by a continuous process of approval and disapproval; the child discovers himself in the conflict of that process. The strength of a parent's punishment does not simply come from the infliction of pain; what hurts is that the child receives pain from those who normally sustain it by their love and approval. As the child learns to negotiate the strange powers that surround it, it receives the most powerful impressions of its own worth and significance from the way in which others regard it; but the child also learns that it has its own thoughts, its own desires, and that it has a privileged access to its own inner conscious world.

The process which begins between the child and its parents only becomes more complicated as the child encounters its peers. Children see the one thing which is hidden from each other – the way they look and move – their manner. Each child only comes to know that indirectly in the response it meets with in others. That may be a source of surprised delight or angry disappointment, but regardless of which predominates there will be a disparity between the child as reflected in the attitudes of its peers, and the child as it perceives itself. On the one hand we live in the regard and attention which others confer upon us. They teach us whether we are liked or disliked, strong or weak, stupid or clever: and yet we also know that their knowledge is always incomplete and often unjust. As long as we live in the good opinion of other people we are also controlled by them. Their praise or blame determines, if not who we are, who we appear to be. Yet even when we have learnt how to elicit the praise we yearn for, we may still deeply resent the price it entails. It is not simply that our self-respect is undermined by the disparagement of others – it is perhaps more deeply damaged by earning praise in ways which we do not respect. Paradoxically the person who lives for the praise of others is humiliated, even when he gains that for which he seeks.

Self-respect demands therefore a measure of detachment, of confidence, of no longer needing to prove itself, and yet the self which seeks detachment will already have been deeply marked by its social experience. It is not as if it has a ready-made, pre-existing identity, to which it can simply retire, away from the expectations and pressures of other people. Instead the person has a long social history which cannot be simply cast aside and forgotten. It has to be understood; we have to learn to tell our story in a way that we can respect.

The heaviest burden which others place upon us is their blame which often not only describes our past, but forecloses our future. To speak of guilt as if it was self-generated or self-induced is misleading. We learn to feel guilty because other people blame us – their recrimination teaches us how to blame ourselves. Once again there is a cruel disparity between the consequences of our actions and our intentions. The outside world only sees the consequences of what we do, and infers our intentions from our behaviour. We alone know what we intended, and indeed how much we were conscious of what we were doing. It is when faced with the desire to attach responsibility, and particularly to blame, that the inadequacy of our language of personal pronouns becomes most obvious. While our language attributes to us a unified, continuous identity which suggests that we have a clearly defined self distinct from that of other people, reality is different. Long after the people who have formed us have died or become socially distant, we carry with us the memory of their voice – their hopes or hostility may have much greater immediacy to us than any present experience. For this reason the process of punishment seldom reconciles its victims to its justice. It is relatively easy to determine who committed a crime, but it is quite different to determine responsibility. Here the simplicity of personal pronouns is often deeply misleading. It is convenient to pretend that only the perpetrator of a crime is responsible for it, because our language ascribes the action to the agent, and it is profoundly disturbing to challenge that. It is perhaps for this reason that we retain prisons, although we know that they neither reform nor deter: because even when we no longer have the confidence to inflict punishment, they do at least protect the logic of our personal pronouns. To revise that logic would not only require that we recognize the carelessness or provocation of the victim: it would compel us to admit that few of us are really responsible for what we do. A husband has a row with his wife, drives off and has an accident. It is his crash in the sense that he is involved in it, but it may well be that the person who caused it is still sitting at home. Maturity demands that we refrain from automatically blaming those who do evil, for the perpetrators of crime are seldom solely responsible, and it is cruelty to pretend that they are. Moreover, it is prudent to suspend judgment, because there may well be times when we too require the same generosity.

Christians are presented with this tension between the social self and the true self by the way in which Jesus is presented in the Gospels. Every Christian reader knows that Jesus is the Messiah, the Son of God. The irony of the Gospels comes from the recurring misunderstandings which that divine identity encounters. It has, of course, the limitation of being presented from the outside, as a story told about Jesus rather than by him. Nevertheless it represents many of the tensions of our own experience. He refuses to be determined by the expectations of his family – the truant child in the temple grows up to be the surly guest at a wedding. He is the object of his family's anxiety, not the fulfilment of their dreams. In the story of the temptations, he is shown declining the expectations of power and popularity, and while he attracts the crowd, he does not hesitate to disappoint it. He refuses to be the consistent miracle worker or the conventional righteous man. He is the prophet who has the temerity to come from Nazareth. He is portrayed as repeatedly seizing the initiative from his enemies, as they seek to define him in ways which will trap him and secure his destruction. Perhaps more painfully he is also shown to refuse the flattery of his friends, and to disappoint the expectations of his disciples. He will not be made a king, or judge disputes, and rejects the description of good. He rebukes the hopes of Peter, the ambition of James and John and is not deflected from his final journey to Jerusalem. He silences the stereotypes with which the demoniacs greet him, and gives to the role of Messiah a quite unlooked for content. Finally he occupies the place of the criminal, without acquiescing in the justice of the proceedings, or in any way modifying his sense of his own identity. This last persona with which human beings try to define him is as misleading as all the rest.

Every reader of the gospel enters into this drama of Jesus' true identity. The Gospels were not written to prove that identity; they all assume Jesus' divine yet hidden identity from the outset. Armed with that secret the reader can enjoy and patronize the misunderstandings with which it is surrounded. The Gospels convince because the Christian reader recognizes in Jesus' story his own.[6] Like his master he is involved in a society which never truly appreciates him. He too has a hidden persona, and derives his true identity not from his family, but from his baptism. The Son is who he is because he is the Son of a divine Father.

God and the Repudiation of the World

For all its language of Father and Son the church is not the family writ large – it represents a radical alternative to the family. The whole modern tendency to present the church in quasi-family terms, family-centred, offering family services, is a betrayal of the Christian tradition. I belong to a family by birth. I do not choose my parents. I receive from them a burdensome inheritance of attitudes and expectations, which I can only partially make my own. By contrast I belong to the church by faith, in which my free consent is crucial. I exchange a set of relationships, which are exclusive, founded in property, and imposed upon me, for a new set of relationships, which I have chosen, which are inclusive and welcoming, in a way which cuts through the barriers and anxieties of possession. It is no accident that churches lose most of their adolescent membership, for a church which imitates the family must expect to be repudiated in the same way that we necessarily distance ourselves from the family that reared us. Clergymen nervous of declining congregations and dwindling revenues, overwhelmed by the institutional apparatus of another age, are tempted to become the professional promoters of 'community': they offer a sense of belonging. They are then hurt and disappointed that the response is trivial. Clubs only nurture clubability. We become people of God, members of the church, not by huddling together for comfort, not by a process of social conformity, but by having the courage to step out of line. Baptism is an act of withdrawal, Exodus, escape. A Christianity which no longer facilitates detachment has ceased to be a means of self-discovery. Good works and togetherness are a quite inadequate substitute.

> Dost thou renounce the devil and all his works, the vain pomp and glory of the world, with all covetous desires of the same, and the carnal desires of the flesh, so that thou wilt not follow nor be led by them?

The God to whom we turn in baptism is a means of repudiating the world. In baptism we withdraw our hearts from the social world around us, and refuse to see ourselves simply in the reflection which other people provide – a vanity so well described by the ageing Rousseau:

> If I could still see in someone's eyes the joy and satisfaction of being with me.[7]

In baptism we no longer look into the eyes of other people in order to discover our true identity. Instead we turn away from that complicated, deceitful social interchange to the God whom we have learnt to imagine. In turning to him we make it possible to separate ourselves from the expectations of those around us. It is the function of that God to give us room to grow. Instead of being hedged around by the demands of other people, with their clear notions of our past,

God frees us for the possibility of a future, which may be quite different from the past. Our friends will always insist that we are who we have been – only in relation to God can we discover who we might become. As long as our minds are preoccupied by what other people will think of us, by our image in their eyes, we can never discover who we really are. My God liberates me from their control, and enables me to begin to be true to myself. This is not to identify God with myself, rather he is the means by which I define myself. The I who turns to God is also the I who has learnt to construct an image of God in his heart. The I who turns to God is the I which has also been marked and distorted by the influence of other people. In turning from them – and all the delights they promise and penalties they threaten – I imagine myself instead in relation to my God. I construct an imagined world in which I and my God are both distinguished and related, in which I imagine myself speaking to God, and discover that the self who speaks to him is a new self. In this way I exchange my old self for a new.

The story of Jesus' divinely-grounded identity in the Gospels is told from the outside, in the third person. For that reason his religious achievement is assumed from the start. We are presented with tableaux, which show him repudiating the various misleading identities which men endeavour to impose upon him. It is, however, a story told by another, in retrospect, when the battle is past and the victory has been won. For those reasons it tends to obscure the uncertainty of the outcome, and the excitement of self-definition. That is to be found not in the Gospels but in the confessions of the saints, written in the first person by people who may be hopeful of victory but are still in the midst of the battle.

God and the Withdrawal of the Self: Augustine

The classic text of this kind is the *Confessions* of Augustine. The neo-platonist in him would have been content to describe his conversion in terms of a gradual turning away from the world of the senses to the contemplation of God, and much of his search for continence is told in this way. What takes his portrayal of himself far beyond such stereotypes is the robust realism with which the social dimensions of the self are described. It is this which makes him a

Christian writer. The famous theft of the apples would have provided a perfect opportunity for a neo-platonist meditation on the moral corruption which comes from a preoccupation with earthly goods. Augustine's account is quite different:

> By myself I would not have committed that robbery. It was not the takings that attracted me but the raid itself, and yet to do it by myself would have been no fun and I should not have done it. This was friendship of a most unfriendly sort, bewitching my mind in an inexplicable way. For the sake of a laugh, a little sport, I was glad to do harm and anxious to damage another; and that without thought of profit for myself or retaliation for injuries received! And all because we are ashamed to hold back when others say, 'Come on! Let's do it!'[8]

The member of the children's gang graduates to belong to a fashionable clique of rowdy students, albeit in his own ambivalent manner:

> By now I was at the top of the school of rhetoric. I was pleased with my superior status and swollen with conceit. All the same, as you well know, Lord, I behaved far more quietly than the 'Wreckers', a title of ferocious devilry which the fashionable set chose for themselves. I had nothing whatever to do with their outbursts of violence, but I lived amongst them, feeling a perverse sense of shame because I was not like them. I kept company with them and there were times when I found their friendship a pleasure, but I always had a horror of what they did when they lived up to their name. Without provocation they would set upon some timid newcomer, gratuitously affronting his sense of decency for their own amusement and using it as fodder for their spiteful jests.[9]

In these accounts Augustine recognizes how much of his identity and behaviour stemmed from the company with which he surrounded himself. While he is attracted by the sense of belonging, he resents the way in which he is influenced by others. His profession as a master of rhetoric made him keenly aware both of the excitement and the pressures of an audience. When writing of Hierius, an established public speaker, whom he admired, he is anxious to distinguish the esteem of a rhetor from that of an actor:

I did not admire Hierius in the way that I might have admired a famous charioteer or a popular contestant in the amphitheatre. My feeling for him and others like him was quite different. It was something quite serious, the kind of admiration that I should have liked to win for myself. Why was this? Though I liked actors and openly admired them, I should not have wanted their fame and popularity for myself. I would rather have been entirely unknown than known in the way that they were known. I would rather have been hated than loved as they were. How can one soul contain within itself feelings so much at variance, in such conflict with each other.[10]

There is snobbery as well as honesty in this examination of his youthful enthusiasm, which makes it clear that for admiration to be serious it must be the kind of admiration which he would like to win for himself. Nevertheless he is forced to concede that his admiration for Hierius, however sincerely felt, was entirely socially determined:

I know now, and confess it as the truth, that I admired Hierius more because others praised him than for the accomplishments for which they praised him. I know this because those same people, instead of praising him, might have abused him. They might have spoken of the same talents in him but found fault with them and despised them. If they had done this, my feelings would not have been aroused nor my admiration kindled. Yet his qualities would have been the same and he himself would have been no different. The only difference would have been in their attitude towards him.[11]

He then makes a comment which reveals how he now feels about such instability:

We can see from this that the soul is weak and helpless unless it clings to the firm rock of truth.

When the bishop speaks of truth, he is referring to God who alone can give him consistency and identity.

Augustine does not tell the story of his conversion as if it was simply a matter of acquiring convictions about God, though he goes to some pains to indicate his intellectual development. Although, as I indicated in the previous chapter, he describes his discovery of God in terms which stress God's initiative and responsibility, his account of God's conquest is intertwined with the drama of a divided self. He directly refers this to the influence of reading St Paul:

> From my own experience I now understood what I had read – that *the impulses of nature and the impulses of the spirit are at war with one another.* In this warfare I was on both sides, but I took the part of that which I approved in myself rather than the part of that which I disapproved. For my true self was no longer on the side of which I disapproved, since to a great extent I was now its reluctant victim rather than its willing tool. Yet it was by my own doing that habit had become so potent an enemy, because it was by my own will that I had reached the state in which I no longer wished to stay.[12]

Having by this stage in his life read the Pauline literature, Augustine can explicitly present his experience in those conflict-laden terms: they represent, however, only the culmination of the same wavering ambivalence, which had marked the theft of apples and the fastidious fellow-traveller of the 'Wreckers'.

As Augustine approaches the decisive moment of his story, the intervention of God and the theme of self-discovery become more closely intertwined:

> While (Ponticianus) was speaking, O Lord, you were turning me around to look at myself. For I had placed myself behind my own back, refusing to see myself. You were setting me before my own eyes so that I could see how sordid I was . . . I had known it all along, but I had always pretended that it was something different. I had turned a blind eye and forgotten it.[13]

While modern scepticism sees in religion simply an illusion about God, Augustine attributes to God the destruction of his illusions about himself. Self-deceit, which preoccupies the modern hermeneutic of suspicion, is a notion at the heart of the *Confessions.* If it is right to see in Augustine's God an imaginary being, whom he has himself constructed, it has also to be recognized that paradoxically one of its functions is to overcome self-deceit. It would be anachronistic to complain that he failed to detect his responsibility for his God; the integrity of his achievement is established by the rigour of his self-portrayal.

Although more than a decade separates Augustine's conversion from his account of it, and although the episcopal self cannot speak of the convert without a certain knowingness obtruding, the personal agony, which preceded and doubtless contributed to the crucial resolution, still grips his memory and communicates powerfully to the reader:

> My inner self was a house divided against itself . . . I now found myself driven by the tumult in my breast to take refuge in this garden, where no one could interrupt that fierce struggle, in which I was my own contestant, until it came to its conclusion. What the conclusion was to be you knew, O Lord, but I did not. Meanwhile I was beside myself with madness that would bring me sanity. I was dying a death that would bring me life. I knew the evil that was in me, but the good that was soon to be born in me I did not know . . . I was frantic, overcome by violent anger with myself for not accepting your will and entering into your covenant. Yet in my bones I knew that this was what I ought to do. In my heart of hearts I praised it to the skies. And to reach this goal I needed no chariot or ship. I need not even walk as far as I had come from the house to the place where we sat, for to make the journey, and to arrive safely, no more was required than an act of will. But it must be a resolute and whole-hearted act of the will, not some lame wish which I kept turning over and over in my mind, so that it had to wrestle with itself, part of it trying to rise, part falling to the ground.[14]

This conflict is resolved by the choice of God, which is also represented as the gift of God. It is a mark of Augustine's honesty that although he wants to ascribe all to God, he recognizes that he is the theatre in whom God is at work:

> You converted me to yourself, so that I no longer desired a wife or placed any hope in this world.[15]

It is now time to examine more closely the content of that decision which Augustine recognizes as the work of God. The predominant category that Augustine uses is that of lust, but he has told us enough about himself to make it clear that this is not some abstract or purely psychological tendency; it relates to his most recent mistress, and the wife that his mother has arranged for him. In repudiating lust, he is also repudiating them and their demands. His choice for God is, however, more radical than the purely sexual, it encompasses the whole range of worldly achievement: it enables him to refuse to allow the structures of human society to determine his life and identity. The crisis of conversion is precipitated by a pious tale told him by Ponticianus. It is a story which must have gained much from the high position in the Emperor's court, which Ponticianus held. He recalled an incident at Triers when some members of the imperial staff read the life of St Anthony and like St Anthony himself were instantly converted. It is their contrast between the secular and the religious life, which Augustine still recalls with clarity:

> What do we hope to gain by all the efforts we make? What are we looking for? What is our purpose in serving the State? Can we hope for anything better at Court than to be the Emperor's friends? Even so, surely our position would be precarious and exposed to much danger? We shall meet it at every turn, only to reach another danger which is greater still. And how long is it to be before we reach it? But if I wish, I can become the friend of God at this very moment.[16]

Compared with a life of laborious calculation and uncertain outcome, the religous self has an immediacy which reflects the accessibility of its God. In becoming a catholic Christian Augustine defines himself in a way that he can respect. Who he is is no longer determined by the uncertain result of sexual or political intrigue. He can at last develop an identity independent of both mistress and patron. It would be a mistake to see in this merely a capitulation to the desires of his mother. She may applaud and be delighted to discover her son as an unlooked for monk, but it must have been one of the attractions of that persona for her son, that it was precisely not the future she had planned for him. One may wonder if the convert's celibacy had not called her devout bluff:

> She saw that you had granted her far more than she used to ask in her tearful prayers and plaintive lamentations.[17]

The God to whom Augustine relates himself in his lengthy *Confessions* with its many questions is never a God with whom he directly identifies himself. Nevertheless God's intervention and Augustine's decision are intimately related. Everything depends on Augustine's act of will, but it is an act of will which God gives him. In this way God becomes the means by which Augustine defines himself:

> Let me know you, for you are the God who knows me; *let me recognize you as you have recognized me*. You are the power of my soul; come into it and make it fit for yourself, so that you may have it and hold it *without stain or wrinkle*. This is my hope; this is why I speak as I do; this is the hope that brings me joy, when my joy is in what is to save me.[18]

As long as Augustine lives in the regard of other people, he is miserable, because they do not allow him to be who he is. His conversion is a repudiation of the self that others impose upon him. Instead he attends to the God who lives in his imagination. As we have seen he cannot recognize his creative responsibility for that God, but he does repeatedly recognize that he is both the creation and the beneficiary of that God. As he speaks to God he defines a self he can affirm; the praise of God which resounds throughout the *Confessions* is also the affirmation of its author.

God and the Withdrawal of the Self: Anselm

To place the *Proslogion* of Anselm beside the *Confessions* of Augustine may seem a curious juxtaposition. Until recently commentators on Anselm had concentrated on chapters 2–4, which contain the origins of the famous ontological argument for the existence of God. That is to treat him as an anticipation of the scholastic theology that came after him. It has been the achievement of the Benedictine scholar Anselm Stolz to place the argument in chapters 2–4 in the context of the whole work, and so to set the *Proslogion* in a tradition of mystical theology derived from Augustine. In this the relation between the self and God is fundamental to the entire work.

The *Proslogion* begins in a way which is quite different from what its preface might lead us to expect. Anselm does not take us into his confused search for an idea which eludes him, instead he begins by commending to himself, and by implication to the reader, a process of withdrawal:

> Come now, little man,
> turn aside for a while from your daily employment,
> escape for a moment from the tumult of your thoughts.
> Put aside your weighty cares,
> let your burdensome distractions wait,
> free yourself awhile for God
> and rest awhile in him.
> Enter the inner chamber of your soul,
> shut out everything except God
> and that which can help you in seeking him,
> and when you have shut the door, seek him.
> Now, my whole heart, say to God,
> 'I seek your face,
> Lord, it is your face I seek.'[19]

The self is urged to separate itself from 'its daily employments', and its usual preoccupations are gently deprecated as 'weighty cares' and 'burdensome distractions'. 'Seeking God's face' is prepared for, even if it is not equated with, this act of repudiation. As in the *Confessions* God's presence is assumed from the outset, as the real audience of words which we only overhear.

There follows a long lamentation to God, which establishes both a relationship between the soul and God, and a distance between them, which it is the purpose of the *Proslogion* to overcome, in so far as that is possible:

> By what signs, under what forms, shall I seek you?
> I have never seen you, O Lord my God,
> I have never seen your face.[20]

Repeatedly Anselm uses the imagery of the lover's search with its sweet interplay of seeking and finding:

> What shall your servant do,
> eager for your love, cast off far from your face?
> He longs to see you,
>> but your countenance is too far away.
> He wants to have access to you,
>> but your dwelling is inaccessible.
> He longs to find you,
>> but he does not know where you are.
> He loves to seek you,
>> but he does not know where you are.[21]

Here distance and intimacy are balanced in a way no human love can imitate. Throughout the lamentation Anselm never doubts the reality of God's attention; he may not see God, but God always sees and hears him. Equally the love of God can survive a degree of inaccessibility, which would be fatal to human love. While human love, however crossed, clings to a memory of the face of the beloved, the soul has no such memory of God.

This distance from God ensures that the withdrawal of the self is not the calm and serene experience which the opening words of the *Proslogion* seem to promise. Instead the religious quest involves Anselm in contradictions which are as radical as those of Augustine's divided self:

> What have I begun, and what accomplished?
> Where was I going and where have I got to?
> To what did I reach out, for what do I long?
> I sought after goodness, and lo, here is turmoil;
> I was going towards God, and I was my own impediment.
>> I sought peace within myself,
> and in the depths of my heart I found trouble and sorrow.
>> I wanted to laugh for the joy of my heart,
>> and the pain of my heart made me groan.
>> It was gladness I was hoping for,
>> but sighs came think and fast.[22]

Throughout this first chapter Anselm is endeavouring 'to arouse the mind to the contemplation of God'. Only the experience of God can deliver the soul from the contradictions it suffers, and the later chapters of the *Proslogion* are an anticipation of that deliverance. It is fascinating to see the literary art with which Anselm's prayer at the outset begins to resolve the difficulty it has created for itself:

> Teach me to seek you,
> and as I seek you, show yourself to me,
> for I cannot seek you unless you show me how,
> and I will never find you
> unless you show yourself to me.
> Let me seek you by desiring you,
> and desire you by seeking you;
> let me find you by loving you,
> and love you in finding you.[23]

In prayer the self who seeks is answered by the God who shows. On the one hand Anselm appears to surrender his power of initiative, on the other he is upheld by God. The love of the self for God is a pledge of God's love for the self. God and the soul, which at first appeared so distant, are represented as enjoying an unsuspected reciprocity. The search of the soul is sustained by the God whom it seeks. The condition of the search is also its goal, a movement which the literary form of the *Proslogion* itself exemplifies.

The Continuing Mystery: The Self and the Unknown God

I have argued in this chapter that in praying to God I withdraw myself from the identity which social life provides and imposes upon me, and begin to achieve a new identity. In prayer I am not only creating the God who lives in my imagination, I am also recreating myself. On this account the primary function of the notion of God is the redefinition of who we are. The self is both the agent of prayer – the person who prays – and also the agenda of prayer – that which prayer seeks to change. At first I necessarily derive my sense of who I am from other people: they talked me into using language and so becoming a person. Nevertheless their picture of me was inevitably inadequate. They knew what I looked like; they might have a very clear view of what I had been and done. They did not know my dreams; their knowledge only obscured their understanding of what I might become. In imagining a God who defies definition, who transcends every category which we are tempted to apply to him, we ensure for ourselves an unlimited horizon. We preserve the mystery of our own personality from all those who would claim to read us like a book.

In this respect it is instructive that in the course of the *Proslogion* Anselm was driven to modify his description of God as 'that than which nothing greater can be thought'. Having explored its implications he recognizes in chapter 14 that he remains unsatisfied with it:

> O my soul,
>   have you found what you were looking for?
>   I was seeking God,
> and I have found that he is above all things,
> and that than which nothing greater can be thought.
>   I have found him to be
>   life and light, wisdom and goodness,
> eternal blessedness and the bliss of eternity,
>   existing everywhere and at all times
>   If I have not found my God,
> what is it that I have found and understood
>   so truly and certainly?
> Why do I not experience what I have found?
>   Lord God,
>   if my soul has found you,
>   why has it no experience of you.[24]

The definition of God with which Anselm begins proves too restrictive. He finds it necessary to extend it in a way which threatens to undermine the adequacy of thought and rational definition:

> Lord, you are then not only that than which nothing greater can be thought; you are something greater than it is possible to think about.[25]

It is this theme which dominates the second part of the *Proslogion*. Anselm approaches it in a prayer, in which the ignorance of the self and the knowledge of God are no longer seen as contrasts, where one overcomes the other; instead the consciousness of the soul's darkness is a tribute to the light of God:

> O Lord my God,
> my Creator and my Re-creator,
> my soul longs for you.
> Tell me what you are, beyond what I have seen,
> so that I may see clearly what I desire.
> I strive to see more,
> but I see nothing beyond what I have seen,
> except darkness.
> Or rather I do not see darkness
> which is no part of you,
> but I see that I cannot see further
> because of my own darkness.
> Why is this, Lord?
> Are my eyes darkened by my weakness,
> or dazzled by your glory?
> The truth is, I am darkened by myself
> and also dazzled by you.
> I am clouded by my own smallness
> and overwhelmed by your immensity;
> I am restricted by my own narrowness
> and mastered by your wideness.[26]

The knowledge of God is a consciousness of ignorance. It does not yield a clearly defined sense of the self with which we can rest content, and say I am such and such a person. After every partial act of self-definition, attention to God reminds us of what remains unsaid.

For this reason the work of religion is never done. The task of self-knowledge is never complete, just because what we call self-knowledge is in reality self-definition. While we live the self has continually to be defined anew. No sooner have we disentangled ourselves from the demands of one audience than we encounter the expectations of another. Towards the end of the *Confessions* Augustine speaks not of his past but of his present:

> O Lord, you who alone can rule without pride since you are the only true Lord and no other Lord rules over you, there is a third kind of temptation which, I fear, has not passed from me. Can it ever pass from me in all this life? It is the desire to be feared or

loved by other men, simply for the pleasure that it gives me, though in such pleasure there is no true joy. It means only a life of misery and despicable vainglory. It is for this reason more than any other that men neither love you nor fear you in purity of heart. It is for this reason that *you thwart the proud and keep your grace for the humble*. This is why, with a voice of thunder, you condemn the ambitions of this world, so that *the very foundations of the hills quail and quake*. This is why the enemy of our true happiness persists in his attacks upon me, for he knows that when men hold certain offices in human society, it is necessary that they should be loved and feared by other men. He sets his traps about me, baiting them with tributes of applause, in the hope that in my eagerness to listen I may be caught off my guard. He wants me to divorce my joy from the truth and place it in man's duplicity. He wants me to enjoy being loved and feared by others, not for your sake, but in your place.[27]

The ancient art of rhetoric, like today's public relations, involved the study and control of an audience. The ageing bishop is under no illusion as to how close he remains to his younger, secular self. Perhaps he reconciles himself too readily to the office he holds, for he recognizes that it is his public persona as bishop that brings him into the most persistent temptation. His conversion to God has continually to be renewed.

7

The Love of God and
the Values of Men

Teach me, my God and King,
In all things thee to see;
And what I do in anything
To do it as for thee!
This is the famous stone
That turneth all to gold;
For that which God doth touch and own
Cannot for less be told.

George Herbert

The Values of the Religions of Power

Much of the confusion which surrounds religious values arises
from a misleading conception of value. Wherever religious values
are conceived as being those permanent qualities underlying the
changing phenomena of a religion, we are still using a concept of
value derived from the gold standard. It is not simply secular
economists, who would doubt the adequacy of such a model, the
religious texts themselves challenge it. At the heart of the Judaeo-
Christian tradition is a preoccupation with covenant, with an
exchange or bargain between God and man. In that tradition values
are not detached platonic ideas inviting our ascent and realization;
the values intrinsic to such a religious transaction are the benefits
which it promises. This demands that we look at religious values in a

quite different way from moral values. Moral values are concerned with behaviour and disposition. Religious values also involve behaviour and disposition, but we fail to understand them properly if we concentrate on the commands of a religion: those are not its values, they are only its conditions. They are the price that has to be paid in order to acquire what is valued.

So in our society the real crisis of Christian values is not to be found in changing sexual habits or the exhibition of racial intolerance, the breakdown of marriage or indifference to the poor. The crisis in Christian values is found in the implausibility of heaven. Without a convincing account of its reward, its promise, Christianity becomes merely ineffectual nagging. It fails to motivate, and it is that failure which is at the heart of secular indifference.

As long as we concentrate on the demands which different religions make, they seem to represent a bewildering variety. If instead we pay attention, not to the conditions of the religious transaction, but to the benefits which it envisages, we perceive a remarkable degree of convergence. Ancient Judaism and paganism alike, when seen from this perspective, had far more in common than their different observances might suggest. Both shared and articulated the goals of the societies which they comprised. As religions of power they were harmoniously adapted to the needs of the societies which produced them. Preoccupied by human weakness they reflected a prevailing consensus about what was desirable, if difficult to obtain. Many of their values were therefore cheerfully secular – the prosperity of society and the individual, victory in battle and preservation from invasion, good health, fertility, protection from injury and accident. It needs no highly educated religious sensibility to appreciate such benefits. The God of power was praised for providing such blessings. One might indeed say that he was prized, as the means to those ends. The pressure of contrary experience only very gradually transformed such expectations. This life might cease to be the place of such rewards, but the end of time or the life beyond the grave offered essentially identical gratifications. The tomb furniture of Egyptian graves is a vivid example of such transferred hopes: kitchens, dancing girls and dice. Faced by such tangible expectations the Christian heaven might be judged anaemic.

In many of its forms Christianity has been little different from ancient Judaism and paganism – a religion of power-sharing the same secular values. It has perhaps only been different from its predecessors in being more evasive about the benefits it offers – at times holding out the prospect of rewards in this life, at other times confining its privileges strictly to the hereafter. This cannot convincingly be represented as a decline from primitive purity. The Gospels themselves abound in confusion and equivocation in this respect, as the example of St Matthew makes plain.

In the abstract Christian values are usually seen as hostile both to money and to pride: this has been given its most arresting presentation in the poverty and humility of the Franciscans. It therefore comes as something of a surprise to find that in Matthew's Gospel Christian values are repeatedly asserted in terms derived from the same values that Christianity challenges. The teacher who replies with the stern warning that 'Man cannot live on bread alone; he lives on every word that God utters' (Matt. 4.4) is nevertheless portrayed as satisfying men's material hunger (14.20f.; 15.36). It may be easier for a camel to pass through the eye of a needle than for a rich man to enter the kingdom of God' (19.24); nevertheless Jesus' status and significance are demonstrated in costly financial terms. At his birth the wise men bring him treasure – gold, frankincense and myrrh (3.11). His death is prophesied by the most extravagant anointing (26.1–13), which might well outrage the susceptibilities of many of his modern followers, as it did his historic ones. Similarly humility is advocated by one who 'did not come be be served, but to serve' (20.28), but he attracts the attention of his audience in the most surprising terms. His teaching in this Gospel abounds with kings (18.23; 22.1; 25.34) and masters (10.24; 15.27; 20.1; 21.33ff.; 24.45f.; 25.14–30), and has a keen sense of social place not only in this world (23.6f.) but in the world to come (5.19; 10.40f.; 18.1ff.; 20.20). It may glory in persecution and dwell on Jesus' eventual repudiation but it also surrounds him with attentive crowds and responsive faith.

Matthew's Gospel belongs inextricably to a society preoccupied by social and economic distinctions, and would be largely unintelligible without those concerns. The fascination of that which is in short supply – fame and money – sold the gospel long before Fleet Street added sex to the mixture to sell tabloids. The parable of hidden treasure is the stuff of the modern newspaper:

> The kingdom of Heaven is like treasure lying buried in a field. The man who found it, buried it again; and for sheer joy went and sold everything he had, and bought that field (13.44).

The story appeals to our greed and envy. Today photographs of the treasure and the lucky owner would focus both the one and the other. Jesus' parable must have begun its life as a story from the bazaar, but it is used in the first place to commend decisive, effective action. Every reader can enjoy the same good fortune if he displays the same energy and courage. Moreover, the hiddenness of the treasure in the parable helps to make more plausible the invisible, imaginary treasure in which the gospel deals. The process is curious: first the reader is persuaded to imagine himself as the possessor of an invisible, heavenly treasure; and then on the strength of that imaginary good he can even pity and patronize the actual possessor of such goods. A famous passage from the sermon on the mount illustrates this progression:

> Do not store up for yourselves treasure on earth, where it grows rusty and moth-eaten, and thieves break in to steal it. Store up treasure in heaven, where there is no moth and no rust to spoil it, no thieves to break in and steal. For where your treasure is, there will your heart be also (6.19–23).

At first the teaching seems to condemn the desire to accumulate wealth, but in reality it is the unsatisfactory nature of earthly treasure that is dwelt upon. Instead the reader is encouraged to accumulate treasure in an imagined, heavenly world where earthly anxieties have no place. This is presented as an act of prudence appealing to the very motivation which is being challenged.

Exactly the same contradiction is found in the teaching on enduring shame and avoiding earthly praise. Humility is commended on the basis of a motivation that the truly humble should have outgrown:

> The greatest among you must be your servant. For whoever exalts himself will be humbled; and whoever humbles himself will be exalted (23.12).

Faced with all the disappointments and conflicts of social life the reader is encouraged to imagine another world where all that matters is the regard of Jesus or God:

> Whoever then will acknowledge me before men, I will acknowledge him before my Father in heaven (10.32).

The reader is being lured to invest heavily in an invisible, imagined world which will more than compensate him for any inconveniences in this one.

The values which Matthew asserts are not only part of a transaction between man and God, they also involve a transaction between the religious leader and his followers. He proclaims the availability of unseen benefits. An invisible king of total power and knowledge, keenly interested in all our doings, will reward and punish unerringly. His favour in his heavenly court is presented as all that matters, his treasure is as inexhaustible as his torments are endless. Modern Christian exponents of a more spiritual and disinterested morality can only be taken aback by this conversation between their spiritual leader and his most prominent disciple:

> At this Peter said, 'We have left everything to become your followers. What will there be for us?' Jesus replied, 'I tell you this: in the world that is to be, when the Son of Man is seated on his throne in heavenly splendour, you my followers will have thrones of your own, where you will sit as judges of the twelve tribes of Israel. And anyone who has left brothers or sisters, father or mother or children, land or houses for the sake of my name will be repaid many times over' (19.27ff.).

Later in the story Judas' complementary reward is also lovingly recounted (27.3–10). This notion of reward is articulated not so much by describing its splendours, as contrasting it with the punishment which is its alternative. The wailing and gnashing of teeth (8.12; 13.42; 22.13; 24.51; 25.30) help to reconcile the reader to the most drastic measures·

> If your hand or your foot is your undoing, cut if off and fling it away; it is better for you to enter into life maimed or lame, than to keep two hands or two feet and be thrown into eternal fire (18.8).

Repeatedly in this Gospel the reader is encouraged to lose money and reputation in order to obtain these things on the heavenly level. This cannot be divorced from the position of the early Christian leaders and the demands they were obliged to make on their followers. Their reference to a heavenly court and its treasure implicitly conveyed the impression of their own privileged access to it and the possibility of making such goods available to others. Much is made of the manifest poverty of Christ's representatives (10.9f.), but the rationale for such poverty is not always perceived. It is the occasion of generosity, an insistent if silent appeal for financial support. Payment for healing and exorcism is forbidden (10.8), but that is not to prohibit the appreciative gift. We should not forget when we read in this Gospel of the insistence on the divestment of wealth (6.24; 19.21), that such divestment requires recipients. The early Christians were ready to part with the devalued earthly resources to gain a more lasting credit; they also had to risk ridicule and abuse in order to secure high standing in the heavenly court. In this way their leaders secured control of considerable financial resources, and ensured that their followers would be proof against any negative social pressures.

In so far as Christianity was conceived in these terms, it was utterly dependent on the objective existence of the God who alone could reward such sacrifice. Those who have paid such a high price will not welcome the suggestion that their investment is in a totally fictitious realm. It is the desperate conviction of rash speculation which every gambler will recognize.

Losing our Heart to the World

The complacent rationalist will doubtless be impatient with such an implausible transaction, thinking it madness to part with tangible goods for the satisfactions of an imagined world. In so far as the Christian is only another more sophisticated worshipper of the God of power such a negative judgment is correct. If the Christian religion represents no challenge to the values of the world, but simply looks to God to deliver them – then all that is at stake is the ability of God to do this, and then the most destructive scepticism is justified. In so far as Christians look to their God for such benefits in this life that must be the final verdict. The resort to an imagined heaven should not, however, be dismissed so totally. It is not merely Christians who in our society part with large sums of money for imagined benefits. The gambler's dream of the big win, the pornographer's sexual fantasies, the imagery which glamorizes so much of our consumption, also belong to an imagined world, and seldom comes cheap. Such behaviour is by no means entirely irrational. It enables people to rise above the unequal distribution of good fortune. If this was only used by the rich and successful to defuse envy it would be repellent; but self-administered it may mean the beginning of self-respect. At least it refuses to acquiesce in the world as it is, and depends for its success on a highly active imagination in a world where material resources are scarce and status uncertain. Often we betray that imagination by refusing to take it seriously unless or until it is realized. We focus on the objects of imagination and then return to the inequalities and oppression of the actual world and confirm them. But the person who has begun to live in his imagination may become aware of his own creativity, that he is only able to bestow value because he already possesses it. In that way alone can we cease to be the slaves of our desires.

The secular atheist has no quarrel with the values of the religions of power, he merely denies that they are an effective means of securing the benefits they seek. Medicine replaces prayer as a means of cure. Fertilizer produces better crops. Prosperity is secured by intelligent economic management, and peace by prudent maintenance of the means of military defence. Risk can never be entirely eliminated, but it can be sensibly evaluated and managed. In this way the religions of power have seemed increasingly redundant. The religion of peace is much more disturbing to such assumptions because it challenges that consensus about what matters; it sees in those values themselves the origin of conflict and destructiveness. It subverts them by inviting us to examine them more closely.

The consensus between the religions of power and the values of common sense rests on an uncritical evaluation of certain material things as good. The most enduring and remarkable example of this is gold – a phenomenon to which the advocates of unrestricted historical relativism give too little attention. Many other things, however, are conceived as having intrinsic value; so that happiness and fulfilment are envisaged in terms of their possession. It is this which lies at the heart of the advertiser's art. On such a view value is intrinsic, it resides in the object which the person is thus encouraged to possess. What is consistently repressed is any awareness that the person is contributing to the value which is placed on the object. Although his imagination is being engaged, he is discouraged from becoming aware of this, for to become aware of the contribution which we make to the value of what we covet is to threaten the whole transaction.

In religious terms this was expressed in Feuerbach's notion of projection, which lies at the heart of *The Essence of Christianity*:

> The personality of God is thus the means by which man converts the qualities of his own nature into the qualities of another being, – of a being external to himself. The personality of God is nothing else than the projected personality of man.[1]

Mediated through the writings of Marx and Freud this awareness of the contribution which we make to our God has been widely disseminated. At the same time the insight has tended to be confined to the sphere of religion. So the modern atheist may dismiss God as the product of his imagination, and yet remain curiously uncritical about the value of his love affairs.

The process of projection, which Feuerbach used with such power and originality in his understanding of God, should not be confined to the sphere of religion. It was first elaborated to understand secular love. In *De L'Amour*, published in 1822, Stendahl analysed love in such a way that made it clear that the qualities prized in the beloved were bestowed by the lover:

> Leave a lover with his thoughts for twenty-four hours, and this is what will happen:
> At the salt mines of Salzburg, they throw a leafless wintry bough into one of the abandoned workings. Two or three months later they pull it out covered with a shining deposit of crystals. The smallest twig, no bigger than a tom-tit's claw, is studded with a galaxy of scintillating diamonds. The original branch is no longer recognisable.

What I have called crystallisation is a mental process which draws from everything that happens new proofs of the perfection of the loved one.[2]

Stendahl develops this highly subversive understanding of love with characteristic wit and sensitivity: it has nevertheless devastating implications for any objective view of the value which the lover perceives in his beloved, as this passage of conversation illustrates:

Madame, the young officer is discovering qualities in you that we who have long been your friends have never seen. For example, we could never perceive an air of tender and compassionate kindness in you. Since this young man is German the most important quality in a woman, for him, is kindness, so he immediately reads into your features an expression of kindness. If he were English he would see in you the aristocratic and LADY-LIKE mien of a duchess;

With typical irony he then adds:

but if he were myself he would see you just as you are, because for a long time it has been my misfortune to imagine nothing more attractive.[3]

Seldom can the flattery of love have been so delicately parodied.

It would be a mistake to limit such an analysis of value to the emotional heights of romantic love, where emotion may seem as overwrought and unreal as in religion itself. Instead I will content myself with an example of a more mundane kind, provided by a less fastidious writer. Victor Hugo in *Les Misérables* gives this account of a doll in the eyes of a child. First he places the article in its objective context:

The last of the stalls, exactly opposite the tavern door, dealt in bric-a-brac and glittered with trinkets, glasswork, and wonderful metal contrivances, and in the front, against a background of white drapery, the stallkeeper had set a large doll nearly two feet high, clad in a dress of pink crepe, with a wreath of gold fronds on its head and with real hair and enamel eyes.

Then Hugo provides its social evaluation:

This marvel had been on display all day, to the ravishment of all passers-by under the age of ten, without any Montfermeil mother having been rich enough, or lavish enough, to buy it for her child. Eponine and Azelma had spent hours gazing at it, and even Cosette had dared to glance at it now and then.

Hugo now takes us into the child's mind:

> But now when she came out of the inn, tired and wretched though she was, she could not restrain herself from crossing the narrow street to examine that prodigious doll – 'the lady', as she called it. She stood entranced, not having seen it so close before. The stall to her was like a palace, and the doll was something more than a doll. It was a vision of delight and splendour, of wealth and happiness flooding with a dreamlike radiance the squalor of her own bleak world. With the innocent and sad shrewdness of childhood, Cosette reckoned the distance separating the doll from herself. One would need to be a queen or at least a princess to own anything so magnificent. She considered the beautiful pink dress, the soft, fair hair, and thought, 'How happy that doll must be'.

The novelist is well aware of the religious implications of his picture and shares them with the reader:

> She could not tear herself away from the stall, and the more she gazed the more she marvelled. It was like Heaven. There were other dolls behind the big one, and these to her were fairies or angels, and the owner, pacing up and down at the back of the stall, was near to being the Eternal Father himself.[4]

This description of a child's doll is a perceptive account of how things acquire value. In the first place, there is the artful presentation of the object, emphasizing its size and uniqueness. Here Hugo presents the doll with the detached eye of an adult, perceiving the way a gimcrack article is being cleverly sold. Then he gives an account of its public and monetary worth: measured by the attention of the children, and the prudence of their parents. When Hugo describes the doll in the child's eyes, the doll becomes endowed with quite new qualities – 'the doll was something more than a doll'. The child sees the value as residing in the object; the author and the reader, however, know who has provided the 'delight and splendour' which the child sees in the doll. At the same time the child's perception of the doll's value involves an act of fascinated humiliation. It may flood 'with a dreamlike radiance the squalor of her own bleak world', but immediately she calculates the distance which separates her from such an object. Because it is so precious, it cannot be hers. The value with which she has endowed the doll only confirms her desperate perception of herself. In this way Hugo reveals the alienation and self-humiliation involved in all our notions of intrinsic value. We bestow value on what is outside us: in so doing we depreciate ourselves and can only regain our self-respect by acquisition. We thus condemn ourselves to recapture a value which we too carelessly mislaid. Cosette is conscious of her valuation of the doll, but she is innocently unaware of what she is contributing to that process.

The other advantage of using a doll to examine the process of human valuation is that it makes it much easier to acknowledge the reality of boredom. In the novel the doll is abandoned with regret, but we know that we grow out of dolls, we become bored with them. The reality of boredom is probably the phenomenon which the common sense account of value finds it most difficult to acknowledge. All the goods which the religions of power promise are only beguiling in their absence: once we have them and cease to be preoccupied by the anxiety that we might lose them, we take them for granted, they cease to interest. Behind all the excitements and ecstasy of romantic love is the dread of boredom associated with possession. We do not repossess the values from which we have alienated ourselves in the process of acquisition; instead we discover the emptiness of the transaction. We project value on to something else or another person, but once we gain that thing or person, we discover that the value has eluded us. We are disappointed. So we discover that we have a heart, by losing it; but once we have lost our heart to the world, it does not give it back to us

Disappointment and in human terms recrimination are not accidental misfortunes: they are the corrolaries of our belief in intrinsic values. It is usually easier to blame the object rather than to re-examine ourselves. In marriage we repudiate the other partner:

we blame him or her for not living up to our expectations, and so look round for a more satisfactory screen on which to project our illusions. Secular love is in its nature repetitious: it accepts no responsibility for its disappointment. Instead it seeks delight in the hitherto unexplored. This is the subject of William Law's satire in *A Serious Call to a Devout and Holy Life*. Having described the careers of Flatus and Feliciana, who seek ever new forms of distraction, he ends with these reflections:

> If you was to see a man dully endeavouring all his life to satisfy his thirst, by holding up one and the same empty cup to his mouth, you would certainly despise his ignorance. But if you should see others of brighter parts, and finer understandings, ridiculing the dull satisfaction of one cup, and thinking to satisfy their own thirst, by a variety of gilt and golden empty cups; would you think that these were ever the wiser, or happier or better employed, for their finer parts?[5]

We may be willing to accept such an account of purely material goods; but people we tell ourselves are different. It is the supreme achievement of Flaubert's *Sentimental Education* that it does not flinch from acknowledging the truth that our affections are equally empty. Surveying his emotional life in retrospect the hero remembers an escapade of his youth in which he and a friend fled embarrassed and unsatisfied from a brothel: 'That was the happiest time we ever had'.[6]

The God who Transcends the World

The flaw in so much religious education is that it is marked by a terror of the process by which we learn to love God. It is so preoccupied by the dangers of sin that it attempts the forlorn task of trying to preserve innocence. So many of its prohibitions seem designed to protect the young from the world, and perversely only enhance its attractions. Most sadly God becomes a matter of boredom. The majority of the children who have been carefully brought to church Sunday by Sunday and given 'a good Christian education' think in their teens that they already know all there is to know about God, and that excitement and fascination lie elsewhere.

That is probably the inevitable consequence of attempting to teach people to love God, before they have tried loving anything else. Such a religion will only attract the timid and the cowardly, and even they will resent the collusion of religion with their fears. The young are often fully justified in seeing the religion which their elders offer them as little more than a conspiracy to deter them from growing up. Sometimes it is far from scrupulous in its endeavours to undermine their self-confidence. It reduces the parable of the father's generosity to the sour comment – I told you so – as the prodigal surveys the prospect of pigs' swill.

We do not learn to love God by a premature withdrawal from the world; that only creates envy and glamorizes the experience we have not had. Instead we learn to love God only by trying to love the world. We must first surrender ourselves to the beauty we perceive in it, endeavour to realize the ambitions it arouses, and lose our hearts to the objects of our love. Only in that way do we learn that we have a heart, in the religious and personal sense. It is not through being nagged by parents, or school-teachers or clergymen that we become dissatisfied with ourselves. Our restlessness begins when we start to bestow value on something other than ourselves. The process of yearning and disappointment is the crucial preparation for learning to love God. We must not try to inhibit the yearning by anticipating the disappointment – that way we only learn at most a cautious prudence, which keeps life safely at a distance. Only those who have loved and hoped with all their hearts can undergo the enlightening process of disillusion. It is easy and unrewarding to be cynical about the goals which others have set themselves. To face the emptiness and boredom involved in our own choices is a quite different discipline.

Bestowing value on things and people other than ourselves, we become dissatisfied with ourselves, which is the hunger at the centre of the religion of peace. Acquiring things or even possessing other people does not satisfy that hunger, but nevertheless it is an essential preliminary. As long as we see ourselves defined by what we lack, we can always dream that acquisition and possession would satisfy us. The reality of having things and possessing people is the opportunity to learn that our hunger is left unassuaged. We tell ourselves that if only we could do something, or acquire something, or if someone loved us, then we would be different, content and happy. Only the granting of the wish breaks its spell – not by satisfying us, but by showing us that we remain the same – hungry and unfulfilled. I have already indicated that the secular response is simply to try again or to turn to some new pursuit. There are enough possibilities to occupy any life.

The religious person responds differently. Instead of simply repeating the exercise or changing the object, he tries to learn from his experience of disillusion. He does not blame the inadequacy of the object of his love – instead he questions the nature of his love, the process by which he came to attach such value to a thing or an achievement or a person. He discovers in the language of religion a detachment of value from the objects with which it is usually associated, and he now possesses the experience which makes it possible for him to use that language with conviction. It no longer represents an escape from engagement with the world, it expresses the reality of that engagement. The attribution of Ecclesiastes to King Solomon is doubtless an historical fiction, but it is entirely appropriate to the viewpoint it expresses. It speaks of the experience of wealth, of fame and power, of sexual satisfaction:

> I undertook great works; I built myself houses and planted vineyards; I made myself gardens and parks and planted all kinds of fruit-trees in them; I made myself pools of water to irrigate a grove of growing trees; I bought slaves, male and female, and I had my home-born slaves as well; I had possessions, more cattle and flocks than any of my predecessors in Jerusalem; I amassed silver and gold also, the treasure of kings and provinces; I acquired singers, men and women, and all that man delights in. I was great, greater than all my predecessors in Jerusalem; and my wisdom stood me in good stead. Whatever my eyes coveted, I refused them nothing, nor did I deny myself any pleasure. Yes indeed, I got pleasure from all my labour, and for all my labour this was my reward. Then I turned and reviewed all my handiwork, all my labour and toil, and I saw that everything was emptiness and chasing the wind, of no profit under the sun (Eccles. 2.4–11).

This is no Manichaean condemnation of the world as evil: it is simply a recognition that we have a hunger which the world does not satisfy.

So the most worldly of the Old Testament books has always commended itself to the ascetic tradition of Christianity.

The value which we had once attributed to objects, to achieve-ments, to people, we were in fact alienating from ourselves in a way which we could not subsequently recover. The objects of our search either eluded or bored us. Instead as religious people we learn to attribute value to God alone. That is the implication of the First Commandment:

> The Lord our God is the only Lord; love the Lord your God with all your heart, with all your soul, with all your mind, and with all your strength (Mark 12.30).

In doing so we are not celebrating a source of supernatural power. We do not value God as God, because he made the world or because he promises its blessings. We find our good in God alone, because only the God who lives in our imaginations can sustain the burden of our hopes and satisfy the depths of our longing. Whatever value we place upon the world – we lose for ever. If the object does not escape us, the joy we associated with it does. In prayer we learn to attribute value only to the God, whom we construct in our imaginations. The value we place upon him, we do not lose, because he is ours. We have only to attend to him to appropriate the glory with which we clothe him.

Prayer on this account is the triumphant art of the human imagination. A person stripped of everything except the power of utterance retains this inalienable dignity which needs no human audience to confirm it. The person who has learnt to find joy in the invocation of God has tasted eternal life. Those who are still consumed with envy for what they have not possessed will see in such prayer merely dishonest compensation. They will continually dis-parage the God who only lives in the hearts of his worshippers, as an unsatisfying illusion. They will compare that God unfavourably with what they regard as the tangible joys of this life. Such a God they will say does not exist: they will only exchange real goods for a God of whose objective existence they have no doubt. Those who have tasted what are called the good things of life will, like the fictitious Solomon, see things differently. Religion only begins when envy has been silenced by boredom and disillusion. Envy impoverished by the value which it has attached to the world assumes that 'the good things of life' bring joy. Solomon with the benefit of experience speaks differently:

> It is a gift of God that every man to whom he has granted wealth and riches and the power to enjoy them should accept his lot and rejoice in his labour. He will not dwell overmuch upon the passing years; for God fills his time with joy of heart (Eccles. 5.19f.).

Once we have shared that awareness of the vanity of all that exists, we will not spurn the God who lives in the hearts of those who have learnt to love him.

Secular values are accompanied either by frightened satisfaction or bitter dissatisfaction. In the alternation between those moods, the self is continually humiliated, enslaved to the values from which it has alienated itself. Perhaps this is why the craving of the drug addict is so offensive to our respectability. It reveals in the starkest form the humiliating logic of all our secular desires. Instead we hope to repress it with Presidential advertising and unleash all our powers of law enforcement against it. We cheerfully construct societies which humiliate many of their members and then object when some of them prefer to humiliate themselves. By contrast the person who learns to pray, to love God, to place in God his hope, his trust, his joy uses his imagination creatively. His dreams are no longer dominated by objects which he can only hope to possess, but which mock his actual life. When I invoke God, I am being truly creative. No image is being imposed upon me. I am not projecting values on to things or people, which will debase me. In prayer, in relation to the God of my imagining, I develop a self I can respect. In praising my God I learn the value of my imagination. The person who has learnt that art will think the world well lost.

Human Freedom and the Reversal of Values

The process of learning to love God, which I have described, may seem a travesty of traditional Christian teaching with its emphasis on the objective existence of God the Creator. It will be objected that to confine God to our consciousness, to make him the construction of our imaginations, the recipient of our values rather than their source, is not only inadequate but blasphemous. To such objections my first reply must be that whether blasphemous or not, it is true, because the arguments for God's objective existence are unconvincing. On such a view our God must inevitably be the work of our imagination. Instead, however, of denigrating such a God, I would suggest that we learn a new respect for our imaginative life. Indeed on this account that is the challenge of learning to pray. The child is rich in imagination, but quite unskilled in using the world. So much of our education is only an attempt to repress the imagination of children and deserves all the hostility it attracts. The adult disparages the child's ready imagination and demands that it be replaced by the skills necessary for survival. It is the achievement of prayer to undo that grim exchange. In prayer the child in each of us is born anew.

It is instructive to compare this process of learning to love the God of our imagination through disillusioned secular loves, with the process described by Augustine in the *Confessions*, for in many ways the process which he describes of coming to love God is indistinguishable from the one I have outlined. Augustine crowns the story of his life with an examination of the carnal delights of the senses and the spiritual gratifications of curiosity, pride and human glory. The process of disillusion goes hand in hand with a growing consciousness of God:

> You have walked everywhere at my side, O Truth, teaching me what to seek and what to avoid, whenever I laid before you the things that I was able to see in this world below and asked you to counsel me. As far as my senses enabled me to do so, I surveyed the world about me and explored both the life which my body has from me and the senses themselves. Next I probed the depths of my memory, so vast in its ramifications and filled in so wonderful a way with riches beyond number. I scrutinized all these things, and stood back in awe, for without you I could see none of them, and I found that none of them was you . . . But in all the regions where I thread my way, seeking your guidance, only in you do I find a safe haven for my mind, a gathering-place for my scattered parts, where no portion of me can depart from you.[7]

The doctrine of God's creation of the world out of nothing in Augustine's hands functions as a means of explaining both the attractiveness of created things, and the disappointment which their love necessarily brings. He gives this expression with characteristic poignancy:

> I have learnt to love you late, Beauty at once so ancient and so new! I have learnt to love you late! You were within me, and I was in the world outside myself. I searched for you outside myself and, disfigured as I was, I fell upon the lovely things of your creation. You were with me, but I was not with you. The beautiful things of this world kept me far from you and yet, if they had not been in you, they would have had no being at all.[8]

Created things elicit our love, because they are the work of God, they disappoint us because they are not the God who alone can satisfy us. Only the creative activity of God conceals the void from which creation is rescued.

The agony of Augustine's theology in the *Confessions* lies in his wavering conviction that God does really satisfy. His theory of creation tells him that that should be the case, but his own experience is fleeting:

> Sometimes you allow me to experience a feeling quite unlike my normal state, an inward sense of delight which, if it were to reach perfection in me, would be something not encountered in this life, though what it is I cannot tell. But my heavy burden of distress drags me down again to earth. Again I become a prey to my habits, which hold me fast. My tears flow, but still I am held fast.[9]

For all his claims about the joy of God, he remains in terrifying uncertainty as to the outcome:

> When at last I cling to you with all my being, for me there will be no more sorrow, no more toil. Then at last I shall be alive with true life, for my life will be wholly filled by you. You raise up and sustain all whose lives you fill, but my life is not yet filled by you and I am a burden to myself. The pleasures I find in the world, which should be cause for tears, are at strife with its sorrows, in which I should rejoice, and I cannot tell to which the victory will fall.[10]

It is therefore both the strength and the disappointment of the *Confessions* that it is so ruthlessly honest about the inadequacy of Augustine's religious experience. So often it seems merely to haunt him by its absence.

All the values with which Augustine had first invested the world, he comes to attribute to his God, but it would seem that he was almost as unhappy in the one love as the other. In terms of present experience the joy of his God was as uncertain and as transitory as any other happiness. It is difficult to avoid the impression that he nurses such expectations of an extraneous God, because if not a disappointed lover, he was still a deeply frustrated one. Instead the rapture of the lover is replaced by a pupil's respect for the discipline of a grim schoolmaster – relentlessly punishing and occasionally rewarding. The divine pedagogue provided an example for the human bishop. There are, however, times when he speaks with an immediate conviction. Then the theories of creation and Creator are left behind, and instead we enter the unique experience which his religious imagination has made possible:

> How sweet it was all at once for me to be rid of those fruitless joys which I had once feared to lose and was now glad to reject! You drove them from me, you who are the true, the sovereign joy. You drove them from me and took their place, you who are sweeter than all pleasure, though not to flesh and blood, you who outshine all light yet are hidden deeper than any secret in our hearts, you who surpass all honour though not in the eyes of men who see all honour in themselves. At last my mind was free from the gnawing anxieties of ambition and gain, from wallowing in filth and scratching the itching sore of lust. I began to talk to you freely, O Lord my God, my Light, my Wealth, my Salvation.[11]

Here the values he has detached from the world he joyfully appropriates as he attributes them to his God.

Augustine would of course have referred the divine sweetness which he experienced in his imagination to a metaphysical source, for which he would have denied any responsibility. I have no argument with his imaginative picture of his experience. In so far as Augustine invites us to make it our own, I would want to share it. My only reservation is that I would recognize my own responsibility for that decision, and wish that Augustine had also been able to recognize his contribution to the God in whom he delighted. I believe that it is entirely possible to share his experience, while questioning the metaphysical rationale which he provided for it. Our love of God has no more need of an existing object than Stendahl's lover depends upon the beauty of his beloved. It is enough that our imaginations have been fired. Indeed I suspect that Augustine paid a high price for the attempt to objectify his God which demanded that he conceal from himself his own creativity. If he had been less passive in his understanding of blessedness, his love of God might have been less clouded, less preoccupied by the distance which continued to separate the human lover from his divine beloved, a distance which threatened the very love which demanded it. For in many ways the ageing bishop was a figure of tragedy rather than enlightenment, harassed by business, embittered in controversy, resorting to compulsion, haunted by a divine vision he is unable to recapture, compensating himself in the elaboration of doctrine and the defence of an ailing institution. Perhaps as we look at the faces of the modern episcopate we see that this pattern is still with us.

Yet however much he may subsequently have betrayed it, Augustine here gives classic expression to the distinctively religious conception of human freedom. Finding his delight in a transcendent 'sweetness', he is 'free from the gnawing anxieties of ambition and gain, from wallowing in filth and scratching the itching sore of lust'. Enjoying in his imagination a transcendent goodness, he is able to leave behind him his old obsessions with external goods which humiliated him when he failed to obtain them, and filled him with anxiety when he possessed them. No longer projecting value on to external objects or people, he ascribes them to the God of his imagination – my Light, my Wealth, my Salvation. In so far as he is conscious of that God he appropriates the values he attributes to him. This gives him a unique freedom, because it removes him from the possibility of reward or punishment. The rewards of this world no longer have any value, its punishments arouse no fear. The whole apparatus of human control is thus made powerless. Augustine has come to share the victory of his crucified master.

The Love of God and the Joy of the Soul

In the previous chapter I argued that in the religion of peace the self ceases to be the manipulator of a God of power, and becomes instead the agenda of religion. We pray, not to change God or the world, but to transcend ourselves, to discover a true identity. Hand in hand with this process there is a transformation in our understanding of God. God is no longer a supernatural means to secure our secular ends – instead God has himself become the all-sufficient goal – the joy of the soul. It is in this respect that religious and political activity are so radically different. Political goals are necessarily achieved by a variety of means which will be different from and may seem inconsistent with the promised ends. Political wisdom is concerned to discover the means which are appropriate to the end in view. Religion is concerned not with achieving particular ends by various means, but with the evaluation of the ends themselves. In religion we seek that which is worthy of our love and can sustain that love.

In this search for the true good, religion comes to repudiate the distinction of means and ends, for it is the mark of real good, that the goal and the journey are indistinguishable. Meditating on the experience that it is better to travel hopefully than to arrive, the religious man realizes that for him the way, the truth and the life are indistinguishable. His God is no longer the extraneous power who answers his prayer. In the act of prayer we receive our reward. We begin by looking on prayer as a means, and God's answer as the end: slowly we come to recognize that in prayer the asking and the finding are one. As we construct in our imaginations a picture of the good we seek, we have begun to appropriate that good. For what the religion of peace promises is the joy that is to be found only in prayer. In prayer to God we seek joy and discover it.

This is the imaginative process which Anselm's *Proslogion* so beautifully articulates. His prayer begins in the urgent seeking of God:

> You have invited us to cry out, 'Help us':
> I pray you, Lord, let me not sigh without hope,
> but hope and breathe again.

Let not my heart become bitter because of its desolation,
    but sweeten it with your consolation.
When I was hungry I began to seek you, Lord;
    do not let me go hungry away.
I came to you famished;
    do not let me go from you unfed.
Poor, I have come to one who is rich,
    miserable, I have come to one who is merciful;
    do not let me return empty and despised.
If before I eat I sigh,
    after my sighs give me to eat.[12]

It ends in a grateful expression of joy:

My Lord and my God,
    my joy and the hope of my heart,
    tell my soul if this is that joy
    which you spoke to us about through your Son,
'Ask and you will receive that your joy may be full'.
    For I have found a fullness of joy
        that is more than full.
It is a joy that fills the whole heart, mind, and soul,
    indeed it fills the whole of a man,
    and yet joy beyond measure still remains.[13]

The careful arguments and elaborate rhetoric of the *Proslogion* present this as a drama, a powerful movement as if from earth to heaven. Yet the reality is different. At every moment of the *Proslogion* the joy, which is acknowledged at its end, is being anticipated and exerts its influence, as much by the sense of its absence as by the affirmation of its presence.

To those who are seeking what it appears to promise – a rational argument for the existence of God – it is baffling and infuriating: a snake which bites its own tail. What Anselm has achieved is not a convincing argument for the objective existence of God, but a classic example of the way in which the religious imagination works: learning to appropriate a joy it already possesses. The achievement of religion is not the discovery of a good we do not possess; it is to overcome distraction, our tendency to lose sight of the good that is ours already. It has been the intention of this book to try to understand why in our prayer the seeking and the finding are inseparable. Pascal in *The Mystery of Jesus* sees to the heart of the matter in a line:

Take comfort: you would not seek me, if you had not found me.[14]

Conclusion

CONCLUSION

The Transactions of Prayer and the Existence of God

The ultimate essence of religion is revealed by the simplest act of religion – prayer; an act which implies at least as much as the dogma of the Incarnation, although religious speculation stands amazed at this, as the greatest of mysteries. Not, certainly, the prayer before and after meals, the ritual of animal egoism, but the prayer pregnant with sorrow, the prayer of disconsolate love, the prayer which expresses the power of the heart that crushes man to the ground, the prayer which begins in despair and ends in rapture.

Feuerbach

The Challenge of Atheism and Indifference

The vitality of the Christian religion depends upon the conviction and integrity with which we can speak of God. Anything which undermines that strikes at the heart of Christianity, and not only makes its future problematic, it makes that problem of no importance. In this respect the militant atheism of Marxism is a mistaken anachronism: its militancy betrays its quasi-religious character. It is not therefore surprising that the triumph of atheism has not been brought about by persecution and repression – that gives the issue an appearance of importance. Martyrs attract attention and recruits. The quiet, relentless indifference towards religion in Western countries is far more eloquent and effective. We do not therefore have to look to the illiberal regimes of Eastern Europe – the collapse of theism is all around us. The tolerance with which the residual phenomena of religion are regarded is evidence not so much of enduring folk religion, as of polite apathy. Church organizations which are largely preoccupied with their own self-preservation are not well placed to speak confidently of God. The irreligious world will have no quarrel with a church sustained by flower festivals and other forms of genteel entertainment. Today many people who have ceased to believe in God and who no longer pray are content in relatively prosperous times to maintain religious institutions for simply nostalgic reasons. As has been noticed the strength and constituency of the Church of England has an embarrassing resemblance to the National Trust. Such is the only future for a church without God.

In drawing attention to the strength and prevalence of atheism and in trying to understand the implications, I am conscious that I have trodden a path which is dangerous for a clergyman and invites misunderstanding. There is a tendency both in the pew and the pulpit to hope that if atheism is ignored it will somehow go away. Indeed that rather pathetic hope is often mistaken for faith. The stubborn reassertion of traditional theism is comforting and makes few demands of either the speaker or the listener. Questioning and reconstructing inevitably disturb and can easily be disparaged as negative and destructive.

Anyone who believes in God must confront the prevalence of atheism. We cannot hope to speak of God with conviction and integrity unless we have listened carefully to our unbelieving contemporaries. If we genuinely listen to their arguments, it would be surprising if our understanding of God remains unchallenged or unchanged. I do not believe that widespread indifference means the end of religion, but I suspect that it points to a rather different religion, in which some aspects of our inherited belief in God will be discarded, and others will possess a new cogency. Conscious of the collapse of theism, I continue to pray, but I pray differently. I believe in God – in this book I have tried to say plainly what I mean, and what I do not mean, when I make that statement of belief.

The Transactions of Prayer

In trying to understand what I mean when I speak of God, I have attempted to examine the way in which our beliefs about God function. I have paid close attention to the transactions which are envisaged in prayer. In this I have been much influenced by Feuerbach who saw so clearly the theological significance of prayer:

> The essential act of religion, that in which religion puts into action what we have designated as its essence, is prayer.[1]

Any reader of this book, who knows Feuerbach, will realize how much of my analysis of prayer has been derived from him. This is particularly true of his awareness of the relationship between prayer and self-consciousness and the importance of utterance in prayer:

> In prayer, man addresses God with the word of intimate affection – *Thou*; he thus declares articulately that God is his *alter ego*; he confesses to God, as the being nearest to him, his most secret thoughts, his deepest wishes, which otherwise he shrinks from uttering . . . Prayer is the self-division of man into two beings, – a dialogue of man with himself, with his heart. It is essential to the effectiveness of prayer that it be audibly, intelligibly, energetically expressed. Involuntarily prayer wells forth in sound; the struggling heart bursts the barrier of the closed lips . . . Concentration, it is said, is the condition of prayer; but it is more than a condition; prayer is itself concentration, – the dismissal of all distracting ideas, of all disturbing influences from without, retirement within oneself, in order to have relation only with one's own being.[2]

Yet however suggestive, I find Feuerbach's analysis of prayer deeply unsatisfactory. He is happy to substitute work for prayer, but the exchange which he envisages is on his own account a denial of human freedom:

> The man who does not exclude from his mind the idea of the world, the idea that everything here must be sought intermediately, that every effect has its natural cause, that a wish is only to be attained when it is made an end and the corresponding means are put into operation – such a man does not pray: he only works; he

transforms his attainable wishes into objects of real activity; other wishes which he recognises as purely subjective he denies, or regards as simply subjective, pious aspirations. In other words, he limits, he conditionates his being by the world, as a member of which he conceives himself; he bounds his wishes by the idea of necessity.[3]

Those who are fired by the almost prophetic zeal of his writing should not forget its bleak outcome.

Moreover, Feuerbach has to insist that the prayer envisaged by the religions of power is the only real prayer:

> Prayer is all-powerful. What the pious soul entreats for in prayer God fulfils. But he prays not for spiritual gifts alone, which lie in some sort in the power of man; he prays also for things which lie out of him, which are in the power of Nature, a power which it is the very object of prayer to overcome; in prayer he lays hold on a supernatural means, in order to attain ends in themselves natural.[4]

I would not of course quarrel with Feuerbach's analysis as a fair description of the way in which prayer operates within the religions of power, but when he refuses to acknowledge the possibility of other forms of prayer, he is mistaken:

> It is only unbelief in the efficacy of prayer which has subtly limited prayer to spiritual matters.[5]

Feuerbach, like other critics of religion, needs to prohibit the adaptation of religion in order to dismiss it.

I have to admit, however, that Feuerbach's account, if not true, is plausible, because in so many of its manifestations Christianity remains a religion of power – indistinguishable from its pagan and Jewish precursors. In the ancient world Jews and Gentiles shared a common religious structure: indeed it was because of their shared assumptions that the conflicts between them were so bitter. In the first place the attention and favour of their God distinguished them from other people. We have already seen how the notion of privilege underlay the Jewish notion of divine providence, but the Greek cities and the Roman republic and empire had the same hope of their gods.

It used to be claimed that only Yahweh was a God of history, but Greek and Roman examples belie this; moreover, there were clear limits to the syncretist universalism of hellenistic religion. Where possible Romans may have preferred to assimilate local deities into their own pantheon, leaving the privileges and status of the traditional priesthoods untouched, but the price of that accommodation was submission. Wherever the local gods were used to sustain resistance, as among the Jews and Celts, repression was savage, and in the case of the Druids successful. Romans like Jews rejoiced in the favour of their divine patrons, because their identity was a privileged one – the centre of a great empire, successfully dominating their nearer neighbours, and repelling more distant ones.

Jews, however, had much more in common with the religions of the Gentiles than they liked to admit, for the vaunted difference between the idols and Yahweh was far less significant than Jews supposed. Certainly there was a difference – Gentiles used a wider variety of artistic means in the portrayal of their gods than Jews allowed themselves. In particular Gentiles created physical representations of their deities and invested those representations with the significance and power of the god. Jews eschewed such direct representations, and concentrated instead on verbal and ultimately literary portrayals for which they consistently failed to see their responsibility. It is as if a modern American should dismiss the orchestrated attention given to Miss Liberty as idolatry, and yet see no problem with saluting the flag. Jew and Gentile used rather different materials in their theological constructions: their purposes were embarrassingly similar.

For ancient religion in both its Jewish and its Gentile forms was concerned with power. Like the gods of the pantheon, Yahweh could be expected to intervene in the affairs of men. The divine was conceived as the source of the power that human beings possessed and a reservoir of power for future use. In polytheism the different concerns of men – victory, prosperity, health, fertility, attractiveness etc. – were devolved to particular gods, while Yahweh monopolized all power to himself, but in both religious structures there was the desire to appropriate power over the natural world and over other human beings. Humanity was seen as weak, often helpless. The gods were invoked to supply what men lacked. To this Yahweh was no exception.

Popular apologetic has tended to contrast the ethical concern of Judaism with the moral confusion and degeneracy of paganism, but that is both to disparage Gentile religion too harshly and to exaggerate the ethical nobility of the Jewish religion. If no other ancient religion seems to have had the same legal apparatus and development as Judaism, that reflects its literary, scribal character after the Exile. It was often ritualistic rather than moral in its emphasis. Furthermore, if some of the stories of the gods are licentious, the God of Israel was portrayed as capable of savage cruelty: and while the Gentile religions subjected themselves to the moral scrutiny and ridicule of later hellenistic philosophy, no such process seems to have taken place within Judaism with regard to their God of holy war. In fact in both religious structures the control of behaviour, particularly of public, ritual observance was central. It served both to identify adherents and to express the dominance of the religious and political authorities. Impiety was considered dangerous to Gentile society just as sin threatened the safety of Israel. In both there existed people whose prestige was enhanced by transmitting and enforcing ancient patterns of behaviour and ritual.

In both religious traditions the invocation of the divine served to disguise human responsibility. We have seen how that process worked in the prophetic religion of the Jews which created the paradox that the same people who saw so clearly the human responsibility for idolatry, were quite incapable of acknowledging their own responsibility for their account of God. This contradiction warns us of the difficulty of achieving honesty about our own religion. We may ruthlessly criticize the faith of others, and yet remain quite naive about our own. We should therefore be cautious in our interpretation of ancient paganism. Jews may have seen the machinations behind imperial religion, while those who propagated it had quite different perceptions. It seems that the troubled end of the Roman Republic precipitated a religious crisis not unlike that of European Christendom after 1914. Some Romans were certainly aware of the political advantages of religion in ensuring popular consent and conformity, but we should be wary of attributing to them a uniformly cynical motivation. The convenience which arouses our suspicion would have provided those involved, not with grounds for doubt, but for conviction. To us in retrospect – who cannot share their social experience – the imperial cult seems artificial and contrived. We forget that it was associated with a long period of prosperity and security. To many the imperial cult must have seemed the proper acknowledgment of experienced good fortune, and a means of ensuring that it would continue. The benefits of the empire would have provided objective evidence that the imperial gods were real. Equally its crisis in the mid third century AD was an experience from which classical paganism never recovered. We may surmise therefore that in their public worship the pagans of antiquity were as serious in their religion as their Jewish contemporaries. In the shared sincerity of their religions, the seriousness with which they took their gods reflected the seriousness with which they took themselves. Neglect of public conformity was in both traditions vigorously punished.

The common religious structure, shared by Jew and pagan alike, promised privilege and power, so that its leaders exercised control over society, while evading any responsibility for their rule. In many of its aspects Christianity is the heir of the same religious tradition. As Judaism offered a privileged identity to the circumcised, Christianity offered to the baptized the delights of heaven, and threatened the unbaptized with hell. Christians, like Jews and pagans before them, looked to their God for power, to save them from their enemies and give them victory in battle, to give protection against accident, to heal disease, to provide plenty and to ensure progeny. Christianity, like ancient paganism, demanded total conformity to its public rituals and achieved through the confessional and the catechism a control of behaviour and disposition as pervasive as that of the Jewish law. Divisive social attitudes, institutional aggression and occasionally downright violence and cruelty were promulgated not as the self-interest of men, but as the demands of the Almighty.

I have spoken of all these things as if they belonged to a past which had vanished; I wish that might be so, but it is not the case. In many of its manifestations today Christianity remains unrepentantly a religion of power. Medieval Christendom may have disappeared or only survive as a pale shadow of itself in the Church of England, but the emergence of the secular state has not robbed clergymen of their political ambitions: the ostensible relationship between church and state may appear more distant, but it remains marked by opportunism on both sides and a continuing irresponsibility on the part of the church. Presidents, elected by the people or imposed by the army, may have largely replaced hereditary rulers, but Christianity is still intimately associated with secular power while remaining relatively untouched by democratic processes. Archbishops may feel free to criticize elected governments and condemn regimes based on a limited franchise: they do not themselves stand for re-election. In congenial situations the church legitimates the social order in return for respect and financial support. Where the regime is unsympathetic the church will gain its prestige by a well calculated and carefully publicized challenge to the authorities. But regardless of whether the church provokes the police or depends upon them, the commitment to secular society has well judged limits. When secular leaders prosper religious authorities court their attention and lend them respectability. However, they take no responsibility for their decisions and only wish to share their successes. They readily disown them in adversity. The religious leaders to whom President Nixon gave such prominence at his inauguration had successfully distanced themselves by the time of his resignation. The dogged devotion with which Archbishop Laud preceded his royal master to the scaffold has not been widely imitated.

In outlining the prayer appropriate to a religion of peace I have made much use of Augustine and Anselm. In them we can see prayer being used to define a new identity and to elucidate our goals. Nevertheless, power remains a considerable interest, both in the practice of their religion and in their conception of God. 'Magnus', great, is the opening word of the *Confessions*, and supplies the comparative on which the whole of the *Proslogion* is built: that than which nothing greater can be thought. Their lives here faithfully exemplified their convictions. Augustine, while not the inventor of state coercion in matters of religion, is its first Christian apologist, finding in the command – compel them to come in – a sinister and unsuspected meaning. Similarly Anselm presided over a church built on the patronage of kings and enjoying a degree of landed wealth difficult now to imagine.

In my account of Augustine and Anselm I have deliberately ignored this dimension of their thought. I can only justify that omission on the basis of the crucified Jesus, whom they claimed to represent. For it has been my argument in this book that his story represents a far more radical critique of the old transactions of prayer than anything put forward by Feuerbach. His broken body is a final answer to all glib claims about the power of prayer to an almighty God; it silences our hopes for special treatment. Those who hanker after an objective, existing God will see in Jesus' death only a God-forsaken man; however orthodox their language they are turning away from the figure of the crucified. The gospel is not the story of an atheist, it proclaims the faith that it is the crucified man, and not the perpetrators of crucifixion, who is the man of God and to whom God truly belongs. The God of Jesus Christ is not therefore a God who gives power to the victorious, but a God who can sustain the self-respect of the victim. In death as in life Jesus gains his identity, not from the attitudes of men, but from his prayer to his God. That prayer did not reward him with this world's goods, it fed him with the bread of heaven, a joy that men could neither give nor take away.

The God who Lives in the Hearts of those who Pray

I have written this book to answer a charge of atheism. If I have conceded more to the arguments of atheists than most of my fellow Christians would allow that is only because I do not think they have the decisive significance that all atheists and most Christians would claim. I do not believe that there exists a God who is

a person without a body (i.e. a spirit), present everywhere, the creator and sustainer of the universe, a free agent, able to do everything (i.e. omnipotent), knowing all things, perfectly good, a source of moral obligation, immutable, eternal, a necessary being, holy, and worthy of worship.[6]

I have tried to show that my reasons for not believing in such a God are not simply philosophical, but religious. The second part of this book on the man of God in a predatory world is therefore fundamental to my vision of God and my understanding of Christianity.

As one might imagine, the objections to the kind of theological revision which I have undertaken are well stated by J. L. Mackie:

> If God is not an objective reality but merely an intentional object, that is, exists only in the believer's mind as do the objects of imagination or events in dreams, then it is misleading to speak of a relationship, and all the more misleading to describe the relationship in terms of 'reliance', 'trust', 'guidance', and 'surrender': how could one sensibly rely upon a figment of one's own imagination? Those who are dissatisfied with the old creeds should change them, not try to do without credal statements. If the other term of the relationship is not God in the traditional sense, then to go on using the traditional names and descriptions, the familiar religious language, carries at least a risk of misunderstanding, and, more importantly, it tempts the believer himself into oscillating between the views he is really prepared to assert and defend and the familiar suggestions and connotations of the language he continues to use.[7]

That warning has been with me throughout this book. I do not think that any reader could fairly complain that I have disguised the extent to which I am prepared to modify the traditional conceptions of God. Nor do I believe that I have underestimated the implications of such a drastic revision. I have certainly tried to avoid resort to a nebulous language of personal relationship to God in Christ of which Mackie rightly complains.[8] Many of 'the traditional names and descriptions' of God must I fear be repudiated, but despite the danger of misunderstanding I am prepared to 'go on using . . . the familiar religious language'. I am prepared to do so because I believe that theology can without inconsistency be self-critical. My confidence is based on the criticism contained explicitly and implicitly in the story of Jesus. The most radical critic of the religion of power did not abandon talk of God, he transformed it.

The God in whom I believe lives in the consciousness of his worshippers. In Mackie's words he is 'not an objective reality but merely an intentional object, that is, exists only in the believer's mind as do the objects of imagination or events in dreams'. I would only question his use of 'mere' and 'only' in this respect. Such language represents a late and surprising tribute to the ancient polemic against idolatry, which consistently denigrated the human imagination. Anselm expressed this traditional point of view in a passage in the second chapter of the *Proslogion*:

> It is one thing to have something in the understanding, but quite another to understand that it actually exists. It is like a painter who, when he thinks out beforehand what he is going to create, has it in his understanding, but he does not yet understand it as actually existing because he has not yet painted it. But when he has painted it, he both has it in his understanding and actually has it, because he has created it.[9]

For a religion that has always contained an element of iconoclasm it is a surprising analogy, but for a religion of power preoccupied by greatness Anselm's conclusion is unavoidable. If we are concerned with the transactions of power the imagined is at the mercy of the actual.

If, however, religion is not concerned with power, but with the consciousness of peace, if religion is concerned with defining a new identity and elucidating that which is worthy of our love, a God who exists primarily in our imaginations is in no way to be disparaged. To describe such a God 'as a mere figment of the imagination' is to beg the question. Certainly we cannot evade our responsibility for him. In that sense 'reliance', 'trust', 'guidance', and 'surrender' must be repudiated, nor can we expect him to intervene as an extraneous power. The God who lives in the hearts of those who pray to him, mirrors the self that invokes him. If we have no difficulty in using the word 'I', we should have no difficulty in using the word 'God'. Both have their existence in the imagination of the living. Both are imagined constructions which gain their content in the use of language in our imaginative life. In that particular sense God exists, just as I do. The only power which such a God can represent is the energy within our consciousness, but that is not to be despised. It may not be the force that moves the stars, but moral courage is not a negligible quality. With the psalmist I can still say – 'O Lord, in thee have I trusted; let me never be confounded' – but the place for such language is the unobserved prayer of the heart, not a Te Deum for victory in St Paul's Cathedral.

Throughout this book I have employed a vigorous contrast between the religions of power and the religion of peace. Often that contrast may have seemed upsetting, destructive and perhaps eccentric. There will probably be some Christian readers who will feel that their faith has only been travestied. For them I will end not with words of mine, but with words of an acknowledged master of the Christian tradition. I shall not pretend that my viewpoint and that of Pascal are identical, but there is perhaps no Christian writer, who has done more to form this argument. In quoting him I am acknowledging a debt, and pointing, if not to an advocate, at least to a witness in my defence:

> There are some who see clearly that man has no other enemy but concupiscence, which turns him away from God, and not (human) enemies, no other good but God, and not a rich land. Let those who believe that man's good lies in the flesh and his evil in whatever turns him away from sensual pleasures take their fill and die of it. But those who seek God with all their hearts, whose only pain is to be deprived of the sight of him, whose only desire is to possess him, whose only enemies are those who turn them away from him, who grieve at finding themselves surrounded and dominated by such enemies, let them take heart, for I bring them glad tidings. There is one who will set them free, I will show him to them, I will prove to them that there is a God for them, I will not show him to others. I will show them that a Messiah was promised to deliver them from their enemies, and that one has come to deliver them from their iniquities, but not from their enemies.[10]

Notes

NOTES

Preface

1. *The Cost of Authority*, SCM Press 1983, pp. 282–84.
2. Ronald Preston, in *Christian Statesman*, No. 27, June 1983, p. 17.
3. *The Cost of Authority*, p. 13.
4. Ibid., pp. 15f.

Introduction

1. Andrew Louth, *Discerning the Mystery*, Oxford University Press 1983, p. 4.
2. D. Z. Phillips, *The Concept of Prayer*, Routledge and Kegan Paul 1965, p. 158.
3. D. Z. Phillips, *Religion without Explanation*, Blackwell 1976, p. 152.
4. Ibid., p. 181.
5. J. L. Mackie, *The Miracle of Theism*, Oxford University Press 1982, p. 228.
6. Augustine, *Confessions*, translated by R. S. Pine-Coffin in Penguin Classics 1961, 1.9, p. 30.
7. Ibid., 8.3, p. 162.
8. Ibid., 1.9, p. 30.
9. Phillips, *The Concept of Prayer*, p. 28.
10. All references to the Bible are taken from the New English Bible © The Delegates of the Oxford University Press and The Syndics of the Cambridge University Press, 1961, 1970.
11. Augustine, *Confessions*, 9.4, p. 186.

1 The All-Seeing Eye

1. Emil Brunner, *The Christian Doctrine of God*, Dogmatics Vol. 1, Lutterworth 1949, p. 263.
2. Ibid., p. 264.
3. Ludwig Feuerbach, *The Essence of Christianity*, 1854, p. 215.
4. Paul Tillich, *Systematic Theology*, Vol. 1, Nisbet 1968, reissued SCM Press 1978, p. 309.
5. Keith Ward, *The Concept of God*, Blackwell 1974, p. 184.
6. F. R. Tennant, *Philosophical Theology*, Vol. 2, Cambridge University Press 1930, pp. 173–79.
7. George Orwell, *Nineteen Eighty-Four*, Secker and Warburg 1949, p. 5.

8. Ibid., pp. 6f.

2 *The Lord of History*

1. Emil Brunner, *The Christian Doctrine of Creation and Redemption*, Dogmatics Vol. 2, Lutterworth 1952, pp. 8f.
2. Benjamin Whichcote, *Works*, Aberdeen 1751, Vol. 4, p. 346.

4 *The Man of God in a Predatory World*

1. *Phaedo*, 118, translated by Hugh Tredennick in *The Last Days of Socrates*, Penguin Classics 1959, p. 182.
2. See J. L. Mackie, *The Miracle of Theism*, Miracles and Testimony.
3. *The Republic*, II, 361. Cf. Simone Weil, *On Science, Necessity and the Love of God*, Oxford University Press 1968, p. 94.
4. Ibid., 362.
5. Andrew Louth, *Discerning the Mystery*, p. 94.

5 *The Credibility of God and the Responsibility of Man*

1. Ludwig Feuerbach, *The Essence of Christianity*, translated by George Eliot, 1854, p. 13.
2. Ibid., p. 269.
3. Ibid., p. 12.
4. Ibid., p. 184.
5. Athanasius, *De Incarnatione*, 46, translated by a Religious of CSMV, Mowbray 1953, pp. 83f.
6. David Brown, *The Divine Trinity*, Duckworth 1985.
7. Peter Brown, *Augustine of Hippo*, Faber and Faber 1967, pp. 174f.
8. Ibid., p. 167.
9. Augustine, *Confessions*, translated by R. S. Pine-Coffin, Penguin Classics, 1961, 1.1, p. 21.
10. Ibid., 4.16, p. 89.
11. Ibid., 7.7, pp. 143f.
12. Ibid., 8.12, p.177.
13. Ibid., 9.8, p. 194.
14. Ibid., 1.20, p. 40.
15. Ibid., 10.2, p. 207.
16. Ibid., 3.6, pp. 60f.
17. Ibid., 13.38, p. 347.
18. *The Prayers and Meditations of Saint Anselm*, translated by Benedicta Ward, Penguin Classics, 1973, p. 238.
19. Ibid., p. 242.
20. Athanasius, *De Incarnatione*, 54.
21. *The Tome of Leo*, 4, translated by T. Herbert Bindley, *The Oecumenical Documents of the Faith*, Methuen 1950, pp. 226f.

6 The Lover of God in Search of the True Self

1. Feuerbach, *The Essence of Christianity*, p. 25.
2. Ibid., p. 31.
3. Ibid., p. 274.
4. Ibid., pp. 39f.
5. Ibid., p. 155.
6. See *The Cost of Authority*, pp. 194–98.
7. Jean-Jacques Rousseau, *Reveries of the Solitary Walker*, translated by Peter France in Penguin Classics 1979, p. 141.
8. Augustine, *Confessions*, 2.9, p.52.
9. Ibid., 3.3, p. 58.
10. Ibid., 4.14, p. 84.
11. Ibid., 4.14, pp. 84f.
12. Ibid., 8.5, pp. 164f.
13. Ibid., 8.7, p. 169.
14. Ibid., 8.8, pp. 170f.
15. Ibid., 8.12, p. 178.
16. Ibid., 8.6, pp. 197f.
17. Ibid., 8.12, p. 178.
18. Ibid., 10.1, p. 207.
19. Anselm, *Prayers and Meditations*, p. 239. Cf. Ps. 27.8.
20. Ibid., p. 240.
21. Ibid., p. 240.
22. Ibid., p. 242.
23. Ibid., p. 243.
24. Ibid., p. 255.
25. Ibid., p. 257.
26. Ibid., p. 256.
27. Augustine, *Confessions*, 10.36, p. 244.

7 The Love of God and the Values of Men

1. Feuerbach, *The Essence of Christianity*, p. 226.
2. Stendahl, *Love*, translated by Gilbert and Suzanne Sale in Penguin Classics, 1975, p. 45.
3. Ibid., p. 287.
4. Victor Hugo, *Les Misérables*, translated by Norman Denny in Penguin Classics 1980, p. 347.
5. William Law, *A Serious Call to a Devout and Holy Life*, 1729, chapter 12.
6. Gustave Flaubert, *Sentimental Education*, translated by Robert Baldick in Penguin Classics 1964, p. 419.
7. Augustine, *Confessions*, 10.40, pp. 248f.
8. Ibid., 10.27, pp. 231f.
9. Ibid., 10.40, p. 249.
10. Ibid., 10.28, p. 232.
11. Ibid., 9.1, p. 181.

12. Anselm, *Prayers and Meditations*, pp. 242f.
13. Ibid., p. 265.
14. Pascal, *Pensées*, p. 314.

Conclusion: The Transactions of Prayer and the Existence of God

1. Feuerbach, The *Essence of Christianity*, p. 193.
2. Ibid., pp. 122f.
3. Ibid., p. 123.
4. Ibid., p. 193.
5. Ibid., p. 124.
6. R. Swinburne, *The Coherence of Theism*, Oxford University Press 1977, p. 2.
7. J. L. Mackie, *The Miracle of Theism*, p. 4.
8. Ibid., p. 3.
9. Anselm, *Prayers and Meditations*, p. 244.
10. Pascal, *Pensées*, translated by A. J. Krailsheimer in Penguin Classics, p. 110 (269).

Index

INDEX OF BIBLICAL
REFERENCES

INDEX OF NAMES